Travellers With Two Hats

Renee Duke

Print ISBNs
Amazon Print 9780228626329
Ingram Spark Print 9780228626336
B&N Print 9780228626343

BWL Publishing Inc.

Books we love to write...
Authors around the world.

http://bwlpublishing.ca

Copyright 2023 by Renee Duke
Cover art by Pandora Designs

All rights reserved. Without limiting the rights under copyright reserved above, no part of this publication may be reproduced, stored in or introduced into a retrieval system, or transmitted, in any form, or by any means (electronic, mechanical, photocopying, recording, or otherwise) without the prior written permission of both the copyright owner and the publisher of this book.

Dedication

To travellers everywhere, young and old.

Acknowledgements

As always, I would like to thank my editor, Susan Anderson, and my beta readers, Linda Rogers, S.D., and M.D. for their proofreading and input regarding the original manuscript, and, again, as always, my family for their ongoing support and encouragement.

Table of Contents

Chapter One 7
Chapter Two 13
Chapter Three.. 19
Chapter Four 25
Chapter Five 33
Chapter Six.. 42
Chapter Seven 49
Chapter Eight 55
Chapter Nine 61
Chapter Ten... 68
Chapter Eleven 75
Chapter Twelve.. 85
Chapter Thirteen 90
Chapter Fourteen 99
Chapter Fifteen.. 109
Chapter Sixteen 119
Chapter Seventeen 129
Chapter Eighteen 139
Chapter Nineteen 144
Chapter Twenty... 153
Chapter Twenty-One 159
Chapter Twenty-Two................................. 165
Chapter Twenty-Three 171
Chapter Twenty-Four................................ 178
Chapter Twenty-Five................................. 184
Chapter Twenty-Six................................... 189
Chapter Twenty-Seven 194
Chapter Twenty-Eight............................... 200
Chapter Twenty-Nine................................ 204
Chapter Thirty... 211
Chapter Thirty-One 219
Chapter Thirty-Two.................................. 225
Chapter Thirty-Three 231
Chapter Thirty-Four................................. 236
Chapter Thirty-Five.................................. 241

Chapter Thirty-Six 248
Chapter Thirty-Seven 256
Chapter Thirty-Eight 266
Chapter Thirty-Nine 273
Chapter Forty 279
Chapter Forty-One 288

Chapter One
Preparations

I met Ellen Blair when we were both thirteen, not long after my family moved from Wantage, a small English market town in, at that time, Berkshire, to the small Canadian city of Kelowna in British Columbia. The latter's school district having not yet embraced the concept of middle schools, it was our first day at Dr. Knox High School. According to her, I looked a little lost, so she came over to say hello. She also claims it took her several days to get used to my British accent. Even to the point of saying she only worked out my name from seeing it on a notebook. But I'm sure I wasn't *that* unintelligible. I mean, it wasn't as though I was speaking Cockney, Scouse, Broad Yorkshire, or one of the other regional dialects many non-Brits, and even some Brits, find challenging.

Once communication became firmly established, it didn't take us long to discover we had mutual interests in many things, among them a desire to journey around the world as soon as we graduated. Other friends had similar aspirations, and we were going to make a group of it.

Years change things, of course. After half a decade of talking about this proposed trip, the time finally came when we had to start seriously planning it. And found that, not only we were the only ones in our friend circle still eager to go travelling and/or in a position to do so, but that our world tour would, for practical (read: financial) reasons, have to be just a European tour. We were by then eighteen, and that five years of comfortable familiarity is probably all that kept us from severing relations entirely when the rigours of travel became too much for us. We had some minor spats before we even set out, started bickering in earnest in Vancouver, and carried on until we returned home with our friendship having somehow managed to withstand the strain. We were hardly ever in discord before making the trip, and weren't afterwards, but the inevitable frustrations and inconveniences of being in foreign lands brought out the worst in both of us.

Of course, one reason Ellen and I fought so much could have been because we were both the youngest child of older parents, with our closest siblings some distance from us in age, hers even more so than mine. Used to having them (the siblings) give in, or be made to give in, to us, we did not tend to give in to each other.

* * *

Our travels now confined to Europe, Ellen and I began to read up on prospective destinations and their various attractions. Since Rick Steves, being three years younger than us, and Bill Bryson, being only a year older than us, had not yet started penning their highly regarded travel books, and Tony and Maureen Wheeler had not yet made the trip that sparked the Lonely Planet series, we had to get our information from the—then—most recent versions of *Fodor's Europe*, Arthur Frommer's *Europe On $5 A Day*, and travel memoirs like Andrea Kenis's *The Single Girl's Guide To Europe* (1969), Janet Gillespie's *Bedlam In The Back Seat* (1960), Ruth Mckenney and Richard Branston's *Here's England* (1955), and Cornelia Otis Skinner and Emily Kimbrough's *Our Hearts Were Young And Gay*. The Skinner/Kimbrough one was first published in the 1940s, but harked back to a trip the authors took in the 1920s, making the Europe they visited as far removed from the Europe we visited as ours is from the Europe of today.

In reading the more up-to-date guides and memoirs, it soon became clear that even a European tour could not be as extensive as we would have liked. Virtually all of Scandinavia was beyond—way beyond—our means, and travelling around any of the countries that lay behind the Iron Curtain was, for political reasons, both unappealing and somewhat difficult. We therefore focussed on 'the rest' and spent hours making and remaking itineraries reflective of our joint and individual interests, a pastime that triggered a few of those minor spats before we even started the trip.

At that time, Ellen's future career plan was to be an archaeologist rather than the librarian she eventually became.

"Pompeii!" she said at one point. "I absolutely have to go to Pompeii."

"Why?" I asked, more to annoy her than anything else, since I'm a history buff too. "All that's there is a bunch of old buildings that were once covered in lava."

"That's all?" Ellen squeaked incredulously. "That's *everything!*"

On another occasion, it was the different tourist meccas the United Kingdom had to offer which caused conflict. Having lived there, I'd been to some of them, but not always at an age where they'd made much of an impression—something Ellen found difficult to fathom as she didn't believe it was possible for someone to have been in such a tremendously historic place as, say, Winchester Cathedral, and paid no attention to the architecture and atmosphere. (I was four.)

"London!" she said rapturously as we discussed our must-visit list for England. "There's *so* much to see in London! I want to go the British Museum, Buckingham Palace, Trafalgar Square, Piccadilly Circus, Westminster Abbey, and—"

"—and Hampton Court and the Tower of London," I said. "So, moving on, we—"

"Wait!" Ellen interjected. "I forgot the National Gallery. That should be on the list too." When I pointed out that she'd already expressed a desire to go to Trafalgar Square, she said, "Yes, yes, but I'm talking about the National Gallery."

"The National Gallery is *on* Trafalgar Square."

"Oh."

But working out ways for us to take in everything we wanted, or even most of what we wanted, sometimes proved difficult. And for me, frustrating.

"You shouldn't let this sort of stuff bother you," Ellen said after one of my bouts of ire over some glitch in plans. "I don't." (This would change.)

"I know!" I snapped. "You just sit there, either nodding or sighing. Why can't you give me some *helpful* input once a while?"

"Because you're more capable. You're the one with all the travel experience. Naturally it's better if I leave things up to you."

She didn't always leave things up to me, however, and that invariably led to argument. The above complaint notwithstanding, I liked to do things my own way and I really was the travel veteran. Ellen's only travel experience lay in short trips to two Canadian provinces and three American states. I, however, had crossed the Atlantic several times, gone on that school trip to Austria, and been to, or through, every Canadian province except those in the Maritimes. That made me the recognized seasoned traveller and I occasionally (okay, *more* than occasionally) tried to flaunt my superior knowledge in ways that, quite justifiably, annoyed Ellen.

Her occasional flat-out impracticality served to exasperate me just as much, however. Over at her house one afternoon during the midst of packing, I picked up a huge tube of toothpaste and held it aloft.

"Why on earth are you taking this?" I inquired.

"We're going to be gone over two months," Ellen said defensively.

"Two months? The Jolly Green Giant® couldn't use this up in two months."

She took it anyway.

* * *

Getting ready for our trip was not just wish lists, route planning, and the accumulation of supplies. Not being spontaneous, take-things-as-they-come types, we craved the security of knowing we had a roof over our heads everywhere we went. In the days before websites, making reservations involved snail mail, and turned out to be a more complicated procedure than we expected. We could only afford to stay in youth hostels, and wanted to be sure we had confirmed places in every town or city we were going to. That meant getting replies from the proprietors before we left, and in order to get replies, we had to enclose an International Reply Coupon (IRC) with each request so the recipients could exchange them for stamps at any post office in the world. Unfortunately, one IRC only allowed for a reply by sea mail. We had to hear back faster than that, and a post office official said an air mail reply would take two or three IRCs. These cost 15¢ each, and since we were mailing out thirty-five inquiries, this promised to be expensive. He didn't know the exact rate of exchange for the various foreign currencies involved and told us to try a bank. But all that the people there could suggest was for us to enclose money orders, which were 50¢ each.

Discouraged, we went to a café to get ourselves some soft drinks. There Ellen dug out a pen and began to list our alternatives on a napkin.

(a) Buy three International Reply Coupons for each hostel: $15.75 plus $5.25 postage for a total of $21.00.
(b) Buy money orders for each hostel: $17.50 plus $5.25 postage, for a total of $22.75.
(c) Fill out the yellow forms some hostels had provided—use unknown.
(d) Write a scathing letter to someone, somewhere, denouncing the unfairness and inefficiency of everything.

Results of (a) and (b): bankruptcy. Results of (c): as unknown as the forms themselves. Results of (d): to whom, and what good would it do anyway?

We wound up going back to the post office, mainly to find out just what IRCs did and if multiple ones really were necessary. They were, so we bought twenty of them. The rules only allowed us ten each, which created another problem, as we required over a hundred in order to ensure air mail replies.

In the days that followed, International Reply Coupons became our top priority. The ten-per-person limit forced us to make repeat visits to the main post office and go round all the sub-post offices in the area as well. These were considerably more flexible about the ten-per-person limit but usually only had about fourteen on hand because people hardly ever asked for them. My father and I cleaned out two such outlets and our wallets (mostly his) in one afternoon and used up a lot of gas in the process. Between us Ellen and I did manage to obtain all the coupons we required, and possibly all such coupons in the district.

Chapter Two
More Preparations

Once reservation requests had been set in motion, we returned to planning where to go and what to see so that I could put together a day-to-day schedule.

"Er, there's something I forgot to tell you," Ellen said when I finally held up a neatly typed list of dates and places. "That wedding we're going to is earlier than I thought."

The groom, Jeb, was a friend of Ellen's whom she knew through her church. He was a Canadian, but met his bride, Elsje, on a visit to Holland. It was there they were getting married, and we were invited to the wedding.

"Aaaghrrr!" I cried, dramatically ripping the schedule to pieces.

After I came up with a new one, we turned our attention to the wedding present we had for Jeb and Elsje. It was a two-tier porcelain cake plate, and, uncertain as to the best way to transport such a vulnerable item halfway around the world, we had it in and out of its box a number of times.

"Why don't you just give it to them before they leave for Holland?" Ellen's mother suggested.

For some reason, we hadn't thought of that.

* * *

We then had to take care of those crucial travel requirements known as immunizations. Summoning our courage, Ellen and I and went down to the local health unit to update our smallpox vaccinations and ask what else, if anything, we should have. Back then, proof of immunization against smallpox was still required by almost every country in the world, just as covid ones would come to be. We were told a smallpox vaccination was the only one that was absolutely mandatory for Europe, but the nurse said we could also have a series of typhoid and tetanus jabs if we wanted to. Well, we didn't *want* to, but felt we probably should. We got our smallpox vaccinations and went back for our first typhoid-tetanus shots two weeks later. The nurse on duty that day didn't think they were really necessary, and after she described what they did to recipients, we didn't think they were really necessary either. Going out, we met Jeb and Elsje. She was there for the second of the shots we'd just declined, and her still red and swollen arm reinforced our belief we could manage without them; the sight reminding me of some of my English school chums making moan about their school-bestowed typhoid injections at a time when I and a few others in our form were too young to get them, as pupils had to be fourteen and our birthdays were later in the year. And, by the time I *was* fourteen, my family was in Canada, where schools did not administer that particular inoculation.

* * *

Next up: home and native land identification. This being the time of the increasingly unpopular Vietnam War, we'd heard that young Americans travelling in Europe were not always well-received there and were advised to make sure no one would mistake us for Americans because of our accents. Well, because of Ellen's accent. Mine was, and some claim, still is, debatable. To Canadians, it's a British accent, to Brits, it's Canadian, so I suppose it must be a cross between the two. Sort of a mid-Atlantic accent. To offset the problem, we got maple leaf badges for each arm of our jackets, and Canadian flags for what I'd always hitherto called rucksacks but was informed by Ellen were packsacks. (We had similar debates over such words as flannel vs. washcloth, basin vs. sink, and the proper pronunciation of aluminium and laboratory.) Deferring, here, to her, the *packsack* flags were sewn on, and proved quite durable. The same cannot be said of the ones on our flight bags and gadget bags. These were merely stickers and began to peel off halfway through the trip.

Our flight bags were for all those things we might happen to want on board the aeroplane, and the gadget bags for our cameras and a vast quantity of film cartridges (slide format), flashcubes, and other accessories. I'd started taking photos with my family's old Kodak Brownie® box camera when I was about eight, but had received a Kodak 126 Instamatic® as a graduation present and was pleased to be able to just pop film cartridges into that and not have to wrestle with the film rolls of an earlier era. Even if—lacking the sophistication of the digital cameras I would later come to own—the number of shots that could be taken with Instamatic film cartridges was capped at thirty-six, and the cartridges themselves had to be taken somewhere to be developed. A process that took several days before one-hour photo labs came into being.

Regardless of our individual intonations when speaking our native language, when it came to the ones spoken in Europe, Ellen and I were either completely ignorant of them or on an equal non-fluent footing. We'd both taken French and German in school, with me having a bit more of a background in French than she did, as English schools began instruction at a younger age. German, we'd only studied for a semester, with each of us attaining about the same level of incompetence. Knowing ourselves to be incapable of carrying on any foreign-language conversation that went much beyond the weather, pens belonging to aunts, and, maybe, simple directions, we felt the purchase of a multi-language phrase book was an absolute must, and bought one without knowing that the 'useful phrases' it contained were seldom going to be useful.

We bought other things too. Such as a money converter—an infinitely more worthwhile investment than the phrase book—and items like collapsible cups, mini first aid kits, and two large, fabric-covered, metal canteens. The lighter, compact, and, it must be said, less environmentally friendly, plastic water bottles of the future were not around at that time, and those metal water holders gave their contents a metallic taste. They were also heavy and cumbersome when full and even when not full were still somewhat cumbersome. Although I dare say they could have served admirably as weapons, should we have happened to required them.

Our packsacks were purchased by our parents, who vetoed all the nice, stylish, nylon ones with external aluminium frames that were becoming increasingly popular, and went for two identical, old-fashioned, but what they believed to be sturdier and more durable canvas and leather models. Sturdy they were—and had to be since they were destined to dragged around railway stations, thrown onto trains, thrown off of trains, wedged in doors, and banged up and down stairs with monotonous regularity—but comfortable they were not. Besides being fairly heavy all by themselves, they didn't ride as high as the framed ones, or have hip belts to distribute some of the weight from our shoulders, the straps for which were not even padded and cut into our flesh. But of this we were blissfully unaware until later.

* * *

In the course of planning our trip we often ran into things our parents, atlases, encyclopaedias, maps, and travel brochures couldn't fully explain. To obtain answers, we spent a lot of time visiting the travel agency through which we'd booked our flight. So much so, I'm sure the poor man who'd drawn us as clients cringed every time we came through the door.

Gap years were not as common then as now, so our time-frame for fitting in everything we wanted to do before moving on to higher education was limited. And because it *was* limited, we wanted to know how long it would take us to travel from one city to another, with an aim to cutting down on travel time as much as possible by taking night trains over the longest distances. Here our travel agent was most helpful, his calculations only proving wrong on one occasion, and that was due to some trouble on the line that turned a nine-hour train trip into a twelve-hour one.

Most of the land journeys we took were made by train, our use of this form of transportation made possible by the Brit-Rail and Eurail passes our parents insisted on us having because they didn't want us hitch-hiking. In 1971 these passes were $55 Canadian for twenty-one days of second-class travel in Great Britain and $180 for two months of first-class travel in Europe—the only transportation costs we didn't pay for ourselves out of what was then our life savings. But the passes were greatly appreciated, and we made good use of them, even though our passports show little evidence of that. Much to our disappointment, they were only stamped in the U.S.A., England, Holland, and Spain.

Our families' concerns went beyond hitchhiking. We may have been looking forward to the trip, but I doubt our parents were. Quite frankly, I don't think either my mother and father, or Ellen's widowed mother, considered us capable of dealing with a totally different way of life all on our own for close to three months. We were, after all, still underage, and had absolutely no experience of life outside the nest— especially thousands of miles out of it. We, of course, cavalierly waved their objections away with the typical adolescent attitude that it was time they realized their 'babies' had grown up and were perfectly capable of standing on their own two feet. Looking back, however, I think it might have been better if we'd been a little older, as we responded to obstacles in typical adolescent fashion—we got mad and blamed everyone and everything but ourselves. We also didn't do some of the things we might have tried if we'd been old enough to dare venturing into new experiences. Except for kids travelling in chaperoned school groups, and a couple of others, most of the young people we met in Europe were three or more years older than we were, and even some of them expressed concerns about our embarking on a European fling so young. After some of the hair-raising stories we heard from them, and later, at home, from people who'd come back from similar trips, we still marvel that nothing that awful happened to us.

    I'm sure our parents would have been happier if our first venture towards independence had been carried out a little closer to home but, in a way, it was better, as we couldn't yield to the temptation of running home to them with every little problem. We had to make a go of it on our own because (a) we had no choice, and (b) we had our self-respect to consider. Mostly reason (a) however.

Chapter Three
And, We're Off!

According to DNA testing, both Ellen and I are, except for a small percentage of French, German, and an even smaller percentage of 'other', pretty much solidly British, Scottish, and Irish, making the British Isles our ancestral homeland. Even so, I considered England more my homeland than hers because *I'd* actually lived there. I also personally knew most of the relatives I was going to be visiting, whereas she'd never met any of hers. Having been informed of our arrival time, two of mine (my mother's twin sister and her husband) were going to be waiting for us when the aeroplane delivered us to Stansted Airport.

They, and several other family members, lived practically next door to Heathrow Airport, but our charter flight went into Stansted Airport over an hour's drive away. The charter flight was with Transavia Holland, a low-cost subsidiary of KLM, and the chartered aircraft a Boeing 707 called the *Princess Irene*—in honour of Princess Irene of the Netherlands rather than passenger Irene Duke of England/Canada. As was common practice then, it had been booked by some kind of organization, in this instance, a sports-minded one called the North American Cycle and Athletic Association. Being completely inept at any sport you care to name, Ellen and I didn't belong to it, but it's unlikely many (if any) of our fellow travellers did either.

The flight was out of Seattle in the United States, and to get to it we first had to get to Vancouver, almost two hundred and fifty miles away. Nowadays, the Okanagan Connector allows buses to transport people from Kelowna to Vancouver in just four or five hours, but the old route—the only one available in 1971—took considerably longer and led us to choose to take the Greyhound® night bus. Ellen went ahead of me and stopped off in Langley to visit relatives before catching the bus again a few days later, when I was aboard. But not all of Greyhound's night buses stopped in Langley, and the first one I was on *didn't* stop there, as I discovered when, prompted by premonition, I asked the driver about this during a stop in Penticton. He told me I'd have to change buses when we came into Hope around five o'clock in the morning.

    I've never been a good sleeper (not *ever*, as my parents knew all too well) so I was awake when we got to Hope. I got off the bus and stood outside the Hope depot waiting for my next bus to arrive. Whilst there, I saw the teacher who'd taught Ellen and me his native tongue (German) back in high school. A young teacher who'd livened up instruction by having us sing Bavarian drinking songs and telling us the most useful phrase we'd ever learn was: "*Wo ist die badezimmer?*" He was headed for Mexico, via Vancouver, and at that hour of the morning, mutual recognition took a moment or two, but we exchanged greetings before he got on the bus I'd just got off.

    I changed buses too, and tried to ignore the new driver's cheerful speculation that Ellen wouldn't be able to join me on it as planned because stopover passengers were generally required to switch over to another line. She did get on at Langley, however, and we got into Vancouver just after seven o'clock. In keeping with its nickname of Raincouver, rain was falling hard.

The land on which Vancouver now sits is the traditional territory of the xʷməθkʷəy̓əm (Musqueam), Sḵwx̱wú7mesh (Squamish) and səlilw̓ətaʔɬ (Tsleil-Waututh) peoples, who doubtless had a different name for their portage route between Burrard Inlet and False Creek. Once Europeans moved into the neighbourhood, the newcomers followed their usual practice of coming up with names that held relevance for *them*. There is ongoing debate amongst scholars as to whether or not Vikings ever made it to what is now the West Coast of Canada, but Spanish explorers definitely fetched up there in 1774 and by the April of 1794, English explorer George Vancouver was doing survey work in the area. Work so appreciated by those who were to become the powers that be that they would later name both an island and a mainland city after him. The city started out as Gastown in acknowledgement of a talkative local tavern-keeper known as Gassy Jack but went on to become a fast-growing settlement named for British diplomat, Granville George Leveson-Gower, second Earl Granville. Due to the proximity of what had, since 1849, been called Vancouver Island, people coming into the area knew more about George the explorer than George the diplomat, so in 1886 the name was changed yet again, with Granville being retained for the main street for old times' sake, and later used for a bridge, shopping district, and Sky Train station as well.

Coming into Vancouver's bus depot, we'd seen several taxi cabs at a stand just outside it and, eager to get one out to the airport bus terminal, we gathered up our luggage as best we could. The chartered buses going to Seattle Airport weren't scheduled to leave until eleven o'clock, but we thought it would be best to go straight to our departure point whilst cabs were available and we could be sure of getting there on time.

Heading for the cab stand at a rapid pace, we discovered that the packs we had, up until then, always had help with, were heavy and extremely difficult to run with. (We had yet to learn how much running with them we were going to be doing. Or how many of the things we'd taken with us weren't nearly as necessary as we thought they were. In addition to clothes, most of which *were* necessary, we had a lot of items that could, and should, have been omitted from our supply of 'essentials'.)

We also discovered that the cab stand wasn't where we thought it was. That was because we'd somehow got turned around and gone in the wrong direction, something we'd find ourselves doing quite often in the weeks to come. But we eventually located it, and got to the airport bus terminal around eight o'clock.

We had breakfast at a café on the next street, then returned to the terminal and watched it fill up with other people headed for Seattle. A great many were young people travelling in twos or threes, who, like ourselves, planned to go on to Europe from England. At least, that is what we deduced from the number of Canadian flags prominently displayed on everything they had, an indication that they'd received the same advice about making their national identity clear.

Our official itinerary from the travel agency stated that the buses to Seattle would leave at *exactly* eleven o'clock which wasn't quite accurate as eleven o'clock came and went with no sign of them. When they finally arrived, Ellen and I boarded the last one, which got moving some twenty minutes later.

In Seattle, we and our fellow passengers got off the bus and made our way to where luggage was being weighed. The scales showed Ellen and I each had close to thirty pounds in our packs. That was well within the checked luggage limit though, so we relinquished them to the tender mercies of the luggage handlers and tried to find our check-in point, a search that took us sundry places before we were finally directed to it by an airport official.

Upon checking in, we were told our departure had been delayed for half an hour due to airport congestion. But the airport had shops, among them bookshops, and we each added the latest *Star Trek* book to the weight we were carrying, little knowing that the unrestrained acquisition of books was just beginning.

When our boarding call came, people with the highest numbered seats got to go on first. Ellen and I had low numbers and, with neither of us able to claim the travellers-with-small-child(ren) pre-boarding privilege that would be mine in later years, we were among the last to board.

Our flight—a night flight—took off just after five o'clock. Ellen had never flown at all before, even domestically, and with one exception, all my Atlantic crossings had been on ocean liners. That exception was when my family made our last move between England and Canada and a dock strike compelled us to fly instead of going by ship as we usually did. Up until the very day of travel, my brother Peter—the younger of my two brothers—and I had been excited at the prospect of this new experience, but on the appointed morning suddenly became somewhat apprehensive about this new experience. My mother, who was no heroine when it came to flying, had at least travelled by air twice before, and claimed she'd had a much better time doing so by herself, when she'd only had to deal with her own trepidations.

I'd also experienced airsickness on that flight, and since Ellen didn't know how she'd react to being on an aeroplane, we'd taken the precaution of swallowing Gravol® tablets before take-off, and so were okay in that regard. But not in others. In 1971, very few airlines provided non-smoking sections, let alone non-smoking flights, and Transavia Holland was not one of them. Much to the disgust of our militantly anti-smoking selves—me because I'm allergic to smoke, Ellen because she plain doesn't like it—we were in the vicinity of more than one nicotine addict, one of whom smoked cigars. But there wasn't much we could do other than endure it.

I have food allergies, too, and because the evening in-flight meal was mostly comprised of items I had to avoid, I did not partake of it. Neither did Ellen, who was concerned that the tablet she'd taken would not keep her from feeling queasy if she ate something.

After finishing the books we'd bought, we tried to settle down for the night. But sleep pretty much eluded us, and the lack of it did not put us in peak mental condition for filling out the landing cards a stewardess handed round after breakfast the next day.

A couple of hours later, we began our descent into Stansted Airport. Ellen offered up several comments as to what the landing process was doing to her stomach but I was too concerned with what it was doing to my ears to worry about stomachs, hers or mine. A painful downside to air travel I've yet to find an effective remedy for.

Chapter Four
Home To The Homeland

Despite the shambolic responses on our landing cards, we went through Customs without any difficulty. After having our passports checked, we simply collected our luggage, walked through the door marked 'Nothing To Declare', and went out to scan the crowd waiting for incoming passengers. Almost immediately, I spotted my aunt and uncle, who were right up front. My aunt said they'd asked an official to tell the two young girls with Canadian rucksacks that Auntie Betty and Uncle Bill were waiting for them, a message we'd not received. As stated before, there were a lot of young people on the flight with Canadian flags on their coats and luggage, so this information had probably been conveyed to two girls who were still making mental lists of both sides of their respective families and wondering where along their genetic lines they could lay claim to an Auntie Betty and Uncle Bill.

As soon as we were clear of the airport, the two-storey brick houses and occasional thatched-roof cottage began to take on a familiar shape to me, and a fascinating one to Ellen. Even that much represented history to her, but of course, Britain's history goes much, much, further back than that. Anthropologists believe humans made their first appearance there about five hundred thousand years ago. These eventually formed themselves into various tribes and went about their various tribal ways until the Romans invaded in 43 AD. Julius Cæsar did make a try for it in 55-54 BC, but the locals didn't take to the idea and pushed that first wave out. After 43 AD—and, from here on in, any date not followed by BC should be taken as being AD—the Romans held sway until around 410, at which point most of them withdrew from Britannia and Europe's Angles, Saxons, and Jutes moved in. In time, the Angles and Saxons became as one and, except for some trouble with Vikings, reigned supreme until the Norman Conquest of 1066. Aside from Germany's temporary World War II seizure of the Channel Islands from June, 1940 to May, 1945, no subsequent invasion of Great Britain ever proved successful. Well, there was a little incursion by French troops in 1797, but it only lasted two days and didn't really amount to anything.

Not long after leaving the airport, Ellen and I realized we'd left without sending our parents the requested (read: mandatory) telegrams regarding our safe arrival. We'd also forgotten to change any money. My aunt said we could do both in Rickmansworth after we found a place to have lunch. Located at the edge of Greater London, Rickmansworth is the present-day blend of what was once 'Ryckmer', the personal name of a local Saxon bigwig, and 'worth', which meant some kind of homestead. Before that, the place appeared in the Domesday Book as Prichemaresworde, the type of tongue-tripping mouthful common to Saxons. Regardless of how much they resented the Norman Conquest—and they resented it a lot—their descendants did at least get some decent names out of it. And not just for places. Some Saxon-era personal appellations, such as Ashley and Kendra, and Alfred and Edward, proved acceptable enough to Norman ears to last down through the centuries and remain popular even unto today, but most failed to catch on with the Normans, and even Saxons eventually stopped bestowing things like Hrothwaru or Scowyrhta on innocent infants.

In Rickmansworth, we stopped at a quaint little eatery that was probably once a tavern, but getting there took a while. Mostly because we kept getting lost, a not unusual occurrence for road travellers in England, and something my father did almost everywhere we went. Not that Ellen and I minded. Jet lag was taking hold and all we really wanted was, as Uncle Bill put it, "a good long kip". But, as is common with jet lag, we'd got our second wind by the time we arrived in Iver, a village that's been around since before the Conquest and takes *its* name from either the Anglo-Saxon word 'Evreham', meaning 'place by the brow of the hill', or from Sir Roger d'Ivry, a friend of—in feudal times—the area's sole owner, Robert D' Oyly. I personally favour the latter. This Robert came over with William the Conqueror and, after reaping much reward from helping him defeat King Harold II's forces at the Battle of Hastings, became such a powerful nobleman it was said that "none durst oppose him". So, if he wanted it named for his friend, I'm sure it would have been. Nor was he the place's only intimidating inhabitant. Six centuries on, England's repressor of all things enjoyable, Oliver Cromwell (1599-1658), had a farm in Iver, which must have had a bit of a dampening effect on the neighbourhood.

Auntie Betty, Uncle Bill, and their son Frank resided with my widowed birth grandmother (Nan) in the Iver hamlet of Thorney, and my mother's oldest sister, Lucy, and her husband Arthur were just up the road.

Several of my relatives lived in towns and villages within Greater London. Once we'd visited the Iver-based ones we went to nearby Sipson to have supper with my mother's sister, Dorothy, the person with whom we were staying. After supper, Auntie Dorothy's son Michael, his wife Lesley and their two small children came by, and Ellen put a telephone call through to one of her English cousins in Chelmsford to find out what arrangements should be made for the next day, when she and I were to separate and spend time with our respective kinfolk. Being once again under the influence of jet lag, she hung up with no real certainty of what was what, but did know she had to find out which train would get her to Paddington Station in London by eleven o'clock the next morning, so Cousin Frank drove us down to West Drayton station to check out train times to Paddington.

We then went to visit my mother's sister Hilda in Uxbridge, another place with two possible name origins: one associated with the seventh-century Wixan tribe, the other with an ancient bridge across the River Colne. Ellen used Auntie Hilda's telephone to ring her cousins back to complete arrangements and with those settled, we went out sightseeing in Windsor with Frank and Auntie Betty. As it was evening, the streets were, not surprisingly, fairly quiet and, also not surprisingly, completely free of the pigs that centuries earlier had been allowed to wander freely around town gobbling up offal and other rubbish; a practical feeding and street cleaning system Windsor's porcine-prejudiced authorities put a stop to in 1635.

Windsor Castle wasn't open, so we had to be content with walking around the outside of it. We did see the Changing of the Guard though. The first time I'd attended that ceremony—which also takes place at Buckingham Palace in London—was as a very small child. According to Auntie Betty, neither I nor Frank, who's the same age as me, had been overly interested, and spent most of our time squabbling about who was going to ride in the pushchair. I didn't remember that, but did, and do, recall being delighted by the kilted soldier doll and the *Teddy Bears' Picnic* book that Uncle Bill bought me in Windsor, and Peter being equally pleased with the car-carrier Dinky toy® purchased for him, most probably in Daniel's, the well-known department store down Peascod Street.

After the Guard had changed, a woman took up the popular tourist pastime of trying to get one to speak to her. Like thousands before her, she failed to get a response. Eventually the guard started walking up and down, either as part of his regular duties or simply to get away from her.

After that we strolled down the hill and over the bridge to take a look at Eton College, with Ellen also looking into the window of every antique shop she saw. By the time we got to the college, jet lag had returned, and I was at that point of jet lag induced exhaustion in which I didn't really care very much about anything and would have gone on walking to the ends of the Earth. Fortunately, we went back to Auntie Dorothy's with me still possessed of enough sense to go to bed.

* * *

Weary though I was, I still woke up about one in the morning, and again at half past eight, when Auntie Dorothy roused Ellen so she could catch the bus to the train station—with instructions to meet me in Trafalgar Square at half past three the next day.

Because Auntie Dorothy ran a shop and had to go to work, Lesley came by later to take me to Nan's for lunch. After lunch, Auntie Betty and I caught a bus to Uxbridge and went to see Auntie Hilda again, where I learned her kids still had the same tortoises they'd had when we were all much younger. They also still had the two goldfish I'd bequeathed them when I left England five years earlier, which meant the hardy little creatures had survived what must have been a stressful fifty-mile car journey home with their attentive new owners. The year before that, one had survived an even more stressful sixty-mile coach journey from London to Wantage after I won it in a hoopla at a fairground that I and several Sunday School classmates went to after ducking out on a—to unappreciative pre-adolescents—somewhat boring affair called the MYD 21 Celebration Party at Alexandra Palace that our teacher had taken us to. (And if you're wondering how I can possibly remember the name and location of this function, I come from a long line of hoarders and still have the ticket.) The plastic bag this fish was in sprung a leak and, having smuggled it onto the coach to avoid awkward questions as to our earlier whereabouts, my friends and I had to transfer it to a paper cup that, with all the coach's twists and turns, had considerably less water in it by the time I got home than it had upon starting out. Obviously toughened by these harrowing experiences, neither it nor the other one had fulfilled Auntie Hilda's expectations of them expiring from her offspring's neglect once the novelty wore off. On the contrary, they appeared to be in the peak of health. The same could not be said of my cousin Christine, who was off school with a throat infection, so Auntie Betty and I didn't stay long.

From there we went into Uxbridge to do some shopping. My mother had requested a jar of a particular face cream she'd used when we lived in England, and although I couldn't find that, there were still one or two things I required for my trip, and getting them gave me my first experience working with Britain's recently implemented decimal money instead of the pounds, shillings, and pence system I'd grown up with. A system that dated back centuries and one I rather resented the loss of after having gone to all the trouble of learning how to do sums in it at school. Nor did 50p (fifty pence) have the same solid ring to it as 10/ (ten shillings) had had. Or seem to go as far.

In the evening, Uncle Bill, Auntie Betty, and Nan took me out to Runnymede, a water meadow along the River Thames, and the place England's King John signed the Magna Carta on the fifteenth of June, 1215. Latin for 'Great Charter', the Magna Carta was to become the base document for many later ones designed to ensure rights and freedom for all, but, much like the covid 'freedom' protestors of our own era, the twenty-five barons who forced King John to affix his name and seal to the original were really only interested in *their* rights and freedoms, and it took a while—as in, centuries—for the benefits to trickle down to 'all'. And there is a strong possibility the lead baron, Robert Fitzwalter, and his son-in-law, Geoffrey de Mandeville, had another reason for wanting to curb the power of Big Bad John, who'd had Fitzwalter's comely young daughter, Fair Maud, imprisoned in the Tower of London simply because he 'wanted' her, and, when spurned, had her poisoned. Medieval fathers and husbands tended to take that sort of thing rather badly because, paternal and marital affection aside, it impinged upon their *honour*.

The Magna Carta has always meant more to Americans than to UK inhabitants and it was the American Bar Association that, in 1957, erected a memorial to its signing. But that memorial is not the only commemorative structure on that site. In 1953, Queen Elizabeth II unveiled a memorial to Air Force servicemen lost in World War II (one of them Auntie Dorothy's husband, Danny), and in 1965 unveiled a memorial to U.S. President John F. Kennedy that was built on land donated to the U.S.A. for that purpose. Since it was raining, Auntie Betty and Nan stayed in the car, but Uncle Bill and I tramped over the fields to view all the above memorials, with me counting the steps up to JFK's to see if there really were fifty of them as claimed. (There were.)

On the way home we got some real English chips from a real English Fish 'N Chip shop, complete with scrumps—the batter 'extra' I'd been deprived of in Canada, even though our local chippy was very good. I had long missed those, and after devouring this mini feast, returned to Auntie Dorothy's and went to bed.

I woke up at four in the morning and, having nothing better to do, indulged in a bit of homesickness until I fell asleep again and, surprisingly, did not reawaken until half past ten, when the telephone rang. And, with Auntie Dorothy at work, rang, and rang. As telephones didn't sound like that in Canada, and we hadn't had one when we lived in England, it took me a while to figure out what it was. When I did answer, it was a wrong number. I then went back to bed and slept until noon, an achievement I could only attribute to jet lag.

Chapter Five
First Stop—London

    I spent some of the next morning with Auntie Lucy, her daughter Frances (known to the family as 'Bun'), and Bun's little daughter. After lunch, Auntie Betty and I headed for Paddington Station in London to meet Uncle Bill, who worked there, and go on to Trafalgar Square via the London Underground. As a tiny tot I'd neither liked, nor disliked, riding 'the Tube' during my first visit to London, but Peter (then nine) wouldn't go back on it for love or money, and our mother tried both. She always assumed it was because he didn't like being on a noisy vehicle hurtling through the bowels of the Earth, but in recent years he told me it was the *escalators* he objected to, a method of people-moving that was non-existent in our little town. I didn't find them in any way alarming, but I was still small enough to be picked up and Mum was, in all probability, holding *me* during our ascents and descents.

    We found a bench and waited for Ellen to arrive. When she did, I handed Auntie Betty my camera so she could take a picture of us sitting on one of the four twenty-foot long, twenty-two-foot high, bronze lions standing guard at the base of Nelson's Column, the bronze having been supplied by melted-down cannons from ships defeated at the Battle of Trafalgar. Differing from each other in only small ways, these majestic beasts were, over a lengthy period of time (1858 to 1867) sculpted by the acclaimed animal artist, Sir Edwin Lanseer, who got the commission after stone ones by another animal artist, Thomas Milnes, were deemed unsuitable. Then, as now, these impressive leonine symbols of England—which legend says will awaken if Big Ben ever chimes thirteen—practically invited people to climb up and have their pictures taken atop them. And many people have, but not us. In spite of me pulling and Auntie Betty pushing, Ellen failed to reach a lion, so the photo only shows me seated between the paws of one and Ellen standing below me, as far up on its plinth as she could manage. Today I doubt either of us would be able to achieve even that.

Later, Ellen and I headed for the Holland House youth hostel, with everyone in the same Underground carriage certain to have been harbouring uncharitable thoughts about us and our big, unwieldy, packs.

We weren't quite sure where the hostel was when we got off at Holland Park station. Accompanied by two other hostel seekers, we wandered from pillar to post for some time before we found it and joined the many young travellers there within. So many that the place was fully booked, thus justifying our having had the forethought to make reservations.

One of the Kensington area's first fancy residences, Holland House started out with the name Cope Castle, even though it wasn't really a castle, but rather an early seventeenth-century private home built for King James I's Chancellor, Sir Walter Cope, The Parliamentarian forces that occupied it during the English Civil War probably didn't go in for a lot of revelry, but in the nineteenth century, members of the Whig party frequently met there, and it was quite the social centre. In the following century the house took such damage from World War II incendiary bombs that only the south front and east wing were salvageable, but salvaged they were, and served as a youth hostel from 1958 to 2014.

After checking in and surrendering our youth hostel membership cards to a warden—common practice in most hostels—we went to the room indicated on the piece of paper we'd been handed and divested ourselves of our packs. Looking around, Ellen noticed a plug-in with a sign that said, 'For Shavers Only', and we shortly afterwards heard distinctly male voices coming from the room across the hall.

"You don't suppose...?" I ventured. "We can't have been put in the boys' section, can we?"

"I don't think so. We followed directions in the only obvious way there was."

"Maybe it's mixed accommodations on this floor."

"Mixed dormitories?" Ellen replied in horror.

"No, just male and female ones on the same floor."

And that was indeed how it was. There weren't any locks on the doors either, so we had to trust that our fellow travellers would behave like gentlemen and stay on their own turf.

As night fell, we learned the light in our room wasn't working. The warden we reported this to said that he'd get it fixed, so we went back to the room and waited. And waited, and waited, until Ellen felt obliged to go downstairs and reissue the repair request. This time he came and put things to rights.

Once he'd gone, we got ready for bed and secured our valuables for the night, something almost every big city hostel we stayed at advised people to do, in order to avoid falling victim to thievery. Ellen was such a heavy sleeper, even the most butterfingered thief would have had no trouble making off with her money, passport, travel passes, and traveller's cheques, plus her pillow, blanket, and maybe her as well. And even though I was a light sleeper, I didn't believe in taking chances. We placed all our money and documents in our gadget bags and put the gadget bags between our feet at the bottom of our sheet sleeping bags. The latter had been made by our mothers and were, unquestionably, the heaviest and bulkiest items we carried, but all hostels required them, and hiring them at each one would have been prohibitively expensive. I think they are now usually referred to as sleep sheets or sleep sacks and are probably much lighter and more compact than ours were.

Before long, the other inhabitants of our five-bed dormitory room came in and we all settled down to sleep. Or tried to. A noisy group of uncouth youths in the next room gave Morpheus tough competition, and yelling at them and banging on the wall did no good whatsoever. Around one o'clock in the morning a delegation of four of us went out to complain in person, our other roommate having somehow managed to achieve a sleep state and maintain it through both the loudmouths and our comments. Unfortunately, access to the disturbers-of-the-peace's room could not be gained from our part of the hostel so we all went back to bed and fumed until they eventually shut up.

* * *

We rose reasonably early and went out on the town. Having been to London several times, I wasn't as excited about it as Ellen, and she shouldn't have been either, because this was not, I repeat, *not*, our day.

It began harmlessly enough with the duty we'd been assigned. Regulations set down in our YHA (Youth Hostel Association) handbook stated that each YHA member staying at a hostel was required to carry out housekeeping duties as directed by a warden. These duties, when fulfilled, had to meet the warden's expectations or be subject to a do-over. Some wardens had high expectations, but most didn't, often assigning the same task to a number of young guests to increase the chances of getting it accomplished. This requirement-of-stay tended to be enforced more in UK hostels than those on the Continent, and I think even the UK ones stopped allocating them a few years later.

Our duty at Holland House was to sweep out the common room. As soon as we finished, we set out for Trafalgar Square to visit the Canadian embassy, Canada House. Embassies and hostels were the places we'd arranged to have people write to us when we were 'on the road', and we wanted to see if there were any letters for us.

There weren't, so we made our next stop a travel agency to see about booking ferry passage to Ireland and the Continent. And it was there that our day really began. We'd planned to go from Fishguard (Wales) to Rosslare (Ireland) on the eighth of July. This was fine. We'd also planned to go from Dublin (Ireland) to Heysham (England) on the twelfth of July. This was not fine. The twelfth was a Monday, and the Irish ferries did not run on Mondays. Aware that, on the twelfth, we had to be out of the Dublin hostel and into a hostel awaiting us across the sea in Arnside, all we could do was book passage for the thirteenth (they did run Tuesdays) and keep our fingers crossed that Dublin would keep us and Arnside would forget us. After changing some traveller's cheques for the necessary funds, we got our Irish ferry tickets and went upstairs to get tickets for a ferry over to the Continent and a hovercraft back. After a considerable—and, as it turned out, unnecessary—wait we were told to go to the British Rail office, which handled such things straight from ports.

Before arriving at the British Rail office, we were approached by two men with cameras who, alerted by the flags on our gadget bags, seemed delighted that we were Canadians and wanted to take our pictures with nearby Piccadilly Circus in the background. (The fact that Piccadilly Circus was not a real circus had come as somewhat of a disappointment to me and my primary school classmates when our teacher took us to London to be on two segments of *Five O'clock Club*, a children's television programme to which most of us were devoted. And yes, I still have that ticket, too.) At first, Ellen and I both thought the men were fellow Canadians who just wanted a picture. Even when they asked for our names and addresses, we figured they wanted them for, well, souvenirs or something. They'd taken us both to one side by this time, and when the one I was with started talking about "just a note—a note for the four", I twigged that he was a street photographer. I hastily declined, saying I was a poor, penniless, youth on a tight budget and escaped. But I knew what a 'note' was. Ellen didn't. She got taken for £4, then worth close to $14 Canadian. Appalled at having been talked into spending so large an amount in such a fashion, she wailed that the guy had even *sounded* Canadian. The photos did, however, arrive at her home not long after our return.

At the continental ferry ticket office, we ran into more difficulties. The night boat we wanted to take to Holland—and because of hostel reservations, *had* to take—was booked solid as regards second class passage. The best they could offer us was the dubious privilege—at extra cost—of going first class.

That sorted, Ellen and I went and sat down to sort *ourselves* out.

"Well," Ellen said after a bit, "Now where should we go to spend our money?"

Being now short of money, we stopped at a bank to cash some (more) traveller's cheques before wending our way back to Trafalgar Square. There we bought as much lunch as we thought we could afford: one small, unripe, apple for Ellen and one small, tasteless, banana for me. We then headed for Buckingham Palace, but when we got there, discovered that tourists were not allowed inside. That they are nowadays is only due to the extensive damage

Windsor Castle sustained in a fire in 1992. Repairs had to be funded *somehow*, and throwing Buckingham Palace open to the paying public seemed as good a way as any. And proved such a popular—and lucrative—summer attraction that the practice still goes on during the ten-week period that the British monarch usually spends in Scotland each year. But being barred from that most regal dwelling came as no great surprise to us. We'd resigned ourselves to it being that kind of day.

Turning our weary footsteps through St. James Park, we went past the pond and on and on in search of a public toilet, also known as a public convenience or a WC (water closet). For some reason, all the ones we came across were closed, and when we eventually found some temporary ones, did so at the same time as a party of three women and what seemed like six dozen little girls, which made for a lengthy wait.

From there we went to Westminster Abbey. At that time, the abbey was still free to enter and at least nothing unpleasant or frustrating happened to us *there*.

We then caught a bus to Charing Cross Road to while away the rest of the day in its bookshops. Specifically, the famous Foyles one, but of course any others we happened upon as well. At some point we thought we'd missed the stop and got off before reaching the right area, leaving us to find it on foot using only bibliophile instincts and the directions of passers-by. A London bobby told us Charing Cross Road was "Just up there on your right. You can't miss it." He was wrong. But someone else we asked simply took us there, which was very nice of him, as it was back in the direction he'd come from.

Upon reaching Foyles bookshop, we were almost too weary to go in, but only *almost*. The Foyle family's book business got its start in 1903, when teenaged brothers, William and Gilbert Foyle, failed their civil service exams and, apparently unwilling to take another crack at them, sold their textbooks from their parents' house. Encouraged by the bounty reaped, they opened an actual bookshop in Cecil Court, near Leicester Square, in 1904, and in 1906 moved to a Charing Cross location from which they proceeded to expand exponentially. A rather eccentric person, William Foyle did not have books arranged alphabetically or even by category, with many of them sitting in stacks on the floor as well as on shelves, a system his daughter Christina—an even more eccentric person who liked to be addressed as 'Miss Foyle' and fired employees at whim—kept to when she took over the business in 1963. In consequence, looking for a book in Foyles really did mean *looking* for a book. We did find some we wanted, and paying for them was a different kind of shopping experience too, as it involved getting an invoice from someone, taking it to someone else to fork over the money, and then going back to pick up the books themselves.

By the time we headed for the Underground, it was five o'clock. Rush Hour. The least favourable time to travel on London's underground railway, or that of any large city.

"I hate this," Ellen muttered as we stood squashed amidst a crowd in one of the carriages.

"Who doesn't?" commented a man who was standing nearby and probably used the Tube every day.

Alighting at the Holland Park station, we set off in search of food to take back to the hostel, as well as an ice-lolly to assuage the thirst I'd been experiencing for several hours. A package of ham and another of chocolate biscuits made for a somewhat sparse evening meal, but it was all we felt we could afford. We consumed the ham and biscuits in the hostel's dining room, and even there, Ellen ran into difficulty. Not being possessed of a 5p piece for the drinks machine, she was forced to go to the reception desk and get change for a larger coin.

Back in the dormitory she expanded on her hatred of, not just the Underground, but basically the whole city—a far cry from how she'd expected to feel about dear old Londinium. She even declared herself ready to take the first offer of transportation home to Canada that came her way, a sentiment with which I was in complete agreement. Being out in the world on our own wasn't proving to be anything like what either of us had expected. Still, we figured the rest of our time in England's capital couldn't be any worse. It just *couldn't*.

Before going to bed, Ellen brought the day to a perfect end by falling off the platform by the washstand.

Chapter Six
Still London

The next morning the hostel did a dormitory shuffle and we were put in a larger one. On the way to it, we passed the common room. Which was not the same room we'd swept out the day before thinking *it* was the common room.

After later sweeping out the right room, we got on the Underground and headed for Madame Tussauds Waxworks Museum. When I mentally converted the 60p entrance fee into old money, it came out as 12/, which I thought a bit steep, but not steep enough to keep me from paying it as I'd been deprived of visiting the place as a child. (There was an extremely long queue the day my family visited, and my father wasn't willing to stand in it.) Since neither monetary system meant anything to Ellen, she didn't care.

The woman for whom the museum is named was originally known as Marie Grosholtz. Born in Strasbourg, France in 1761, she moved to Bern, Switzerland at a young age so her widowed mother could become housekeeper to Philippe Curtius, a Swiss physician and talented waxwork sculptor whose first figures were made for medical students who wanted to study human bodies without stealing cadavers from local cemeteries—a practice the authorities, and society in general, frowned upon. By 1765, Philippe Curtius had moved himself and the Groshotlzes to Paris and branched out into waxwork replicas of the rich and famous, a skill he began to pass on to Marie once she reached her teens. She took to it quite readily, and in 1777 completed the first of her own creations, a waxwork model of the writer-philosopher, Voltaire.

A mere twelve years later, the French Revolution kicked into high gear, and the rich and famous started to become thin on the ground; either because they'd fled the country or because they'd lost their heads to the guillotine. Even so, this decline in the upper-class population did not lead to a decline in demand for Pierre and Marie's services. To encourage widespread approval of the latter reason for the shortage of aristocrats, the revolutionaries ordered wax duplicates of their aristocratic noggins so they could be taken to other parts of the country and waved about for propaganda purposes. (Look! Look! We got another one! *Vive la révolution!*)

The period of French history known as 'The Terror' ended in 1794, the same year Marie's mentor died. He left the business to Marie, and a very profitable business it was, too. But times were still a bit precarious, especially for a now-wealthy woman with no male protector, so she married an engineer named François Tussaud. Unfortunately for her, François did not turn out to be much of a protector when it came to her money and almost brought her to financial ruin. Refusing to allow this to dishearten her, she kept working hard, and, in 1802, was invited to London to exhibit her figures. There she managed to recoup her fortune and later opened a permanent exhibition hall on Baker Street, the precursor to the one Ellen and I visited on nearby Marylebone Road. The second one got hit by a bomb in World War II, destroying a lot of the waxwork figures within, but not, ironically, Adolf Hitler's.

With the exception of the gruesome figures in the Chamber of Horrors, we found the waxworks very much to our liking, and also enjoyed the astronomy show in the planetarium that was added to the museum in 1958.

From there we caught a bus to the London Zoo, another London attraction I hadn't been to before, although I'm not sure why as I'd been to Chessington Zoo with my father and to Whipsnade Zoo with both my parents. But to the London Zoo, no. Even though it was the one I remembered being in the news the most when we lived in England. One such report centred on a golden eagle named Goldie that escaped from durance vile and led keepers, firefighters, and the London constabulary a merry chase for close to a fortnight. The public was delighted, but the unfortunate Muscovy duck he decided to dine on wasn't as thrilled. Neither were the owners of the small dogs he *tried* to dine on when they took them for walkies in Regent's Park. In this he was less successful, as the owners tended to be rather protective, and one, in true British fashion, beat him off with her handbag and had a brolly for back-up. Another occasion on which the zoo was considered newsworthy was when it tried, but failed, to get its female Giant Panda, Chi-Chi, to mate with the Moscow's Zoo's male, An-An. (He was interested, she wasn't.) Ellen and I went to visit both those famous zoo residents, but Chi-Chi was napping, and neither Goldie nor his mate Regina deigned to come out of their shelter. Still, there were other critters to admire, as well as interesting structures like Britain's first walk-through aviary. Designed by Antony Armstrong-Jones (the first Earl of Snowden), Cedric Price, and Frank Newby in 1960-61 and opened to the public in 1965, the Snowden Aviary housed a number of less adventuresome birds than Goldie. A refurbished version of it now houses monkeys.

In the nocturnal animals' enclave, I almost stepped on a small child I hadn't noticed in the dark. My piercing scream was due to the fact that Ellen said, "Look out down there," and I thought an animal had escaped and was right beside me. Illogical reasoning. If there had been an escaped animal right beside me, Ellen would not have been.

On the bus we took back to Baker Street, the conductor took so long to come to us, we thought he'd forgotten to, but he hadn't. London bus conductors have exceeding good memories and are capable of remembering exactly where their passengers get on, and where they want to get off. At Baker Street we again managed to hit rush hour on the Underground, but it was Saturday, so it wasn't too bad. Except that we got on at the wrong end of the route and had to go almost all the way round the line before reaching Notting Hill Gate, where we had to change for Holland Park. That was a long, long ride, but the shops were still open when we arrived at something after six and we were able to buy a small amount of provender to eat back at the hostel. After which I rang Auntie Dorothy to find out if it would be all right for us to drop some of our things off at her house on our way to our next stop. Even at this early stage we were willing to rid ourselves of some of the contents of our packs that we figured we could do quite well without.

We turned in early, about ten o'clock., but like the first night, this one did not prove to be too great a night for sleeping. For one thing, my throat was bothering me, and for another, someone in the new dormitory was snoring.

* * *

My throat was still sore when morning dawned, a sign that even though Auntie Betty and I hadn't stayed around my infectious cousin for long when we were in Uxbridge, we'd stayed long enough for her germs to find me. I didn't really want to get up and, my writer's imagination being quite active even back then, I had visions of Ellen having to leave me in an isolation ward somewhere and go valiantly on with the trip.

Even so, I struggled up, got dressed, and helped Ellen sweep out the common room again before setting off for the Tower of London. I say, 'Tower', singular, because everyone does, even though there are quite a number of them. Originally, however, there was just one, the White Tower, built by William the Conqueror towards the end of the eleventh century and added to by successive monarchs who wanted to make their London stronghold even stronger.

Getting to it cost 15p each and brought home to us just how rapidly Underground fares and tickets to attractions were depleting our London budgets.

A sign outside the Tower said it didn't open until two o'clock on Sundays. It was then only eleven, but that didn't deter a nearby tour guide, who was dutifully telling her party all about the famous fortress from outside of it. Which seemed a bit pointless. I was sure they would much rather have gone in, and wondered why a tour company would bother to take its patrons to a place that was closed.

Temporarily thwarted in our own viewing plans, we took the Underground to Paddington to find out about trains to Stratford-Upon-Avon for the next day. Ellen also rang up the British Museum to see if it was open before she wasted the Underground fare later in the day, and was pleased to learn its Sunday hours were from two-thirty until six.

Returning to the Tower, we joined the queue of people waiting for admittance, spending the hour or so that this took complaining about the expense of London, an opinion heartily shared by two American girls behind us. The four of us agreed that limited-budget young travellers such as ourselves basically had to wake up each morning and decide whether to eat or sightsee that day.

When the Tower finally opened, we learned the entrance fee was 10p more than we'd been led to expect, plus another 10p for the Jewel House, so we decided to bypass the jewels. Even without them, we found much to interest us as we wandered around eavesdropping on tour groups whose guides were providing them with titbits of information about the Tower's most illustrious prisoners and the Yeoman Warders that have been its custodians since Tudor times. We also saw some of the Tower ravens that are kept there to guard against the prophecy that if they ever leave, all of England will fall.

After that we went into the White Tower to look at all the armour, shields, and other weaponry therein, as well as the Bloody Tower, which was simply known as the Garden Tower until the bloody fates of some of its inhabitants brought about a name change. The narrow, poorly lit, spiral stairs in that tower struck me as a rather awkward means of access, and must have caused prisoners a bit of worry if they had to navigate them with their hands tied behind them. One slip, and the executioner would have been saved the trouble. By our day, cautionary signs were on display.

When Ellen later went off to the British Museum, I stayed at the Tower for a bit because, although I do like the British Museum, I like the Tower more. I still go round it every time I'm in London, as there always seems to be some new aspect to explore—something else I was deprived of doing as a child when, as at Madame Tussauds, my father refused to stand in a long queue. I don't recall what we actually did do that day, but presumably something.

Before tearing myself away from the Tower, I got an ice-lolly and sat listening to a brass band that was performing there. I then took the Underground to Oxford Circus and walked to the Post Office Tower (now the BT, British Telcom Tower) from there, visiting it a scant three months before Irish radicals attempted to blow it up, and did manage to damage it extensively. In those days, London's streets were almost deserted on Sundays, and it was a bit eerie walking through them. I got a ticket for the lift and went up to the observation tower from which people could view all of London, except, of course, the bits covered by fog—or smog. A view the London Eye/Millennium Wheel now provides.

When I got back to the hostel, Ellen had not yet returned, probably because the British Museum had not yet closed and she was still immersed in its wonders. I sat around feeling unwell and alternating between feeling sorry for myself and telling myself to stop feeling sorry for myself and do something constructive, like figure out how much money I'd spent during the course of the day—money having become my (and Ellen's) primary concern.

Later, Ellen came in to report that the museum had been "absolutely wonderful" before going down to the kitchen to make some tea; the makings of an evening meal not being in that day's budget. Later on, we went down to the hostel laundry to wash some clothes and left them out to dry overnight.

Chapter Seven
Shakespeare Country

Some clothes were still damp the following morning, but since we were leaving, we had to pack them anyway. Picking up our youth hostel cards on the way out, we were pleasantly surprised to get some money back because we'd been charged as senior YHA members and were apparently mere juniors.

At Trafalgar Square. Ellen stayed with the luggage, and I raced to Canada House to collect any letters that might have come for us before we headed to Paddington to get a train to West Drayton. We both had letters, but the officious female there wouldn't give me Ellen's, even though I explained we had a train to catch and wouldn't be back in London until mid-July. Ellen had to pick it up herself and became quite agitated when it took the woman a while to locate one letter amidst hundreds.

"Don't get worked up, dear," the woman said. "I'll find it."

She did, but not in time for us to catch our train, so we had to get the next one and resign ourselves to taking a later one to Stratford.

By the time we got to Paddington, our packs were causing us considerable discomfort and we were almost willing to leave *all* our stuff at my aunt's, not just some of it. From West Drayton we took a bus to the William IV pub near Auntie Dorothy's house. Unfortunately, she was still at work and the house was locked. But Michael and Lesley lived just up the street, so we went there and had lunch before getting down to the business of lightening our load before heading for Stratford. Ruthlessly stuffing everything we didn't really require, or, by this time, want, into our flight bags for Lesley to take down to Auntie Dorothy's later on, we found their removal did provide some weight relief. And the fleece Michael padded the shoulder straps of our packsacks with made the packs not just lighter, but a bit more comfortable when we returned to London.

Back at Paddington we found our platform easily enough but didn't want to take our packs off in case we had to move in a hurry to catch the train. Instead, we tried to just rest on our ankles. Not a sensible position for people wearing packsacks. We both overbalanced and I landed on my back. Getting up unassisted was virtually impossible and I floundered about like a flipped turtle until Ellen, who'd only fallen sideways, regained her feet and rescued me.

When the train arrived, our packs were too big to go up on the racks of the non-smoking compartment we clambered into, so we put them on the table between the seats. Ellen then went to get a tin of Pepsi® and two paper cups from the buffet car, and after she got back, divided it up and handed both cups to me so she could swing her pack onto the seat beside her. A move that resulted in the pack hitting the cups and spilling the contents over me and the unfortunate gentleman in the seat beside me, which I'm sure did nothing for the three-piece suit he was wearing. With true British aplomb he said that was "quite all right" and not to worry about it.

London to Stratford was not a direct route. Before boarding a different train at Leamington Spa, I relived my childhood by buying *Dandy* and *Beano* comics, as well as some boiled sweets to soothe my throat, which was a little worse and starting to make my voice sound raspy. But even the train from Leamington Spa did not take us to Stratford. We had to change again at

Hatton, as did two German boys who, like us, were going to the Stratford youth hostel. Once in Stratford, we all searched for the hostel on the station map but couldn't find it until a guard pointed it out. He told us it was "a distance of some four miles" but said there was a bus we could take if we wanted.

We all did, but because it was already half past six, Ellen and I didn't think the bus would get us to the hostel by seven, when beds were supposed to be claimed, and tried to phone the hostel to say we *were* coming. As was sometimes the way with British pay phones, this one didn't want to co-operate, and in the end, a Canadian expat who'd come from Vancouver in 1951 made his own call and then put ours through for us. The hostel people were very nice, and said they'd expect us when they saw us. The four of us trooped down to the bus stop, getting there approximately two minutes after the last one out to the hostel had gone.

I don't know if the place really was 'a distance of some four miles', but it certainly seemed like it. We didn't all end up going there, though. A group coming into town from the hostel told us there was no room left for male hostellers, so the German boys went down a road marked 'Chalets To Let' to try their luck there.

Ellen and I trudged on towards the hostel. And on. And on. Just as we were considering throwing ourselves down into the nearest ditch for the night, two young men in a car stopped and told us we were heading in the wrong direction for the youth hostel and should turn up the road we'd just passed.

This hostel was an oak-floored Georgian mansion called Hemingford House. Sold to the YHA in 1947, it had once been a private home and later, during World War II, a place used by the Ministry of Supply for, presumably, supplies. There was a bus stop near the gate, and I told Ellen—who always took much longer to get ready each day than I did—that we were *not* going to miss the morning bus. Not even if I had to drag her to the stop half-naked, which she assured me would not be necessary. She, too, had no intention of missing it.

After checking in, we went down to the member's kitchen to have tea and biscuits. Whilst I was engaged in setting our foodstuffs out on a table in the dining area, Ellen went into the kitchen itself to boil a kettle on the gas cooker there. A cooker I'd already said I wanted nothing to do with, due to the childhood trauma of watching a girl in my housekeeping class set her hair alight by placing her head too close to the flames. Our school had both gas and electric cookers, and even though the teacher quickly came to her rescue and she wasn't hurt, I thereafter always made a beeline for an electric cooker on housekeeping day and did not seek to further my culinary knowledge upon moving to Canada, where the course was an elective rather than a standard part of the school curriculum.

Picking up what she took to be the nearest kettle, Ellen filled it with water, and after several frustrating attempts, succeeded in lighting the gas ring. She then placed the 'kettle' on the ring and stood back happily, waiting for it to boil. The only thing wrong with this was, it was a teapot, not a tea kettle. England's aluminium varieties tended to look somewhat alike—something I could have told her, had I been present. But I wasn't, and one of two English girls standing nearby grabbed the teapot off the ring before any damage occurred. She then painstakingly explained the difference between the two pieces of kitchenware to Ellen in as simple language as possible, thinking that she was either a foreigner from Europe or a Canadian francophone. Under the circumstances, Ellen thought it prudent to let her go on thinking so and put on an eager, but bewildered expression. The girl even told her how to make tea. "Fill this big pot with water, put some tea in the little pot and when the water boils..."

The two left as soon as they saw the tea safely brewed and Ellen wandered back to me to relate what had happened.

"Twit!" I said.

"Well, can I help it if they look the same?" she said. "What do they want to have aluminum teapots for anyway?"

"To form a kitchen set."

"Bah!"

After eating, we went back upstairs to read and talk to two Yorkshire girls in the bunks next to us until the whole dormitory turned in about half-past-ten.

* * *

At the bus stop the next morning, a woman told us we'd just missed one, even though I'd chivvied Ellen along relentlessly from our first waking moment. Another came by about half an hour later and, unwilling to lug our packs around Stratford all morning, we paid to leave them in the train station's Left Luggage room and went our separate ways, me, to shop, and Ellen to visit Shakespeare's birthplace, the school he attended (King Edward VI Grammar School), Ann Hathaway's cottage, and all the other places the Bard's admirers flock to. Not being one, I had no desire to join her. I loathed studying his works in school and only attended Shakespearean plays when forced to do so by teachers or, later, the parental obligation to watch my offspring perform in them.

My shopping trip—based on essentials rather than Shakespearean souvenirs and tickets to revered buildings—resulted in some soap for Ellen, more boiled sweets to soothe my worsening sore throat, and two ice-lollies for same. Sitting on a hospital wall sucking on one of the ice-lollies, I watched children in a primary school across the road emerge from the building in twos and go to collect their respective classes' morning milk, which brought back childhood memories of doing the same thing. I never personally took as much as one sip of school milk, but fetching it was a coveted privilege; a privilege that British children older than seven were about to lose. Free milk for schoolchildren started up in the 1940s, and had, to some extent, been available before, but not long after I watched the Stratford tots collect theirs, the programme was axed by Margaret Thatcher, who was then Britain's Education Secretary rather than its Prime Minister—a highly controversial move that got her dubbed 'Thatcher, the Milk Snatcher'. Not entirely fairly, since Prime Minister Edward Heath was actually the one pushing for it, but his name didn't lend itself to a catchy phrase. And Maggie did go on to do some other things that weren't exactly in the interests of the working classes, so I think a less than charitable view of her and her time in office is still warranted.

Ellen and I met back at the train station just after eleven o'clock with her bemoaning the fact that she hadn't been allowed to take pictures inside Shakespeare's birthplace and had to be content with snapping one from without.

Chapter Eight
Wandering Around Wales

Our next stop was Llandovery, in Wales. To get there, we had to go via Birmingham and other places. Birmingham had more than one station, and the one we first pulled into was not the one from which people could catch a train that would connect to a train going to Llandovery. The station master's, "left subway, third right", directions to this other station did little to enlighten us as we didn't know what he meant. After a while it occurred to us that 'subway' might mean a pedestrian subway rather than an underground train subway, but by the time we got to the right station, we'd missed our train. I was too hoarse to make inquiries about the next one, so Ellen did it, and then rang up the Bryn Poeth Uchaff (in English, 'Upper Burnt Hill') youth hostel in Llandovery to say we'd be late. After reaching Directory Inquiries, she asked to be put through to the hostel, saying the address was all in Welsh and she didn't know how to pronounce anything, but would spell out each word. She did so, with the operator occasionally interrupting to ask if she meant 'N' as in 'Nellie' and 'B' as in 'Bob'.

At one point in the conversation, Ellen required another 2p to go on with the call. Throwing open the kiosk, she waved her arms about and demanded the necessary coin, which, luckily, I had. She was almost at the end of the address when the operator said she thought she had enough to go on.

"Wait!" Ellen yelled into the receiver. "There's another word. I don't know what it says, but there's another word here."

She gave it to her, and then offered up some numbers that came after it. At this point the operator started to laugh, finding it amusing that Ellen had laboriously spelled out all those words when she'd had the telephone number all along and only had to phone another department to put through a call for which a number was already known. Ellen was not similarly amused, but did eventually get through to the warden who, after all that trouble (and 26p), said what time we showed up was of little importance as the hostel wasn't full.

We caught a train to Wolverhampton, doubtless bruising several people with our packs as we got on, and bruising them again when we got off to change to a train going to Shrewsbury. On that one we rode in a first-class compartment because we couldn't find any second-class ones, but no one said anything. At Shrewsbury we had to wait three and a half hours for the train to Llandovery, most of which we spent sitting on a bench, Ellen reading, me writing my journal, and both of us forced to listen to a man we figured was either drunk or on something rant about his haversack and tell everyone in his immediate vicinity to shut up. Ellen and I were just about to move to a more densely populated area when another man came and sat down on our bench. Feeling somewhat reassured by this, we struck up a conversation with him and kept it going until he got on a train and, much to our relief, the ranter did, too.

Our own train eventually rolled in and the trip to Llandovery was uneventful. Aside from me having attained a high enough fever to be seeing cute little pictures moving about within the pattern on the back of the upholstered seat in front of us. We arrived quite late at night, and upon stopping at a house to inquire as to the whereabouts of Bryn Poeth Uchaff, were told it was several miles from Llandovery, near a village called Cynghordy. But our informant—a Mrs. Evans—said it could only be reached by a path she didn't think it advisable for us to try to traverse in the dark. At this point, I was possibly not looking too healthy, which might have added to her concern, and she very kindly offered us the use of her caravan for the night, free of charge. An offer we gratefully accepted, along with the cups of tea we drank under the watchful gaze of a spaniel who seemed to have strong doubts about us.

The caravan was in Mrs. Evans's yard, and after showing us out to it, she brought us blankets, and some hot water and salt for my throat, which was by then, really, really sore. After a quick wash, we tumbled onto the caravan's couch beds and even I slept like a log until eight o'clock the next morning.

* * *

Hardly able to believe it was only eight o'clock, we went into town and had breakfast at a restaurant before going to look for postcards. We found some nice ones in a little shop where customers were trying to convince a tearful toddler in a pushchair that his mother had merely stepped out for a moment, and not disappeared off the face of the Earth.

"It's all right, boyo. She's coming back," one man assured him.

From there we went back to the train station to ascertain the times for trains to Cynghordy, but on the way spotted the ruins of a castle and simply had to explore it and take pictures. So did a group of like-minded people who'd just got off a tour bus. Wales has more castles than any other country in the world, and even though Llandovery Castle—built on a hilltop above the River Bran around the beginning of the twelfth century—was never quite as spectacular as some of the thirteenth-century ones put up across the land by England's Edward I, it was obviously grand enough, or strategically placed enough, for Edward to want it. He took it over in 1277 and, except for a short period in 1282, when a Welsh Prince called Llywelyn the Last took it back for a few months, it remained in English hands, with nothing especially noteworthy happening there from that point on.

There weren't a lot of trains to Cynghordy, and the next one wasn't due until mid-afternoon. With several hours still to go until then, we bought some more of what were fast proving to be the main relief for my sore throat (ice lollies) and a 'Thank You' box of chocolates for Mrs. Evans.

After saying goodbye to her, we returned to the train station, where we met two girls who were staying at the hostel we were going to. These girls, Ruth and Alicia, said they could show us the way, so as soon as the train arrived, all four of us boarded it and went to Cynghordy station, a very small station comprised of just one hut.

From there we embarked upon the long, long trek up to the youth hostel, and en route, the conversation turned to my denim cap.

"Where did you get it?" Ruth asked.

I told her it came from a Hudson Bay store.

Alicia's eyebrows went up. "You mean the trading post? We learned about that in school. Do you actually still have such things in Canada?"

"Of course," I said. "My father traded some Klondike gold dust for it."

I'm not sure if they believed us or not.

Our YHA address book said the remote cottage-turned-hostel, Bryn Poeth Uchaff, was two and a half miles from the train stop but I'm quite sure it was five or more, and uphill all the way. And we might not have made it without the help of our new friends, who carried our coats and gadget bags, or the people in a car who came along before we reached the really steep parts and offered to take our packs up to the warden's house, a place called 'Hafod-y-pant'. What that means in English I'm not entirely sure but think it might be something along the lines of house in a hollow. We were somewhat weary by the time we got there, and the hostel was still at least half a mile beyond that, so we left our packs with the warden and just took out basic requirements for the night. Even then, tramping through fields, streams, innumerable insects (flies, horse flies, midges) and a great many sheep was quite an ordeal for people who were not—and were never destined to become—hikers.

We'd initially planned to go into Cynghordy for supplies after we got to the hostel, but the thought of going back down that hill and up again amid all those insects caused us to scrap that idea. Instead, we scrounged cups of tea and some soup and crackers from other hostellers. As the warden had indicated on the telephone, the hostel wasn't full, its present set of guests only being comprised of, in addition to Ruth, Alicia, and ourselves, two boys and two more girls. After eating we all sat in the kitchen talking, with the conversation mostly leaning towards television shows, television stars, the appalling youth of today (other members of it, that is), and whether or not the Queen should get a raise.

We went to bed after attempting some semblance of a wash with ice cold water in the cottage's somewhat spooky twilight-lit washroom. The night was not a great one for me, as I spent most of it trying not to cough and wondering if the strange noises I kept hearing were the spirits of past inhabitants, or the mice one of the other hostellers had spoken of earlier.

* * *

Early the next morning, we went back to the warden's house to collect our packs and get our youth hostel cards from someone. Preferably someone English-speaking. This because Ruth had said that, when she and Alicia had gone there to get milk, the only one around had been an old woman who spoke fluent Cymraeg, but no English, forcing them to obtain their milk through sign language. Fortunately for us, the warden was at home. After retrieving our belongings, we set off down the hill, and found going down almost as hard as going up. I repeat, almost. For most of the journey I set myself a goal in the distance—a bridge, post, house, anything—struggled up to it, collapsed for a while and then went on again. Ellen just followed me, usually some distance behind. We'd long since decided that her inability to keep up with me was due to the fact that her legs were hereditarily short because her ancestors had spent their time stomping around the peatlands of Northern Ireland, and mine were hereditarily long from my Stewart clansmen tramping through the Scottish heather. Although my faster pace could also—and this is more likely—simply have been due to having older brothers unwilling to wait for me. Her siblings had been more accommodating in that regard.

We panted up to the little station a few minutes before the train was due, a feat we'd had our doubts about accomplishing. Passengers had to flag the train down if they wanted it, and we vigorously did so as soon as we saw it coming. The guard told us we'd have to go to Llanelli to get a train to the Irish ferry port at Fishguard, but said he'd tell us where to get off. Not blessed with the memory of a London bus conductor, he forgot, and we breezed right through Llanelli, necessitating a trip back from the next station as soon as we realized this. The train for Fishguard was packed with ferry passengers, but we managed to find seats in a non-smoking compartment containing just two people, an Irishman and his wife who, in the course of the journey, gave us some helpful hints on Irish travel.

Chapter Nine
The Emerald Isle

The small market town of Fishguard was the site of that sort-of-last invasion of Britain alluded to in Chapter Four. In February, 1797, Britain was—by no means for the first time—at odds with France, and pretty much expecting an invasion attempt by French Revolutionaries bent on liberating Britain's poor and oppressed. But the expectation was that this attempt would be made through some large, significant, English port, not a tiny, insignificant, Welsh cove. Not that it mattered. Even though the invading force was comprised of around fourteen hundred men, only six hundred or so were regular soldiers, as France's best fighting men were with Napoleon Bonaparte wreaking havoc on the Italians. The rest were either irregular soldiers or convicts who'd been offered army life as an alternative to prison and were not exactly committed to the cause. More interested in looting than fighting, the 'invaders' came across some wine and were soon too inebriated to stand against the local militia—or probably even stand. They surrendered two days after landing, and Britain's poor and oppressed (of which it had an abundance) remained so.

Our visit was even briefer. By our day, Fishguard's harbour had been in the Irish ferry business since 1906, and we went straight from the train to the ferry, where we set our packs down on the deck and stood by the railing until we got underway. It was a bit breezy, so, scrunching down beside the packs, Ellen read for much of the three-and-a-half-hour crossing and I did nothing in particular except get up occasionally to look over the side and be thankful the sea wasn't being as rough as the Irish Sea is capable of being. There were a lot of children around us, some of whom were crying and the rest running around wildly. I was still three years off of being an aunt, but Ellen was already one, and although she liked her two nieces, aged five and two-and-a-half, well enough, she was not otherwise overly fond of the company of people under the age of fifteen. She did soften towards juvenile members of the human species as she aged, but at that time they did not hold much appeal for her. Whereas I—the future teacher and parent—had always liked children and for the most part got along well with them, so our noisy little ferry mates didn't really bother me.

* * *

The harbour in Rosslare, County Wexford, had also been in the Irish ferry business since 1906, and a train was waiting at the docks to take passengers on to Waterford. We arrived there after all the banks had closed but were able to find a hotel willing to change some traveller's cheques for us so we could board a bus to Kilkenny.

Despite numerous stops, the bus was a fast one and had us roaring through the Irish countryside with a speed fiend driver who took pleasure in rounding corners almost on two wheels. The only other passenger was a little old lady who merely grabbed the bar of a front seat, held on for dear life, and smiled sweetly. Ellen and I just lay back on our packs (nothing could knock us flying with those on), not really caring much about anything. Even when the driver told us the youth hostel was three or four miles from Kilkenny and there was no bus, we remained calm and unconcerned. It was only when he let us off and we started walking, that we became concerned. Especially after someone in a house we stopped at to ask directions said it was five miles to the hostel, and someone in a pub gave us an estimate of six or seven miles. At home, we weren't old enough to go into pubs and Ellen was sure an aunt who belonged to the Temperance Union back in Canada would very much disapprove of us being in one. But we only ordered soft drinks, and even though the pub was also a Bed and Breakfast establishment, staying there would have put quite a strain on our finances.

We pushed on, and after a while, by mutual agreement, held out our thumbs. We knew our parents wouldn't be happy about us hitchhiking, but there didn't seem to be much else we could do. On and on we went, with cars whizzing by, some of the occupants smiling, others waving, none stopping. We speculated as to why and came up with: (a) respectable girls didn't hitchhike in Ireland, (b) they did, but we weren't sufficiently attractive to be deemed worth stopping for, or (c) no one did because the Irish thought walking was good for you.

An hour or so into this ineffectual attempt to get a ride, we started to look around for a telephone to inform the hostel warden that we wouldn't be able to make it that night. We also, as a contingency plan, looked for a field in which to spend it. But finally, a car stopped. It was driven by a woman, which made us feel much better, although, at that point, we weren't inclined to be picky. The woman said she had a daughter who did a lot of hostelling, so that doubtless made her sympathetic. She took us right to the road the hostel was on, and we tottered the remaining distance to a small fourteenth-century tower castle the Irish Youth Hostel Association purchased back in the 1940s.

Foulksrath Castle—the name a possible corruption of that of its builder, Fulco de Frene—was not as large and imposing as the castle-hostel I'd stayed in near Werfen during my school trip to Austria, but still looked rather impressive in the twilight. And must once have been quite a desirable little fortress as little fortresses go, since Oliver Cromwell judged it worthy of being confiscated when he inflicted himself on Ireland three centuries later. By the nineteenth century it had come into the hands of some descendants of *Gulliver's Travels* author, Jonathan Swift, one of whom, Godwin Meade Pratt Swift, patented Ireland's first aircraft in the year 1897. He launched it from the top of the castle by means of a catapult, but the flight was not a successful one and the pilot (his butler) sustained several injuries. I don't know if he handed in his notice after that little episode but could scarcely be blamed if he did.

At the castle-cum-hostel, we signed in and made inquiries about the Kilkenny-Cork buses for the next day. We were told it would be best to hitchhike to Durrow and catch one from there. The idea of having to hitchhike again didn't exactly appeal to us, but both Kilkenny and Durrow were eight miles away. And, from Durrow, the bus was cheaper.

Happy to have arrived, we deposited our stuff by our beds and went down to the kitchen to make ourselves some tea. The milk available had come straight from a cow, and went straight down the sink after we, only being used to pasteurized milk, each took a mouthful of tea. We made some more, and sat down on the kitchen steps to drink it without milk.

"What a damn silly place to have a hostel," said Ellen. "Why in hell do they always have to have them miles and miles from damn silly anywhere?"

Despite her strong evangelical upbringing, she'd been uttering words like 'hell' and 'damn' with increasing frequency ever since London. There, I'd attributed these shocking additions to her vocabulary to her dislike for London in general, and the Underground in particular, but it had since become clear that she was willing to use them wherever, and whenever, she was in a state of discontent.

Once again, I did not have a great night, most of which was spent coughing, having unsettling dreams about being stuck in an attic, and, Ellen claimed, moaning, which I must have been if I disturbed *her* night's rest. But no one else did. Or perhaps I should say, nothing else. Foulksrath Castle is supposed to house some ghosts, one of them that of a young woman whose father locked her up and starved her to death because she was in love with someone he didn't approve of. Another spectre is said to show up at a certain time of year, specifically, November, when otherworldly footsteps and door openings are accredited to a sentry who fell asleep on duty and was thrown from the battlements by an irate Fulco De La Frenne. We were four months too early to be visited by him, but the hapless young woman didn't put in an appearance either.

* * *

The Cork bus didn't leave Durrow until twenty to ten, but thinking it might take amateur hitchhikers like ourselves a while to catch a ride, we were among the first people up the next day. When we went to get our cards from the warden, she gave us a large key and asked us to open the large gate outside for her. We took the key, and tried to fulfil the task, but couldn't even get the door *leading* to the gate open. The warden had to come and help us. She seemed most put out that we couldn't do it, but neither of us had ever opened a castle door before. Such things take practice.

Out on the main road, we started along another road signposted Durrow, stopping a little while later to rest underneath a different signpost. This one informed us we'd come all of a quarter of a mile. Our walking speed left something to be desired, but walking backwards with packs on and our thumbs out wasn't all that easy. As before, cars whizzed by, some of the occupants smiling, others waving, none stopping. Most hostellers we'd talked to had spoken of having almost the first car to come along stop for them, but we were not favoured in the same manner. Eventually, we branched out, with me leading and Ellen trailing behind and occasionally calling out my name so that I'd stop for a while. But having set a goal in my head I generally refused to stop until I reached it.

When a car did stop, we again felt no qualms about taking a ride, as the driver was a priest and, unlike the unfortunate victims of ecclesiastic perverts, we'd never had reason to mistrust members of the clergy. He took us all the way to Durrow and got us to the shop the bus stopped at with time to spare; time we used to purchase some food items and a packet of tissues for what had, for me, now turned into a head cold.

Upon arrival in Cork, the bus conductor told us which bus to catch for the hostel. Two ladies told us when to get off, and we trotted across the street to the Redclyffe Youth Hostel after first going to the Redclyffe Guest House next to it by mistake. The hostel was closed, but we were allowed to drop off our packs before going off in search of more groceries, most importantly milk and sugar, as not all hostels supplied them, and we'd scrounged enough off of other hostellers to feel we really had to start carrying our own.

Returning to the hostel, we checked in and went down to the kitchen to partake of our first square meal in days and then back to the dormitory to get ready for bed. That was when I discovered my face conditioner had leaked out onto my flannel, toothbrush, and everything else in my sponge bag. Forced to dispose of it, I had to trust the teenage curse of acne wouldn't be too much of a problem for the rest of the trip. I then took two pain killers in an attempt to alleviate a headache and went to bed—successfully keeping everyone else with the same idea awake for at least a couple of hours by coughing.

Chapter Ten
More of The Emerald Isle

The next morning, Ellen and I drew the task of sweeping out the dining room, a chore no one appeared to have performed for quite some time if the amount of dust and dirt was anything to go by.

We knew Cork was an historic city in and of itself, having been, among other things, an important settlement for both Vikings and the medieval kings of Desmond and, later on, a refuge for Huguenots fleeing persecution in seventeenth-century France. But its main attraction for us was as a base from which to visit nearby Blarney Castle. Built by the King of Munster (Dermot McCarthy) in 1446, Blarney Castle is, like Foulksrath, just a tower castle, but, thanks to a certain stone set within one of its walls, is somewhat better known. Theories on the origins of the Blarney Stone range from biblical connections to it being half of Scotland's Stone of Scone, but regardless of where it came from, those who kiss it are supposed to gain 'the gift of the gab'. There are several ideas about that too, the most likely one pertaining to the verbosity of one of King Dermot's descendants, who managed to fend off demands that he hand the castle over to England's Queen Elizabeth I by writing her a series of letters full of smooth talk she referred to as 'blarney'. Smooth talk she must have either been impressed by, or amused by, as she let him keep the castle.

Our duty discharged, we went out to Blarney Castle on a double-decker bus, along with a middle-aged American couple, and a twenty-six-year-old fellow Canadian named Hank who worked in Scotland but was holidaying in Ireland. At Blarney, Ellen and I explored the castle's outer walls with them, and then went to the top of the castle and took pictures of each other kissing the Blarney Stone. Official photos were taken, too, but they cost money. Being somewhat acrophobic, I found tilting backwards with the ground far below me somewhat alarming, but the guard held tight.

Performance of this ritual did not, however, result in either of us becoming any more silver-tongued than we'd been before.

Descending by means of the spiral stairs, we explored numerous side chambers before going into a souvenir shop. (To return home with country-specific items for others, or to keep for ourselves as mementos, was something we, at that age, basically looked upon as an obligation.) There we met up with Hank again and went into the village for tea and cakes, for which Hank chivalrously paid.

Back in Cork, Hank and Ellen and I went regular shopping, mainly visiting bookshops. I bought quite a lot of books but was spared having to carry them around Europe as one of the shops was able to ship them to Canada for me. We also stopped at a cinema to inquire about the start time of a movie we'd decided to go to that night. Put on as a fundraiser for the local Variety Club, *The Song of Norway* wasn't being shown until half past eleven and didn't end until two in the morning, so when we got back to the hostel we asked for a late pass. Unfortunately, the hostel had two wardens, one young and one elderly. The one on desk duty was the younger one and, being, in the words of the other, "a wee bit officious", wouldn't give us a late pass, even for a charity do. But after we'd turned away from the desk, the older warden took us aside and told us to ignore his colleague.

"You go out and enjoy yourselves. And you'll not be having to worry about getting back in again. 'Tis me who locks up for the night and I'll leave the window open."

It was a generous offer, and we accepted it. But accepted it somewhat uneasily, because we knew if we were caught trying to enter the hostel after closing time, our youth hostel cards could be retained. And then where would we be? Shelterless! But hey, we were teenagers, a time when rule-breaking holds a certain appeal. Hank, being an older, responsible adult, was decidedly dubious about taking such a course of action, but went with us when we followed the old warden into the kitchen so he could point out exactly which window he planned to leave open. Rule-breaking holds a certain appeal for the elderly, too.

After supper Ellen and I put our pyjamas on under our clothes and went downstairs to join Hank and a young woman we'd met whilst preparing and consuming our supper. She didn't want to go to the film, but did accompany us to a pub, where she and Hank spent some hours arguing about subjects Ellen and I didn't know much about, so we mostly just listened until she went back to the hostel. Hank, Ellen, and I then walked around town until it was time for the show.

Once there we had to sit through a Variety Club trio and the appearance of one of the movie's stars, Elizabeth Larner, before the film even started. Both of which were better than the film. We naïvely thought *The Song of Norway* was going to be something like *The Sound of Music*, but it wasn't. I later read a review in which the film critic said it was 'like being stuck on a railway siding with nothing to read', a statement I thought summed things up quite well.

The film ended at twenty past two, and we didn't sneak into the hostel grounds until something to three. Sneaking wasn't easy with Hank's shoes making resounding clicks on the pavement, and it took us a while to find the door that led to the back of the hostel, where the kitchen was located. The window was open, just as the old warden had promised, but screeched and groaned terrifyingly when Hank opened it a bit more in order for it to allow him passage. He waited a minute or two to see if the noise had attracted any attention and then crawled through, leaving Ellen and I to wait outside, tensely readying ourselves for the great clatter that would announce he'd gone headfirst into the sink. He didn't but the noise his shoes were making was still dangerous.

"Hank, take your shoes off," Ellen hissed.

He did so. After he let us in, we tiptoed through the kitchen and out into the hall, where Ellen tripped over a chair.

"We'd make a hell of a gang of burglars," Hank whispered.

We crept upstairs expecting to see the warden—the young warden—standing at the top of them with his arms folded, smiling sadistically, but by some miracle, he wasn't. We made it to our respective dormitories safely and tumbled into bed, where I allowed myself the coughing spasm I hadn't dared indulge in before.

* * *

The next morning, we set off for Dublin with Ellen periodically complaining that she'd caught my cold. Vikings established Dublin on the banks of the River Liffey around 831 and made it into a prosperous trading centre for all manner of goods, with slaves being an especially sought-after commodity. But the native Irish were living in the area long before the Vikings came, and the city's name comes from the Gaelic term, *dubh linn* (black pool), a reference to the black bog water that drained into the Liffey.

When we got there, a man showed us where the hostel was and told us to be sure to keep to all the rules and regulations because the warden was "something of a stickler" for them.

He certainly was. The very manner in which he signed us in told us that and made us wonder if he was in any way related to the younger warden at the Cork hostel. He even wanted our reservation cards, which were stuffed down in my pack somewhere because no one else had ever wanted anything more than our names.

Assigned to a dorm on the top floor, we had to climb stairs. Many stairs. According to two girls in that dorm, seventy-four of them. They were from Belfast, in Northern Ireland, and were, shall we say...hardened types. Not in any way nasty, but definitely tough. The result, no doubt, of living amidst the violence and oppression besetting their part of the country. Ireland's history had long been filled with violence and oppression, but the most recent conflict, the Troubles, had started up two or three years earlier and were the reason Ellen and I had decided against visiting the North, even though that was where her Irish ancestors came from.

When we went to rid ourselves of the day's accumulated grime that night, we had to wait awhile because the girls' washroom, located two floors below us, was small and the number of girls wanting to use it large. Ellen also gargled with salt water for her sore throat but said it didn't help, something I already knew. We went to bed, coughing alternately.

* * *

The next morning, the warden came around banging on doors with great force and ringing a bell with great zeal. I was already awake, so it didn't startle me overmuch, but did have quite an entertaining effect on the room's other occupants.

"Well," snarled Ellen, "we've had reveille—what time's parade?"

The two girls from Belfast had a few uncomplimentary things to say as well.

Our duty for that day was to sweep off the stairs and landing, a task hindered quite considerably by people running up and down them en route to doing their own chores which, unlike at other hostels, all had to be completed before breakfast.

After breakfast, we went to check on the ferries for our return to England. And it was a good thing we did, since they ran at different times to what we'd been told in London. The rest of the day should have been spent visiting Dublin Castle, Trinity College, and other attractions in the Republic of Ireland's capital city, but wasn't. Neither of us felt very well, and we settled for going shopping for what had become necessary items; such as small food containers for staples like butter and sugar, and a tea towel to use in place of the unsanitary rags available at most hostels for the drying of dishes.

That accomplished, we went to Mountjoy Square, just across from our hostel, and sat in the sun until the hostel opened at five o'clock. Later on, we made ourselves a quick meal alongside some boys who were making a far more elaborate one. Women's lib was still in its infancy, and food preparation wasn't something the vast majority of young male hostellers knew much about, but those who did invariably put together complicated meat and vegetable dishes, complete with dessert. Whereas young female hostellers nearly always opted for simple meals that seldom even involved the use of a cooker.

* * *

The warden and his bell made the rounds again the next morning, but at least it was the last time *we* had to put up with such a rude awakening.

At the train station we went to a wicket and waited for it to open up so we could purchase tickets for the train to the ferry port. And waited, and waited, until told that that which we desired would not go on sale for another hour and a half. To pass the time, we went in the station buffet to have some tea and write postcards, with Ellen treating her mother to a thrilling account of being dangled over a precipice at Blarney Castle.

Chapter Eleven
Bonnie Scotland

Our second traversing of the Irish Sea was rougher than the first, so we spent most of it in the ferry's lounge, out of the wind and rain. By now Ellen was convinced she was extremely ill and said she intended to go to a doctor as soon as we docked at Heysham in Lancashire. I reminded her we wouldn't be arriving until evening, after doctors' surgeries closed, callously adding that I'd had the same thing, and still did, but was managing to muddle along without professional medical care.

At Heysham we found ourselves an empty compartment on a night train going up to Inverness in the Highlands of Scotland. Once inside, Ellen stretched out as though all she required for a deathbed scene was a lily. She suggested putting a plague sign on the door to alert other passengers to the danger of joining us.

No one did, but even with the compartment to ourselves, the seats were none too comfortable. Using our packs for pillows was none too comfortable either. Besides that, it was so cold, we were soon pulling clothes out of our packs to cover ourselves with.

We both woke up several times, but only started to put things back into our packs when daylight came. That was when I found the compartment had a heat gauge, but I can't say it helped much.

"I wonder why all the sheep up here still have their wool," Ellen mused as she gazed out the window.

"Any others we've seen have been shorn for the summer.

"They damn well have to have it to keep warm!" I snapped, shivering.

All in all, our mood was not good. For want of something better to do, we huddled in our respective corners and glared at each other until we got to Inverness, ancient capital of the heathen Picts, whose King, Bridei mac Maelchu, (anglicized as Brude), was converted to Christianity by Saint Columba in 565.

We got to Inverness around eight in the morning, along with a herd of naval cadets whose boisterous departure from the train swept us out onto the platform with them. Fighting our way through the crowd, we left the station and presented the Inverness hostel with the challenge of signing us in just as other hostellers were trying to sign out.

We then took a train to the little village of Kyle on the Lochalsh Peninsula. And, from there, a ferry over to the little village of Kyleakin on the Isle of Skye, in Gaelic, *An-t-Eilean Sgitheanach*, the Winged Isle, from the way its headlands jut out into the sea. Also known as the Misty Isle, the largest of Scotland's Inner Hebrides islands was much closer to the mainland than we expected.

It was raining a bit when we got there, but not enough to stop us going up into the hills to take pictures of one another amidst the heather, bracken, and rocks of Skye, and conjure up mental pictures of Scottish heroes, real and fictional, being chased through the heather, bracken, and rocks in the dark of night. And very sure-footed they must have been because, even in daylight, most of the ground beneath us was wet and slippery.

Coming down from the hills we were accosted by a small, yapping, dog. We ignored him and, eventually, he went away.

Returning to the ferry port, I tried to copy some Gaelic words of welcome from a sign. Whilst I was thus engaged, Ellen wandered down to the ferry and got aboard.

I turned to join her just as the ferry started to chug towards Kyle.

"Get on! Get on!" Ellen urged.

I tried. I really did. I ran down to the edge of the water and jumped up and down in agitation. Trying to jump aboard was out of the question as it had already moved well past any long jump mark I'd ever achieved.

"I'll meet you over there!" I yelled as I stood forlornly on the shore watching Ellen sail away.

Before the Skye Road Bridge opened in 1995, ferries to and from the island ran every few minutes, so I caught the next one. Stumbling sheepishly ashore, I waved to Ellen, who was standing up above the port capturing the moment with her camera.

We didn't get back to Inverness until around half past nine that night, but it was still quite light out and remained so, even at midnight. Which you'd think would have made it easier for the people chasing those Scottish heroes through the heather to have spotted them.

* * *

Before moving south the next day, we paid a visit to Loch Ness, the long, narrow, lake in the Highlands' Great Glen that has been the reputed home of a legendary monster since Roman times, but it was an early biography of Saint Columba that first made written reference to this leviathan. How much that excited readers I couldn't say, but a dozen or so centuries later, the *Inverness Courier* carried an article about a local couple's sighting of a large, scary-looking, creature in the local watering hole, and interest took off all over the world—helped along by a photo of 'Nessie' published in the *Daily Mail* in 1934 and not revealed as a fake until the 1990s. Even then claims to have seen the elusive denizen of the deep didn't diminish and are still going strong today.

We'd been advised that the best way to get to Loch Ness was by bus, but went to the train station beforehand to leave our packs in what turned out to be a non-existent Left Luggage room. There were, however, storage lockers. We didn't think our packs would fit in one, but they did. Both of them. We then wasted more time figuring out how the locker worked and had to run all the way to the bus station. Unnecessary exertion on our part, since ours was twenty minutes late.

The bus took us to Drumnadrochit, a village located about half a mile from Loch Ness and the closest drop-off point available. Having only an hour and a quarter to find it before we had to go back to Inverness and get a train to our next destination, we set off at once. We followed the road for a considerable distance and then, catching a glimpse of the loch across some fields, cut across them, getting snagged on barbed wire fences, stung by stinging nettles, scratched by thorns, and blown about by the wind. Going over the last fence, we also stepped ankle-deep in mud, but at least we got there. I can't say we came out at the loch's most picturesque viewpoint, though, and were only able to search for Nessie for about two minutes before we had to start back for the bus without making his acquaintance.

The wind was against us all the way back to Drumnadrochit, and too strong for us to attain any kind of decent walking speed. Even so, we managed to get to the little shop the bus stopped at about five minutes before it was due. Unaware it had to be flagged down, we went into the shop for postcards and the bus sped past without stopping, leaving us fifteen miles from Inverness, with no chance of catching our train unless we hitchhiked again. But this time luck was with us. Within minutes, a car stopped and a man going into Inverness gave us a ride. He let us out on a side street about ten minutes before the train was due to depart and we raced through the streets of Inverness in the manner of Roger Bannister going for the four-minute mile.

At the railway station, Ellen dashed off to find out what platform our train went from, and I went to retrieve our packs from the storage locker. I waited beside it for a couple of minutes, expecting Ellen to join me. When she didn't, I started to drag both packs out towards the trains, constantly tripping over the one in front of me and getting banged on the heel by the one behind me.

Halfway to the ticket booth I saw Ellen at a point just beyond it, frantically waving.

"It's leaving!" she called out. "It's leaving *now*. Hurry! Hurry!"

Finding it impossible to 'hurry' with two packs, I yelled at her to come and get hers. She raced over and picked it up in her arms, as I did with mine. We charged towards the barrier, barely noticing when the ticket collector—who'd evidently decided against asking us to show our tickets—leapt out of the way. A guard offered to take Ellen's pack, and she threw it and her coat into his arms. He heaved the pack aboard, I heaved mine aboard, and Ellen and I both scrambled aboard ourselves. Snatching her coat from the guard, Ellen managed to shout out a thank you as the train shot out of the station.

Our next destination was Dundee—in Gaelic, *Dùn Dèagh*, meaning 'Fort on the Tay'—where my mother and oldest brother, Ronald, spent part of World War II with some of my father's relatives. Dundee was considered a safer location than her home village of Longcross, which was dangerously close to London, the Luftwaffe's prime target. I'd been to Dundee, too, as a small child, but remembered next to nothing about it. As far as I knew, few, if any, of Dad's kinsmen still resided there, but there were some in his place of birth, the nearby village of Wellbank. Visiting them was our primary reason for going to Dundee, so we were not overly concerned with anything pertaining to the three J's Dundee was famous for: jute (the last mill for which would soon be closing), jam (specifically, Keiller's marmalade), and journalism (the D.C. Thomson & Co. Publishing Company having set up shop there in 1905).

After checking into our hostel, we went straight out again, and upon spotting a police sergeant, asked him how to get to Wellbank. Ellen later admitted to not understanding a single word of his reply, but I'd been listening to the Doric dialect my entire life and had no trouble grasping that we had to get a bus sometime within the next half hour if we wanted to get one back that day. Forty-seven years later, Doric became one of Scotland's official languages, so I suppose I can now claim to be bilingual.

Waiting for the bus, I chatted with a woman who used to live in Wellbank. She didn't know for certain where my father's cousin lived—all I had to go on was Wellbank and the not exactly uncommon Scottish name, Bill Stewart—but she thought he might be the one who'd run a dance hall there once, and the bus driver let us off in front of what she said was *that* Bill Stewart's house.

Fortunately, they were one and the same. I'd never met Bill, his wife Peggy, or their son Billy before, but they knew my father well and welcomed us warmly.

After serving us a lavish tea, Peggy got out photos of my father when he was a little boy. We didn't have any such photos, but I managed to pick him out from his numerous siblings, and Bill gave me one of the photos to take home. He then took us next door to see the house Dad was born in, as well as some of the surrounding farmland and the woods. The woods Dad had told me my great-grandfather used to sneak into and incur the wrath of both his neighbours and certain family members by releasing rabbits from snares because, "the paer wee beastie was squealing".

Later on, Bill showed us some slides of his visit to Canada three years earlier, as well as a few conjuring tricks, taking care to explain that he could not explain them, as he was a member of Britain's Magic Circle and such revelations were not allowed. By then it was too late for us to catch a bus into Dundee, so he and Billy took us back to the hostel.

* * *

Because we had an early train to catch, the warden at the Dundee hostel didn't give us a duty the next morning. We got breakfast at the train station and spent the journey to Edinburgh talking politics with an Englishman in the compartment with us.

Knowing the Edinburgh hostel didn't open until four o'clock, we left our packs at the train station and went up to Edinburgh Castle. The inactive volcano known as Castle Rock gave locals an easy place to defend and fortresses were built atop it from the Iron Age on. The current one is a veteran of some twenty-three attacks, the last in 1745, when Bonnie Prince Charlie and his followers made an unsuccessful bid for it as part of an equally unsuccessful bid to put him on the English throne.

We spent an enjoyable two hours at the castle before going into a café for tea and toast, a combination we'd read visitors were supposed to eat in the birthplace of such Scottish notables as Alexander Graham Bell, Robert Louis Stevenson, and Sir Arthur Conan Doyle. Shortbread was regarded as another Edinburgh must, so we had some of that too, but I was not willing to order that other Scottish staple, oatmeal porridge, a distaste for which I shared with my father. Despite his fierce pride in being a Scot, he hated the stuff and never ate it beyond childhood, when he was forced to.

Thus fortified, we went to see the statue of a Skye terrier that sits atop an animal drinking fountain near the castle. Installed in 1873, it serves as a tribute to Greyfriars Bobby, the famous little dog who faithfully guarded his master's grave for close to fourteen years, day and night, rain or shine, spurning all offers of a comfier home. A tale that, in 1971, was still accepted without question, but has since come under scrutiny. Most particularly, the day and night, rain or shine aspect. It seems there are accounts of him not being at all averse to accepting food and shelter from people living nearby, especially in inclement weather. But if so, who could blame him? Or blame the city of Edinburgh for wanting to keep a good thing going for as long as possible. Victorian era tourists flocked to town to see Bobby manning his post in the churchyard and trotting off to a local restaurant for a hand-out when a gun from the castle sounded the one o'clock time-check. Such actions were crowd-pleasers. So much so that one sceptic, Jan Bondeson, has suggested that, when the original Bobby (believed to have been born around 1856) passed on, another Skye terrier was procured by interested parties and taught to do the same things. His suspicions about this arising from the fact that the much-admired wee doggie doesn't look quite the same in photos and paintings of him dated before 1867 as he does in those dated between 1867 and Bobby's official demise in 1872.

Regardless of how many dogs there were, or how deep Bobby's devotion went, the bronze statue atop the granite fountain is a handsome one and we gave it due admiration before turning our attention to the shops along Edinburgh's main thoroughfare, Princes Street, a tribute to the many sons of England's King George III. He had a few daughters too, but princesses weren't deemed worthy of the same level of toadying.

The first shop we went into was a bagpipe shop to get some chanter reeds for my father, a piper who played, initially, with the Oxford Caledonian Pipe Band, and then with the Kelowna Legion Pipe Band. His Sassenach wife and half-Sassenach children did not share his passion for the instrument—not even Ronnie, who'd been exposed to them at a young age whilst living in Scotland during the war—but I dutifully got them for him and arranged to have them shipped to Canada. I would have liked to have got him a skean dhu (the small dagger worn with Highland dress) as well, but they were over my presents-for-friends-and-relatives budget so I got him a plume for his Glengarry cap instead.

Returning to the hostel, we washed out some clothes and strung a line between the dorm bunks to dry what wouldn't fit on the radiators. We also brought our journals partially up to date. Or, rather, I did. Ellen *started* hers.

* * *

En route to the train station the next day we met an elderly woman and a boy of about twelve who were touring Scotland by motorcycle, an unusual and rather adventurous mode of travel for such a duo. I admired their pluck in attempting it as, at that point, I'd never made more than a few short in-town motorcycle trips as a passenger on my brothers' bikes. In later years I did come to drive a motor scooter, but that, too, was mainly in town, so my admiration for them still holds.

There was no buffet car on our train, but the journey to London involved a stop at Grantham. As we approached it, a guard walked up and down telling people we'd be there long enough to nip out for a cup of tea. Ellen and I were quick to respond to this announcement, and managed to return with our cuppas well before he started yelling for everyone to get back on board. One man claimed the carriages up his end hadn't been told about the stop, and was extremely vexed to learn he no longer had time to get a cup of tea. (Never deprive an Englishman, or, on this occasion, a Scotsman, of his tea.)

Still soured on London, our re-entry brought us no pleasure, and when Ellen went to see if the films she'd taken to a shop for processing had been processed, the place was closed, signalling that our London luck was running true to form.

Towards evening, we boarded the boat train for Harwich and spent most of it reading. At Harwich we proceeded to our ferry, the *Avalon*, but were unable to book cabin accommodation on her. Or perhaps I should say, unwilling, as my Scottish blood kicked in big-time at the thought of paying out £3.50. Instead, we settled down in the *Avalon's* lounge as soon as she set sail. But the lounge turned out to be more comfortable than we'd thought it would be and we had a fairly restful night.

Chapter Twelve
Going Continental

The *Avalon* reached the Hook of Holland early the next morning, and Ellen and I were among the first passengers to disembark in what was once one of the wealthiest countries in the world. Though its official name is the Netherlands, it was, and still is often referred to as Holland because, during the seventeenth century, most of the people who made it one of the wealthiest countries in the world came from the two provinces—Noord and Zuid-Holland—that were collectively known as Holland. This led the people dealing with them to call the rest of the country Holland as well. The name stuck, along with the term Dutch for the language spoken by the people there, and the people themselves; the blame for this lying with the British, who were of the opinion that all Germanic (Deutsch) languages were too similar to rate individual classification, and called all speakers of them Dutch. At some point, the actual Deutsch language became known as German and its speakers Germans, but, for some reason, Nederlanders (their own name for themselves), and the language spoken by them, remained Dutch.

As soon as we'd had our passports stamped, we headed for the Amsterdam train, stopping only long enough to get our Scottish money converted to Dutch money. The train could not get underway until all the ferry passengers had disembarked but, armed with our newly validated Eurail passes, we got aboard and waited about an hour to get going on what Ellen and I considered the truly European part of our European trip.

The city of Amsterdam was built around a dam in the Amstel River towards the end of the thirteenth century. By the seventeenth century it was a major trading centre with the canals initially dug as a form of defence now primarily used to transport all kinds of merchandise. For the nonce, however, we were only interested in transporting ourselves from the train station to the youth hostel.

The first people we asked for directions didn't speak English, but when I showed them the address in our YHA address book, we managed to get the gist of what they were saying about the way in which we should go. A fruit vendor directed us a little further, and just as we were despairing of ever getting beyond that point, three Dutch hostellers came along and led us right to the place, using a somewhat, for Ellen and me, disconcerting route, as we had to pass through a part of town containing a high number of sex shops. Some said so in English, others didn't require a translation as to the nature of what they were selling—that being all too clear from what was on display in their windows. I didn't think my daddy would have felt too happy about his baby walking along those streets. And, to be honest, his baby and her travelling companion didn't feel too happy about it either.

Unable to sign into the hostel until later in the day, we left our packs in the basement and returned to the main part of the city to take a canal boat tour with a guide who kept up a running commentary in Dutch, English, French, and German. Repeating the same thing, multilingually, every hour for eight hours, five days a week, didn't strike me as a job I'd like, even if I'd been capable of it, but she didn't seem to mind.

After that we went into a restaurant. Upon securing a menu with English translations, I ordered two teas and a chicken and chips platter. This was ofttimes to be our meal combo of choice in Europe, as it was available almost everywhere, did not contain anything I was allergic to, and was the menu item most easily recognized in various languages when translations weren't provided. When the chicken and chips platter arrived, Ellen requested another plate and some more cutlery so we could divide it. The waiter said we couldn't do that but relented when I said I could never eat it all myself. But Ellen had to *hire* the cutlery.

After eating, we wrote some postcards and went to the post office to get stamps, our trek there periodically interrupted by forays into interesting shops. Regular shops, not the racy kind. Some were bookshops, and even had books in English, offering us temptations we thought we'd be safe from in Europe. In this we were wrong, because Europe positively brimmed with English book shops designed to play havoc with our carefully made budgets. But I must admit that it's kind of nice to browse through my bookshelves now and think, *I got that in Rome*, or, *oh, yes, I remember finding that in Paris*.

Ellen was also in pursuit of a piece of the Delft Blue pottery Holland is renowned for. Made in the city of Delft since the seventeenth century, it started out as an imitation of the Chinese pottery Dutch merchants had hitherto had to buy from intermediaries at great expense. They didn't like this much and weren't all that thrilled about having to pay homage to the Chinese Emperor either. They therefore welcomed the home-grown substitute destined to become popular all over Europe and beyond. One shop we went into had a wide selection of Delft Blue and other lovely, but extremely breakable, objects, and we had to be very careful where we swung the shopping bags we were carrying. Shops like that are hard on parents, and we observed an American man with three kids—aged about twelve, nine, and four—quietly having a nervous breakdown. He finally grabbed the youngest one and said, "Timmy, Timmy, give me your hand!"

At the post office, we couldn't figure out how to work the stamp machines. Neither could several other tourists, but within a few minutes, a man came by with some sheets of stamps and sold everyone the correct ones. A side-line to his regular line of work, perhaps.

Back at the hostel, signing in required us to answer a lot of questions: occupation, birth date, birthplace, passport number, and heaven knows what else. Once we found our dormitory, we made up our beds, sorted out some things we'd bought, and placed our packs in the lockers provided. Locks cost money, but seemed like a good idea, so we each got one. Before going to bed, I got into conversation with an American girl from New York who told me I spoke English 'real well'. From this I could but assume she'd heard me speaking French to another hosteller a short time before—almost certainly something simple, such as answering a question as to where the kitchen was—and thought that was my own first language.

I smiled and said, "Thank you."

* * *

At seven the next morning, Ellen and I were already awake, but for those who weren't, the lights above us came on and rock music blared over the intercom amid snarls from the room's inhabitants:

"How jolly uncivilized!" (English)

"Someone throw something at it!" (American)

"*Nein, nein! Zu laut!* (German)

"*Sacre bleu!*" (French).

And similar sentiments uttered in other languages.

As was to occur in most European hostels, we were not assigned a duty before signing out and, being naturally lazy, did not ask for one.

Holland was one of the places we were expecting to get letters. Wanting to collect them before we moved on, we caught a tram we'd been led to believe would drop us off near to where a number of foreign embassies were located.

It didn't. We were to discover that embassies were seldom in city centres, but instead hidden away in distant reaches—possibly to discourage foreign visitors from running inside with the local police on their heels, like in the movie *Don't Drink The Water*. Pack-laden, we had to walk quite a way. Even when we did get to the general embassy area, we couldn't find Canada's, and every person we asked had a different idea about where it was.

Where it was, as it happened, was in The Hague, so we never did get to it, and, for all I know, our letters might still be there.

Thus thwarted, we abandoned Amsterdam for Maastricht, where we had to change trains for Luxembourg. The woman in the compartment we chose condescendingly pointed out that that particular compartment was First Class. We politely—but borderline smugly—pointed out that we were, too, courtesy of our Eurail passes.

Chapter Thirteen
Moving Inland

En route to Luxembourg, we noticed a multi-language sign telling passengers not to lean out the window. Translated into English, those in French and German simply issued the command, 'Do not lean out the window'. From what we could tell, the Italian and Spanish warnings were phrased much the same way, but the English one said, 'It is dangerous to lean out the window', English speakers seemingly being regarded as people who required a *reason*.

Our only stopover in the Grand Duchy of Luxembourg was its capital, also called Luxembourg. The original name for the part of the country the city occupies was Lucilinburhuc, meaning 'Little Fortress', presumably a reference to the little castellum built on a rocky promontory above a river (the Alzette) in Roman times and acquired and renovated by Siegfried, Count of Ardennes in 963.

While little remains of the fortress, both the city and the country of Luxembourg are in good condition; perhaps watched over by the legendary Melusina, a mermaid whom Siegfried is supposed to have fallen in love with without realizing she was a bit 'fishy'. His lack of perception is said to have been due to the fact that, as in the way of mermaids wishing to abandon their aquatic surroundings for life in royal castles, she appeared to him in human form. In that guise she bewitched him, married him, and bore him seven children. She did have to revert to her natural state sometimes, however, and chose Saturdays, when hubby honoured her request that she be allowed to enter a tower and keep to herself for a time. After a few years, he got curious as to why this was so important to her and, peeping through the tower's keyhole, beheld the tip of her long, scaly tail as she lounged in a bath. Her secret discovered, she flopped over to the window, dove into the river below and disappeared. In reality, Siegfried was married to Hedwig of Nordgau, and none of their offspring were reported to have had any particular affinity for water. But the story of Melusina lives on, and in 2015, a Luxembourg artist, Serge Ecker, used 3D printing to create a purple statue of her that now sits on the banks of the Alzette.

We plotted our course to the Luxembourg youth hostel from a large map in the train station, but outside the station could not find any of the streets we'd written down.

Marshalling my limited knowledge of French, I went over to a woman and said, "*Pardon, madam, le Montée de la Petussé, s'il vous plait?*"

"Oh, gee," she said, with a decidedly American accent. "Do you speak German, or Spanish, or..."

"English?" I prompted helpfully.

"Yeah!" she said, adding, "Oh!" as realization struck.

I thanked her anyway and found a native Luxembourger to whom I could put the same question. I received simple enough directions to get us started and another inquiry got us as far as a cobbled street where, being laden with packs, we kept tripping over several of the cobblestones. But we no longer had to ask our way, as the area was heavily posted with YHA signs. A practice we thought all youth hostels should follow.

Once again, we had to fill in lengthy forms, and decided it would be a good idea to commit our passport numbers to memory rather than having to keep digging them out every place we went. Each dormitory had a name and ours was Marie de Zorn, in honour of the seventeenth-century founder and benefactress of a hospital run by Luxembourg's Sisters of St. Elizabeth. After we'd made up our beds, we went looking for a souvenir shop so Ellen could buy a Luxembourg-themed charm for her bracelet. In addition to the little crests we bought in every country we visited, she tried to collect culturally appropriate charms. A collection she managed to add to with a greater degree of success than I had with the type of collection I'd decided on. That was supposed to be culturally appropriate brass ornaments to go with a little brass rocking chair I'd had in my possession for as long as I could remember. Albeit minus the rockers. (I was a destructive child.) But for many years, that collection never got beyond that little English rocking chair and a brass leprechaun purchased in Ireland.

* * *

Early the next morning, the hostel's intercom came on and a female voice said something in German that nobody caught but we assumed meant get up. Fifteen minutes later, this was followed by music, to make sure everyone took the hint.

Waiting for a bus to the train station, Ellen sewed her Luxembourg crest onto her jacket. Sewing and I have never got along, so this was something I had no intention of doing with any of *my* crests, preferring to mount them in a frame upon my return home. When we got to the train station, I suddenly realized we had no pictures of Luxembourg and went out into the street and took one. Having also not written or mailed a postcard I'd bought, I hastily scribbled a few lines to the recipient, banged on a stamp and raced to a post box.

Hurrying proved unnecessary, as the train came in late. When it did arrive, we travelled to Strasburg in the company of two American girls who spent much of the trip popping bubble gum.

In Strasburg there was a different destination card in the window of practically every carriage of the train we had to transfer to in order to get to Freudenstadt, a spa town in Germany's Schwartzwald (Black Forest). Freudenstadt was founded just before the start of the seventeenth century and was originally slated to have to have a castle. Plans for that fell through, but it did acquire the largest market square in the country.

Assuming—correctly—that several of the train's cars were going to be switched around later, we got in one marked Konstanz, the only place we knew was in the direction we were going. At one point en route, Ellen went in search of a buffet car and opened doors onto empty air because a lot of cars had been removed at the last station we'd gone through. Among them, perhaps the buffet car as I couldn't find it either when I went to look. Coming back, I had to pass through a freight car. The doors were open, and with all the jogging and jerking of the train, I got thrown around so much I almost fell out. There were two officials in that freight car—possibly to keep passengers from doing things like that—but neither attempted to assist me.

A little while later a guard came by and started jabbering away at us. By then the train was getting close to our next changing place, and since he was the guard who'd told us, we assumed he was telling us to get off at the next stop.

He wasn't, and we never did ascertain what he *was* talking about. But, believing him to be telling us we'd reached our stop, we got off and found ourselves in Haslach, when we should have been in Hausach. I suppose he could have been warning us not to confuse the two, but, if so: communication failure.

Forced to wait for a train from Haslach to Hausach, we looked for a currency exchange booth but couldn't find one. There wasn't one in Hausach, either, or even a bank close enough to the station for us to get to it before the Freudenstadt train left.

Once aboard, we shared our compartment with an American woman who was touring some of the small towns in Austria, Germany, and Switzerland. We spent the journey talking to her, and even without good conversation, the journey would have been a pleasant one, as it took us though a number of picturesque Schwartzwald villages.

Our arrival in Freudenstadt was not so pleasant. Its train station did not have a currency exchange booth either and we still had no German money whatsoever. An official told us we'd have to take a bus into town and go to the local tourist bureau. Ah, yes, but how to pay to get to a place to get some money when we had no money?

As luck would have it, the woman we'd been travelling with was going into town by bus. She generously paid for us too and refused repayment when we eventually got our traveller's cheques cashed at the tourist bureau.

That late in the day, the bureau only had enough cash on hand to change a $10 cheque and the only $10 cheque we had was in Ellen's secret—as in, secreted in an intimate place—pocket. With no nearby public washrooms in which to discreetly retrieve it, she had to do a great deal of embarrassing twisting and turning before she managed to extricate it and exchange it for Deutsche marks.

Somewhat solvent again, we got a local map with the route to the hostel marked out and arrived just before nightfall.

***

Short though it was, our stay in Freudenstadt gave us the feel of the Schwartzwald we'd been looking for. The next day we moved on to Zürich in Switzerland, known, in ancient times, as Helvetia.

The country's official Latin name, *Confoederatio Helvetica*, reflects the fact that it is a confederation of twenty-six different cantons (administrative regions), with Zürich being the largest. We shared our train compartment with a young teenage girl from Miami and a woman who was acting as her chaperone. We spent most of the trip talking to them and looking at all the sights the chaperone (an experienced traveller) pointed out. The chaperone and I later set off for the buffet car at the other end of the train. When we were nearly there, we were advised to go back because we would soon be coming into the next station and several cars were going to be disconnected. This could easily have led to Ellen and the young girl winding up in Zürich and the chaperone and I heaven knows where, so we hurriedly returned to them.

At Zürich we ditched our packs in Left Luggage, and went to the ladies' WC, where I somehow found myself locked in a cubicle. Turning the handle every which way, I yelled at Ellen and rattled the door until the old woman stationed on the premises to collect token payment came to unlock it, muttering something like, "*dumme Mädchen*" (fool girl). Of Switzerland's four official languages—German, French, Italian, and Romansh—Swiss German is the one that predominates in Zürich, and I must admit the remark was somewhat merited, since it appeared the door's mechanism simply had to be slid sideways.

With me freed from imprisonment, we went to the recently opened underground shopping centre in Zürich's Bahnhofplatz. The idea behind Shopville was to relieve traffic congestion in the area by closing the

Bahnhofplatz to pedestrians and providing them with a safe, attractive, vehicle-free, shopping area in which to...well...shop. But when it opened in October, 1970, it opened amid controversy. Though many locals welcomed it as a move towards modernization, others viewed it as 'too American' and an assault on traditional Swiss culture. Even the name drew condemnation, with some declaring it an English-French monstrosity and other, even less complimentary, things. Despite this, those who chose to open businesses there did quite well at first, but a gradual decline in Shopville's popularity led to it being closed down in 1992 and parts of the Bahnhofplatz returned to above-ground pedestrian use. In 1971, however, the place was still a novelty, and Ellen and I had plenty of company as we made the rounds of its various retail establishments.

Interesting though Shopville was, we didn't spend long there. Having read about Zürich's model railway, we wanted to see it, and were told to take a tramcar out to a stop just before the Zürich Zoo. From there we tried to find the model railway by asking people to point us the right way, but most of them told us it didn't exist.

They were wrong, as proved by the woman who finally did give us directions. We were a bit surprised that so many of the other locals hadn't known their city possessed such an attraction, but looking at it from a more mature viewpoint, I can't honestly say I know every attraction that the city I've lived in for fifty plus years has to offer either.

Zürich's model train display was every bit as charming and detailed as was to be expected in a city with one the busiest railway stations in the world, but since I haven't come across any modern-day references to it, it perhaps no longer exists, or has moved to a different location.

Our next stop was to be Arnhem, in Holland. Having earlier decided to take a night train there, we returned to the real train station and caught a tram out to the Zürich youth hostel to cancel our reservations. A young man told us to take a #7 tram and showed us how to get tram tickets, something we hadn't been doing because there were no conductors aboard to take them and we were unaware that they operated on the honour system, with passengers expected to buy tickets from a machine beside the tram stop. He explained that no one actually checked on this, but inspectors did occasionally come aboard, and woe betide you if you didn't have a ticket. Sort of like transportation Russian roulette, so we'd obviously just been lucky.

Once our hostel business had been brought to a close, we went back to the station to reclaim our packs, and when Ellen opened hers, she found that some peaches she'd bought in Freudenstadt had got squashed and oozed all over her sheet sleeping bag.

Not long afterwards, I noticed two men from Nigeria having language problems with a porter. One asked me if I was going to Hamburg. I said no, but asked what he wanted to know, which was just what time the train left. He and his friend didn't speak any German, but I figured mine would stretch to "*Wen gehen die züg fur Hamburg?*" and upon speaking to the porter, felt inordinately pleased with myself when he understood me, and I understood his answer.

Our own destination was Bäsel, where we had to change trains for Arnhem. In Bäsel we found ourselves with over an hour to spare before the Arnhem train was due out and went to the station buffet with the intention of having supper. Getting a waitress to notice us took a bit of doing, and even when we did, all Ellen was able to request before she darted off again were two cups of tea. She'd evidently taken our tea order though, because just as we were about to walk out, she appeared with it.

We boarded the train five minutes before it was supposed to leave, and, upon finding an unoccupied non-smoking couchette, settled in. Swiss trains had, and mostly still have, a good reputation in the running to time department, but this one was obviously not a *Swiss* train. As the minutes ticked by, we began to wonder if it was ever going to set off. And when the minutes turned into an hour, we began to wonder if we'd even got on the right train. Eventually, one and a half hours behind schedule, it finally started to move, and we thought we were on our way. But we weren't. It was simply moving to another part of the station. Having nothing much else to do, we started in on some food we'd purchased in Shopville, and half an hour later our conveyance did actually get going.

By then it was night-time, and we slept off and on until a conductor came in for our tickets at about quarter past three. We sleepily gave them to him and dozed off again until some other type of official came in and demanded to see our passports. Ellen handed hers over without even looking. She could have been giving it to simply anyone, but said she didn't care, as long as she could return to slumber.

Chapter Fourteen
Holland Homestay

Waking again in daylight, we sat up and talked, our conversation mostly centring around worries about the passing landscape, which seemed rather hilly if we were in, as we supposed, Holland, a country that isn't completely devoid of hills but doesn't have them in abundance. Knowing this, we again wondered if we'd got on the right train and instead of going to Holland were actually heading towards, say, Russia. Without visas. All the long, unexplained, stops and high number of uniformed officials aboard contributed to this notion and prompted me to mentally compose the following letter.

Dear Jeb and Elsje: Afraid we might not make it to your wedding. Don't know how we managed it, but we're somewhere where they wear big fur hats and speak some language we don't understand. The guy across the desk from us, the one with the machine gun, he doesn't think we'll make your wedding, either, and he seems quite knowledgeable. He speaks a bit of English and talks about us going to a place called Siberia for seven years for having no visas. By the way, please contact my brother and tell him to gently break what has happened to my parents and Ellen's mother. Sorry I have to close now. The guy across the desk says I'm writing too much.

A vivid imagination really helps to pass the time on long trips.

Fortunately, our fears were unjustified. The train had just not made as much headway towards Holland as we'd thought. The next stop was Bonn, capital of *West* Germany, thus providing reassurance that we were still within the free world.

We later passed though Cologne, a history-filled city we'd thought about going to. But it wasn't possible for us to stop off everywhere we wanted so we'd sorrowfully taken it off the list. Leastways, for that trip. I did pay Cologne a short, but worthwhile, visit at a later date. The first member of the next generation to visit Europe with me liked it too. Mostly. Bryan was ten at the time, and close to forty years on, my nephew still remembers not just the magnificence of its cathedral, but also being barred from entering a WC because he didn't understand about user fees. And how appalled he was to find an old *woman* in the 'Men's' loo.

Not long after passing through Cologne, a guard came along with an announcement we now recognized as meaning the carriage we were in was going to be disconnected at the next stop and we'd have to move into one that was going all the way to Arnhem. Struggling into our packs, we inched our way down a corridor crammed with a great many other people with the same goal. After watching us get pushed through doors, mashed into corners, and squashed against windows, some Dutch travellers took pity on us and made room for us in a compartment that was, they assured us, going to Arnhem.

The next stop involved another long wait, but everyone had come to expect that on this run. An American boy seated in the corridor said it was his firm belief that select carriages were dismantled and rebuilt at each station. He then went on to warn us about Paris, saying that the people there were mean, nasty, unhelpful, bad tempered, and a number of other things. But the obviously less-than-pleasant time he'd had in *la Ville Lumière* (City of Light) did not put us off going there. Travel experiences differ. We, for example, had negative feelings towards London, but had met lots of people who'd loved it. We did, however, trade complaints with him about the railway officials who'd lied about the time the train was scheduled to arrive in Arnhem. That was supposed to have been around nine o'clock, but it was by then already eleven, and our actual arrival time turned out to be close to noon.

Arnhem was the place from which the World War II Battle of Arnhem (code name: Operation Market Garden) was launched in September, 1944. The plan was to help bring about an early end to the war by gaining control of certain key bridges and opening up an invasion route into Northern Germany. Unfavourable circumstances, coupled with poor decisions by several allied commanders, did not allow that to happen, but the bold move did succeed in liberating parts of Holland. It also deprived the enemy of some of the bases being used to fire V2 rockets at Britain and enabled the Allies to establish bases of their own from which to make assaults on German forces.

Many tourists visit Arnhem specifically because of its war connections, but we were not among them. Our destination was a small town outside of it, home to Elsje and her family. As soon as we got there, Ellen looked for a telephone to inform them of our arrival. With wedding arrangements at their height, she kept getting the busy signal at first, but eventually got through and before long a car drove up containing Jeb, his brother Duane, and a girl named Veerle, who was a friend of Elsje's sister, Grethe.

They took us out to the farm where Elsje's family lived and introduced us to everyone not off doing wedding work. After talking for a while, we went outside with Grethe to see their horses. These were all at the far end of the field, but soon came trotting up when she rattled an oat bucket. During our own supper, Duane announced that, at the *wedding* supper, it was a Dutch custom to have the people in attendance say a rhyme about the bride or groom, depending on which of them they were connected to.

Once these had been composed, we folded wedding programmes until a group of visitors arrived. Wine and lemonade were handed around, and Elsje's family and their visitors did a lot of talking, mostly in Dutch. Duane, Ellen, and I weren't able to follow much of it until Elsje's brother Daan arrived with some of Jeb's Canadian friends and some English got spoken too. Then the visitors went home, Elsje went to bed, and shortly afterwards everyone else turned in too—Ellen upstairs to a room she was sharing with Elsje's grandmother, and me outside to a tent I was sharing with Grethe and Veerle.

Just before the tent's occupants fell asleep, one of the horses whinnied in a manner that sounded like a monkey in the depths of a jungle. With a resigned sigh, Grethe went to see if it had got out. It hadn't, but appeared to be upset about something, so she got her father to go out to it and went back to bed.

* * *

Early the next morning, neighbourhood children decorated the farmhouse's front walk and doorway with flowers. Holland overflows with flowers—many kinds, not just the proverbial tulip—and all the guests travelling to the church with the bridal party were presented with either a corsage or a buttonhole.

As soon as the others in the bridal party arrived, Jeb and Elsje got in the first of three horse-drawn carriages waiting outside. Their parents got in the second and everyone else got in the third, and largest. And then we were off, with the Dutch horses responding to their drivers' tongue clicks just as obediently as a milkman's English horse always had when my brother Peter and his friend John clicked to it to get it to move on to the next house whilst the milkman was delivering his wares to ours. (Peter and John always prudently disappeared before the milkman figured out why the horse had taken it into its head to do that.)

Once the carriages were underway, cars followed; one containing the horses' owners, another the wedding photographer, and still another, Elsje's grandparents, but even with the continual buzzing of flies, I preferred the carriage ride.

In Holland, only civil wedding ceremonies are legally binding, so we had to stop off at a registry office to get one conducted. The wording of it was lost on the Canadians present, as was what the officiator said at the end that made all the Dutch-speakers laugh.

Back en route to the church, the horses decided to mutiny. For a few moments, they just stopped and refused to move, but then started to jump around. It was against just such an eventuality that their owners had tagged along, and the voice of their master must have held power, because the agitated equines immediately calmed down and resumed the journey.

At the church, everyone received one of the programmes we'd folded. Then Jeb, Elsje, and the minster came in and the religious ceremony began, this time with a translator standing by for the benefit of the Canadians present. The hymns (beautifully played by Daan) were not translated, but most were familiar, and the Canadians just pronounced the Dutch words as best they could if they didn't happen to remember all the English words to them.

About halfway through the service, I got a coughing spasm. According to Ellen and Duane, my face turned bright red, my eyes started to water, and when I tried to cough without making any noise, I shook the whole pew. They found this quite entertaining. I did not.

Leaving the church, everyone filed past Jeb and Elsje to congratulate them before going into a nearby hall for pre-wedding supper refreshments. Ellen and I found seats at a table with a non-English speaking Dutch couple and had some tea. Cakes and pastries were circulating as well, but none came our way until Elsje's brother Zeger invited us over to his table so we would know what was being said. The goodies were, however, well worth waiting for.

Later on, Ellen and I wandered outside with Duane and succeeded in convincing him that he didn't really require all of his weight allowance for flying home the following week and could easily take back some of the bothersome little items that were weighing down our packs. When it started to rain, we returned to the hall and saw most of it had been set up for the wedding supper. Daan was the Master of Ceremonies, and during the first course (salad) read out telegrams and got the poems about Jeb and Elsje going.

The poems corresponded to numbers the guests had been assigned. They were supposed to be about Jeb or Elsje when they were the age of that number and be accompanied by a small present related to the incident being recalled. Around seven or eight people did theirs before the soup course arrived and Daan temporarily called a halt. After the soup came more poems, among them one I'd written for Duane about going fishing with Jeb. His present was a fish. Quite real, quite dead, and quite odorous.

The main course was served after all the poems had been read, and as soon as everyone got through that, Daan and Zeger entertained the crowd with the well-known 'Broken Mirror' routine (in Dutch: *De Gebroken Spiegal*). Originally performed in the early 1900s in Europe and the U.S.A. by the Schwarz Brothers—in actuality, the father-son team of Camillo and Carl Robi—variations of it were later used by comedians such as Max Linder and the Marx

Brothers. This skit about a valet who tries to copy all his short-sighted master's movements to keep him from finding out that his prize mirror has been broken proved itself capable of still drawing laughs fifty years later. It was followed by a song, with Daan seated on a wooden goat and Zeger handing him strange things like straw whiskers at intervals.

Dessert was an ice-cream cake, a treat everyone tucked into readily.

From that point on, conversation prevailed until, at last, people began to head home. The horses and carriages had long since departed, so Daan took Jeb and Elsje back to the farmhouse by car and everyone else who'd arrived by carriage had the choice of waiting for cars or returning on foot. The farmhouse was only about two miles away, and since Grethe said she knew a shortcut, Ellen, Duane, and I elected to go with her, as did Zeger, Zeger's wife, Grethe's friend, and Jeb's Canadian friends.

The rain had stopped, but the dark, moonless, night was cool. Walking along wearing just a short plaid skirt and thin, short-sleeved, peasant blouse, I felt a bit chilly, and Duane gallantly lent me his suit coat. Soon afterwards, we took to a grass footpath on which the grass was still wet and the earth muddy. Even so, we were doing all right until Grethe led us onto another path, this one enclosed by trees. That made the going a bit harder and, to help things along, rain started to fall again.

In response, Grethe and all the others at the head of the column quickened their pace, leaving Zeger, Duane, Ellen, and myself behind. Not wanting them to get too far ahead, I grabbed hold of Duane's wrist, Ellen grabbed hold of mine, and the three of us raced after Zeger as he raced after Grethe and company. Unfortunately, this path did not just have wet grass and mud puddles. It had several deep ruts, and we fell into one that Zeger had managed to leap over. Duane, first, me running into the back of him, and Ellen sliding down behind us. This slowed us down, and although Zeger stopped to wait for us, the others didn't, all of them working under the assumption that, like Grethe, Zeger knew the way back to the farmhouse.

And Zeger did know the way, but it involved going onto an even worse path—one that trees grew *on*, not just at the side. One was right beside the deepest, widest, rut we'd yet come across. It was practically a ditch, and even though I caught hold of the tree in time to keep from falling in, Duane *did* fall in. Since I still had hold of his wrist, I went in too. By then Ellen had lost her grip on me, and should have been able to steer clear, but didn't. She tumbled in—flat on her face—just as Duane and I scrambled out and went racing after Zeger, who was again racing after Grethe and the others.

"Wait! Wait!" Ellen yelled desperately. "You haven't got *me* with you. Wait!"

A great crashing through bushes was heard, and she managed to catch up with us.

We tried calling out to attract the attention of our friends up ahead but the only attention we attracted was that of a large, savage, dog from a neighbouring farm. Doubtless alerted to our presence by the yells (Duane's) and screams (Ellen's and mine) brought forth by our plummet into the ditch, it rushed out at us, snarling, snapping, and otherwise threatening to tear us limb from limb. Up until then, I'd never really appreciated the term, 'slavering hound', but this one was definitely slavering heavily, in anticipation of a midnight snack.

"Stay very still," said Zeger—unnecessarily, as none of us were harbouring any delusions about being able to outrun the brute.

Stay still we did, holding our breath in terror until the snarls subsided to a growl and a whistle from the house made our furry assailant abandon its prize and lope back onto its own property.

"That is a very bad dog," Zeger informed us. "Very mean. I meet it before."

"And you came this way *again*?" Duane inquired, unable to believe that the danger of running into the local Hound of the Baskervilles could possibly slip anyone's mind.

Zeger agreed it had been a mistake and suggested we move on before it decided to come back.

After stumbling around a bit more and being hit in the face by several branches, we finally made it to the main road where, not far ahead, we could see the lights of the farmhouse and our companions walking towards it.

This time they responded to our hails, and waited until we caught up to them. But it was not until we were all inside, in full light, that our now bedraggled look elicited gasps.

Zeger and I hadn't fared too badly. Other than his hair being askew and his shoes muddy (features common to all of us), he just had a crooked tie and slightly wet trouser cuffs. And my dishevelment was limited to muddy socks and a headpiece with twigs sticking through it. This was mostly because my blouse and skirt had been covered by Duane's jacket, thus sparing them the mud streaks and grass stains his jacket suffered. Duane himself hadn't been as lucky. His white shirt was in a similar state to his jacket and *his* trouser cuffs were completely soaked. And with mud all over the front of her dress, her scarf torn, and her stockings laddered and caked with mud, Ellen was quite a sight as well. But we'd made it back unchomped, and for that we were thankful.

It then being half past two in the morning, Ellen and I put together everything we wanted Duane to take home for us (our muddy wedding garments among them), and said good-bye to everyone who would not be up when we left for Munich early the next morning. Sleeping arrangements had been changed around, putting Ellen and I out in the tent by ourselves. Ellen had moved her sheet sleeping bag to the tent earlier on, and the family's dog—a much friendlier animal than the neighbours' hellhound—must have liked the smell of crushed peaches emanating from it because, just before we went to bed, he came in and rolled on it, adding his farm dog aroma to the grubby thing.

Chapter Fifteen
Down-and-out In Munich

Grethe had lent us an alarm clock to make sure we got up in time to catch our train and the alarm was a shrill one. It gave me quite a start when it went off, but Ellen did not stir. Annoyed by this, I shook her awake and we went into the house, where Elsje's mother had breakfast waiting.

After breakfast, Elsje's father and Jeb's father took us to the Arnhem train station. An American man who'd been living in Germany for twelve years joined us in our compartment and for part of the long journey to Munich pointed out the Lorelei Rock and other famous sights along the River Rhine. When he got off at Frankfurt, I stuck my head out the window to see if there was a food vendor on the platform. To do this I had to stand on a little ledge, and when the train started up unexpectedly, I got jerked backwards and lost my footing, with my head still wedged in the window. Luckily, no injury resulted, and Ellen soon freed me.

Wales might have more castles than anywhere else, but there's no shortage of them in Germany either. We'd taken an early train for the express purpose of getting to Munich in time to go on a Saturdays-only night tour of Herrenchiemsee Palace, one of the many rural retreats of Bavaria's castle-crazy—and, many believe, just plain crazy—monarch, King Ludwig II. This imitation of France's Palace of Versailles cost more than Ludwig's better-known

Neuschwanstein Castle and Linderhof Palace combined, and is located on Herreninsel Island in the middle of Lake Chiemsee. Like several of Ludwig's expensive building projects, it was unfinished when he died what some historians consider a 'suspicious death' in 1886. It remained unfinished, but the Hall of Mirrors had been completed, and we wanted the palace's night tour as opposed to a day tour because it was only on Saturday nights that the Hall's chandeliers and candelabras were lit and visitors treated to the sight of its mirrors reflecting the glow of thousands of candles.

At Munich we had to chase around a bit to find the tour booth the tour left from. There was a large crowd, and when our turn finally came, we were told the tour had already left, but, since the illuminations weren't due to start for a couple of hours, we could take a train out to what sounded like Brehen and get a ferry over to the island on our own.

As time was limited, I got the woman in the booth to phone the Munich youth hostel to say we'd arrived and ask its wardens to hold our beds for us. She did, but they wouldn't. At *that* hostel, beds had to be claimed personally, so we caught a tram out to the hostel, checked in, and left our packs in its keeping.

Back at the train station, I stopped at its currency exchange booth to get some Deutsche marks, and Ellen went to find out the departure time of the train we'd be taking to Vienna on Monday. The currency exchange was busy and its queue typically European—non-existent. People just stood somewhere and got to the front eventually. I expected Ellen to rejoin me by the time I got there, but she didn't. This was because the clerk in a passenger information centre outside the station was having an argument with a German woman. A long argument, in their native language. Every so often he'd say, "Yes, what is it?" to Ellen, and Ellen would say, "Well, I ..." and he'd go back to yelling at the woman again. When he finally finished dealing with her, he again asked Ellen what she wanted. Ellen stared at him for a moment to make sure he really meant it, then told him and got referred to an information centre inside the station. She then stayed there to ask about the Vienna trains, and I went up to the platforms to find out which one the Brehen train left from. Both pieces of information secured, we looked around the station's shops for a while wondering why so few people in Munich were German. The first five we spoke to were American, French, Spanish, and English. There were a lot of Italian people about too, especially men, and one put his hand on my arm as I passed him in a corridor, removing it only when he was met by the icy 'British look' living in England had enabled me to acquire. Although my Scottish father was of the opinion that Ronald and I both came by it naturally. An inheritance from our Sassenach mother.

Once aboard the train, no one we spoke to seemed to know if it stopped at Brehen. Having time to spare before it started, we got off and asked a guard, who apparently didn't have time for foolish questions, as he just walked away without answering. Moving on to the ticket counter, I explained our concerns about the Brehen stop and getting to our ultimate goal. The ticket seller nodded and engaged the help of at least six passers-by, who all spoke in German and confused us completely. The train did seem to be the right one, though, so we got back on and passed the time complaining about Munich, with Ellen declaring that London no longer topped her 'Horrible Cities I've Been To' list. Munich did. At the time, I agreed, but have been back twice since, and quite like the place.

Soon, two English boys got on, and a map they showed us revealed that the name of the town we were going was Prien—full name, Prien am Chiemsee—not Brehen. Not that pronunciation made much difference. People had seemed to know what we'd said and where we wanted to go. They just didn't happen to know how to get there.

The train didn't get going until after eight o'clock, and as we rode along, it suddenly dawned on us that we'd never be able to get out to Herrenchiemsee and back to Munich before the youth hostel closed at half past eleven. Reluctantly abandoning our plans, we decided to take the first train back to Munich as soon as we reached Prien.

And we would have, but, upon arrival, were told the last train to Munich had already gone. In fact, the last train to *anywhere* had gone, and the station was closing.

Outside the station, a man summoned some cab drivers to help us. There were only two at first, and neither spoke English, so we were unable to follow their rapid discussion of our plight. Finally, an English-speaking one came along and was able to make us understand that we could take a cab to Rosenheim and catch the last train to Munich from there. The cab cost twenty-three marks (around $5), so, at first, we were hesitant. The cab driver pointed out that a hotel would be more than that, and the train station had shut down, so we couldn't stay there. Having little choice, we agreed, and a non-English speaking driver transported us to Rosenheim at a rate I felt must have broken all speed records. But only because, at the time, I had not yet travelled in cabs in Mexico City and Cairo.

At the station, the driver and jumped out as soon as we paid him and ran ahead to try to find us the right platform. The train came in about two minutes after we panted up to it and after making sure we were all right, the driver left, and the train started off.

At Munich East, it stopped for about ten minutes, and that was enough to spell our doom. We arrived at Munich Central Station at half past eleven, the exact time the youth hostel closed. Our Eurail passes would have allowed us to get on a train and ride all night, and if our packs had been with us, we would have bidden farewell to Munich without a second thought, but we didn't know where we'd end up and didn't want to get too far from Munich. Sitting up all night in the train station didn't appeal to us either, but after we'd engaged in a session of shouting at one another and sulking privately for a few minutes, it seemed the best option. We did, at one point, go and look at the station's local accommodations board to see which hotels still had rooms, but decided we couldn't afford them and probably wouldn't be able to find them anyway. A man passing by handed us a card with the name of a 'ladies' hotel' on it and told us the rooms there were quite cheap, but as this hotel was not listed on the board, we didn't want to risk having it be the type of ladies' hotel a naïve Cornelia and Emily had chanced upon in *Our Hearts Were Young And Gay*.

Had we not been so panic-stricken back in Prien, we might have thought to check our YH address book to see if Prien had a youth hostel. If we had, we would have learned that it did, but as things stood, staying right where we were until dawn seemed our safest bet. Unfortunately, we couldn't. Leastways, not in the station itself. At midnight, a guard came along and chased everyone out, saying something about a mission. This caused me to remember a German neighbour telling me about Bahnhofsmissions before I left Canada. These missions can be found in every major German train station and are run by an ecumenical Christian organization that's been providing a variety of social services to people travelling through Germany ever since an evangelical pastor, Johannes Burckhardt, set the first of them up in Berlin in 1894. The neighbour had advised me to go to one if we ran into any trouble, which we certainly had.

With the help of a young man who spoke German better than we did, we explained our predicament to the woman in charge of the Munich Bahnhofsmission.

She showed us into a room with benches and tables and we spent the night there alongside several other women and some children.

Benches do not make especially comfortable beds, but despite this, Ellen did manage to get some sleep. I didn't, and mostly just sat up feeling disgruntled. A baby kept crying, and although I didn't mind him—I figured the kid had legitimate reasons for howling—the elderly woman beside me got on my nerves by periodically letting out an imitative bellow.

* * *

In the morning, we returned to the hostel to get our packs. Even though we'd paid for two, non-refundable, nights at the hostel and had already missed one of them, we decided to go on to Vienna by night train. Being now thoroughly disenchanted with Munich, we thought it best to just spend the day window shopping in and around the train station and taking in any sights in the area that didn't involve entrance fees.

For the next few hours, that's what we did, alternating turns of staying with the packs with turns to go off on our own for a bit. Around noon, two boys in their late teens came up to me during one of my roaming around interludes and, seeing the flag on my gadget bag, asked where in Canada I was from. I told them and, at some point in the course of the conversation that followed, one invited me to join them on a personal tour of Munich. As he had a great tendency to hold my arm with one hand and let the other creep around my waist as we talked, I did not find the offer all that tempting. I muttered something about my friend and I having already made plans for the afternoon and said I'd have to check with her. Undaunted, he and his sidekick followed me back to

Ellen. As we approached her, I hid my face from them with my purse and mouthed, "Help!", a cue Ellen immediately picked up on. Between us, we managed to convince them that we couldn't possibly go with them because we were in Munich with our brothers and were supposed to be meeting them in the station café, oh, any time now. We also tried to give them the impression these brothers stood well over six feet tall, weighed around three hundred pounds, and were very protective of their baby sisters. This was, on all counts, a vast stretching of the truth but it worked. They left, and to add credence to our ruse, we gathered up our packs and went to the station café to get ourselves some tea.

Inside, I swung my pack down and got it caught on a chair. The twenty-something young man at a nearby table unhooked it for me and asked if he could join us at our table. As we got to talking, we discovered his name was Kurt, and he was a Berliner now living in Munich. When Kurt offered to show us around, we agreed. For some reason, we trusted *him* instantly. Granted, the other two might have been just as nice, but Kurt practically exuded nice, and didn't talk with his hands.

As soon as we'd finished our tea, Kurt took us on a short walk to what I assume was the Löwenbräukeller Restaurant. I didn't actually take note, but he said it was one of the largest restaurants in the world and the Löwenbräukeller—established in 1883—fell into that category. He'd already downed a large beer at the station café, but ordered another, equally large, one there. We, however, ordered food, chicken for me and Wiener Schnitzel for Ellen. As well as small-sized beers. Kurt said that, in Germany, we were of age to drink beer, and wanted us to sample *Bavarian* beer, which he deemed the best. I was pretty sure beer, Bavarian or otherwise, was not a drink I would like, but thought I should at least give it a try in the original home of Oktoberfest, the annual and no-longer-confined-to-Munich folk festival in which the consumption of beer plays a significant role. Initially, however, Oktoberfest was a Munich tradition that grew up around a big horse race set up by Bavarian National Guardsman, Andreas Michael Dall'Armi, in October, 1810 to commemorate the wedding of Prince Regent Ludwig (later King Ludwig I) and Princess Therese of Saxony-Hildburghausen.

When our 'small-sized' beers came, they came in foot-high glasses, and although Ellen managed to get hers down, my suspicions regarding how my taste buds would react were quickly confirmed, and I left mine sitting after two sips.

From there we took a cab out to Kurt's apartment. Again, we had no qualms, and none were warranted. A large Bible lay open on his coffee table, and although Kurt poured himself another beer, he made us tea. He then put on some Bach records and under the soothing influence of the Bible and Bach, we discussed Hitler, communism, advertising, and a number of other topics.

Later on, we took a tram out to the lovely palace of Nymphenburg and walked around its massive grounds, with Kurt pointing out its different architectural styles and filling us in on some of its history. Work on this royal summer residence started in 1664 at the behest of the current Bavarian ruler and Kurfürst (Elector) of the Holy Roman Empire, Ferdinand Maria (1636-1679). An Elector was a prince with the right to take part in the election of a new Holy Roman Emperor whenever a vacancy came up, and at one time, Holy Roman Emperors *were* elected, but by the seventeenth century, the House of Habsburg had gained a firm enough grip on the reins of power to have made the title of Holy Roman Emperor pretty much hereditary, and that of Elector pretty much pointless. Ferdinand Maria was still a ruler in his own right though and had Nymphenburg built as a present for his wife, Henriette Adelaide of

Savoy, after the birth of their son, Maximilian Emmanuel (1662-1726). They'd been married for ten years and were beginning to wonder if an heir for Ferdy was *ever* going to come along, and when he finally did, that love of fancy domiciles to which Germanic royals were prone must have made the building of a new palace seem the perfect way to celebrate.

A deer running free in the grounds ran too quickly for me to get a picture of it, but, after Nymphenburg, Kurt took us to a huge park-like beer garden with fenced-in deer that were easier to capture on film. There, he had yet another beer. I'd never really believed all those drinking stories about Bavarians until I met Kurt. He had six or more really large beers in the hours he was with us without giving any sign of being the least bit tipsy. Ellen ordered a glass of root beer, but this turned out to be a glass of real, alcoholic, root beer rather than the soft drink she was expecting, and she didn't finish it.

It was dark by the time we left the beer garden and went back to Kurt's apartment for more tea and conversation before returning to the train station. We wanted to get some food for the trip, but all the station's food stalls were closed so Kurt took us to an underground shopping centre similar to Zürich's and then back up to the station's restaurant to have even more tea. And, yes, he had another beer.

In making a study of the train we were to board, we could only find four carriages marked 'Wien', for Vienna, so we climbed into the nearest one and said good-bye to Kurt, our pleasant afternoon and evening with him having helped mitigate our antipathy towards Munich.

We walked the corridors of those four carriages for some time looking for seats but there weren't any. We spent close to two hours sitting in the corridor before a man and woman got off and we were able to get their seats in a couchette. The other people in it, two men and a girl, helped us put our packs up on the luggage rack, and after ascertaining that we, like them, were not getting off until Vienna, converted the seats into beds so everyone could settle down for the night.

Chapter Sixteen
Vienna And Its Woods

Ellen was tidying herself up in a WC, when we got to Vienna. With a little help from one of the men in our compartment, I slung both our packs off the train and got him to watch them so I could dash off to find Ellen before the train set off again with her on it. My concern regarding this was based on past experience. My mother once got off a train in the early hours of a morning to send an estimated-arrival-time telegram to my father. Taking with her the only kid who was awake—which was, of course, me—she returned to find the train pulling out with her still slumbering offspring aboard. As she pursued it down the platform, the stationmaster assured her the carriages were merely being repositioned and child abandonment charges would not be pending.

The powerful Austrian-Hungarian Empire that came into being in 1867 came to an end in 1918 when Austria became a republic. But only until the twelfth of March, 1938, the date on which soldiers from neighbouring Germany marched in and annexed it. At the time, many Austrians were in favour of *Anschluss* (unification) with Germany, mostly because they thought it would restore the ethnic pride lost in the aftermath of World War I and allow them to enjoy the same economic benefits as Nazi Germany and still keep their autonomy. In this they were wrong. The Germans took charge of everything and everyone. After the fall of the Third Reich, the Allies did likewise, and Austria did not regain its sovereignty until 1955. My school trip took place ten years later, but the capital, Vienna, was not on the itinerary, so I was no more familiar with the city than Ellen was.

We got to the hostel well before its morning closing time and were able to deposit our packs in our dorm before going to the Canadian Embassy to pick up letters. Unlike some we'd been to, this embassy was a modern place, with lifts, carpets, and automatic doors. We both had letters and stayed in the lobby to read them. One from my mother informed me that a letter I should have picked up in Amsterdam's non-existent embassy contained a reply from one of the Paris youth hostels we'd written to. The reply stated that advance payment was required for advance bookings, and without making an advance booking, there was a chance we might not be able to stay there, which was a bit worrisome.

A fellow hosteller had told us a local tour was the best way to view a major city's highlights within a short period of time, so after we'd been to the embassy, we went to a tourist information centre to see if we could book one. Top of the list for places we wanted to take in via a tour was the Spanish Riding School and a performance by its famous equines. Much to our disappointment, it was closed for the summer, with only the stable and riding hall open to the public at certain hours. No tours went there, so we booked a tour of the Vienna Woods instead. Since it didn't leave for several hours, we decided to indulge in the favourite pastime of most teenage girls and go shopping.

Our first purchases were made in a stationery shop, where we got some postcards and a new journal for me, as the one I'd brought with me was close to full. From there we drifted from shop to shop, mostly browsing but occasionally buying. In the course of this, we went down several interesting side streets, and within an hour were totally lost. The directions people gave us confused us even more and we finally had to catch a tram back to where we'd started out from, amazed to find how far we'd wandered.

Even so, we were in good time for our tour. I didn't catch the bus driver's name, but the guide was Hans, an architectural student who reeled off information in both English and German. Upon entering the Vienna Woods, we went past, but not into, Liechtenstein Castle, and then on to the SOS Children's village of Hinterbrühl, which opened in 1956. The first SOS village was set up in the Tyrol in 1949 by a young Austrian medical student and child welfare worker named Hermann Gmeiner, who realized how important a stable family environment was for children left orphaned and destitute by World War II. Concerned, he founded the organization that would eventually establish over five hundred such villages and operate in over one hundred and thirty countries. The Hinterbrühl village we visited is now the largest SOS Children's Village in Europe and considered a model for all the others.

The majority of Hinterbrühl's youthful residents were away on holiday at the time of our visit. We were supposed to return to the bus after viewing one of the temporarily deserted homes, but most people in the group made their way to some tourist-oriented stands to get postcards and cold drinks. Clearly used to this, Hans merely sighed, said, "What can I do?", and started yodelling, which is what he always did when he wanted us. Eventually everyone got back on the bus and we set off again.

Hans's next objective was Heiligenkreuz Abbey, then, as now, the largest Cistercian Abbey in Europe, but not as well-known to the world as it would become in 2008, when seventeen of its monks made a CD of some Gregorian chants and rose to the top of the classical music charts. One of the oldest forms of written music, these sung prayers take their name from the man considered the founder of the medieval papacy, Pope Gregory the Great (also known as Saint Gregory I) who lived from 504 to 604. Heiligenkreuz was built in 1133 and somehow avoided the destruction or dissolution others fell victim to. In consequence, monks have been working and praying in it for centuries, with Gregorian chants forming but a part of their lives. A hard-working order, Cistercians also devote themselves to pastoral duties, manual labour, and religious study.

This time, Hans let his group visit tourist stands *first*, and then took us around the ancient abbey.

From there we went to Mayerling Hunting Lodge. Used more for stalking the fair sex than for hunting, Mayerling was the place a nineteenth-century crown prince, Archduke Rudolf, and one of his (many) mistresses, Baroness Maria Vetsera, died under mysterious circumstances in 1889.

The last stop on the tour was the spa town of Baden, where Ludwig von Beethoven and other famous people once eased their aches and pains in its sulphur baths. We, however, went to the Hotel Sacher and were allowed thirty minutes to get refreshments.

"Great," a middle-aged American who worked in Germany said as he looked out at a veritable fleet of other buses. "All these people, and thirty minutes to get served."

Everyone managed to, however. Ellen and I found a table alone at first, but then a young Canadian couple asked us to join them. He had a beer, she an apple juice, Ellen and I tea, and all of us that lovely chocolate cake the place is famous for—Sacher-Torte. Whatever people had to drink cost seventeen schillings, regardless of what it was. Even though we thought having to pay seventeen schilling (70¢) for a cup of tea was outrageous, it was nice to sit in peaceful surroundings with a three-man orchestra playing.

When the thirty minutes were up, we heard Hans yodelling and went back to the bus, where he counted noses and found four missing. Three of the people to whom they belonged came running up after he'd been outside looking for them and everyone cried, "Shame!" "Shame!", when they came aboard. That still left one unaccounted for, and Hans was about to go out and look for him when he saw him coming.

"Start the bus slowly and scare him," someone suggested.

"Yeah, make him run," said the middle-aged American.

"Don't be cruel," said his wife.

"I can't help it," he said with a fiendish smile. "It's all those years of living as a company boss in Germany. It's made me tyrannical."

The latecomer got on amid boos and we took off. Passing through vineyard-covered slopes, Hans told us that Beethoven composed many famous pieces in the Vienna Woods, which he did not just visit for sulphur baths. He was also very fond of a particular red wine produced in the area.

Back in the city, various stops were made to let people off at, or close to, their accommodation. As we only knew our way via the tram circuit near where the bus had left from, we stayed on until the end, along with the young Canadian couple, the middle-aged American and his wife, and two or three others.

At the youth hostel we dug out some groceries and had our evening meal. I then left Ellen to finish eating and went down to our dorm with the intention of falling into bed. But between talking to two American girls and recording the day's events in my new journal, I was still up when Ellen came in.

* * *

Awakening the next morning, I sleepily asked a nearby girl what time it was.

"Nine," she replied.

"Nine?" I repeated disbelievingly, certain it was only about half past seven at the latest.

But nine it was, and the hostel closed at ten, so Ellen and I were forced to struggle up. That was a later closing time than most, but still required us start the day sooner than we wanted. We got some washing together—one peach-stained, dog-rolled-on sheet sleeping bag, month-long worn pyjamas, and filthy towels—and asked a hostel employee where the nearest laundry was. The man in charge of it didn't speak English, but after a good deal of poor German, no English, and considerable hand waving, we ascertained that we could not wash our clothes ourselves. We had leave them there for him to do. As far as we could tell, he wanted us to come back in two hours, so we went to a café on another street and had tea and pastries for breakfast.

Later on, we found an area of grass and trees in the middle of the road and sat there for a time. But conversation was difficult with cars whizzing by and we thought it might be nice to find a quiet park to spend the afternoon in. After arranging to meet Ellen at a nearby toy shop, I went to look for such a park, and she went back to the laundry for our things.

The reason the toy shop was chosen as a meeting place was that Ellen wanted to get something for her nieces. Its proprietor didn't speak much English, but was very helpful when it came to pointing out which toys were the most suitable for kids their age, and saying whether or not they were made in Austria. Ellen's nieces were unlikely to care, but she felt a present from another country should at least have been manufactured in that country and not in Japan, the—then—chief producer of mass-market goods.

That accomplished, we went to the park I'd found and scouted around for either a WC or a nearby restaurant in which to have a meal, as the latter was sure to have 'facilities' for its patrons. The one we chose also had really, really good food, providing us with one of the best meals either of us had ever had: chicken for me, and some sort of mushroom dish for

Ellen. As well as most excellent service from the owner, a Mr. Kalina.

Moving on to the park, we upset a few people by walking on the grass. "*Verboten,*" they said. One word that, thanks to numerous war movies, we would have understood even if we hadn't taken German in school. (Along with *hande hoch,* which was fortunately *not* said to us.)

An Australian woman at a nearby picnic table asked us what it was that was "*verboten*", and we told her that, near as we could tell, it was walking on the grass. She nodded, saying she and her two little boys, aged eight and five, had got yelled at for playing on it earlier. The boys were in possession of a ball, so Ellen and I took them to a concrete play area, where Ellen overcame her aversion to children long enough for us to play piggy-in-the-middle with them. But they were little and energetic, and we were big and easily exhausted. They were sneaky, too. One time when I was running after the ball, the younger one kicked it out of my reach. Foiled by a five-year-old!

All this activity did not cause Ellen and I to start coughing, so I suppose we must both have recovered from our throat infection/cold by this point. Even so, in about twenty minutes, we were too weary to go on and went back to where the boys' mother was sitting on a bench. She'd been ordered off the picnic table, which in the minds of some old codgers who considered it 'theirs', was not a picnic table, but a chess-playing table.

After we'd talked some more, the kids wanted to play ball again, but we didn't have the energy. I told the older one how to say, "Will you please play with me?" in German, so they could ask people closer to their own age and vitality level. They were too shy to try it at first but did find someone to play with shortly before their mother packed up to go back to their room. Ellen and I stayed where we were for a while, occasionally getting up to take drinks from what we'd first thought was a fire hydrant but came to realize was a water fountain.

The park also had a paddling pool. Too old and mature to cool off in it, we returned to our hostel and asked where the nearest swimming baths were. I knew Austrian cities had such things because the teachers had taken us to one in Innsbruck when I was on my school trip. One of the few places they *did* take us. Clearly ahead of their time, they were firm believers in free-range children and mostly just let us wander around each city on our own during the hours in which the hostels we were staying in were closed.

The aquatic centre recommended wasn't very big, and played host to a number of biting insects, but the water was cool and refreshing enough to be enjoyed by even such poor swimmers as we were, and still are. Although I did once win a beginners' race for my house at an inter-house school swimming gala. Due, no doubt, to the fact that the representatives from the other two houses couldn't swim at all.

Having no towels, we put our clothes on over top of our swimsuits and started off for the tram. On the way we spotted a wine garden with some musicians who were trying to entertain the patrons—somewhat in vain, as I doubt many people could hear them above the roar of passing traffic. We went in and ordered tea. As we were drinking it, I realized I'd left my watch at the swimming desk and had to go back for it.

A rather full day, but a pleasant one.

* * *

The next morning, we went to the Canadian Embassy to change some money and then to a tourist information centre to see if there were any concerts taking place that day. There weren't, leaving us free to shop for souvenirs in general, and some petit point in particular.

We also tried to find the Spanish Riding School, which takes its name from its use of Spanish horses. We knew it was in an impressive-looking building, but there were a lot of impressive looking buildings in the general area and very few signs. And when we did finally come across a Spanish Riding School sign, it said no tours of the place were available until mid-afternoon. As it was not yet even noon, we went into a café, and met an American who told us about a cholera epidemic in Spain. This caused us to race to the Canadian Embassy in a panic to find out what we should do about this. The people there didn't seem overly concerned, but said shots were advisable and gave us the name of a health clinic that was only open mornings. Since we were leaving in the morning, we figured we'd have to wait until we got to Salzburg.

Back at the Spanish Riding School a huge crowd had gathered and we went in with the next English-speaking tour party. The school was established in 1572, at the height of the Austro-Hungarian Empire, and was run from an arena in the Imperial Palace until 1735, when Emperor Charles VI commissioned the winter school building. The grand architecture and beautiful chandeliers of the practice and performance arena was already familiar to us, courtesy of the 1965 Disney movie, *The Miracle of the White Stallions*, which recounted how American forces under orders from their horse-loving general, George Patton, saved the school's famous Lipizzaner horses from being seized by the Nazis towards the end of World War II. Born dark, Lipizzaners—the name coming from the stud farm near Lippizza/Lipica in Slovenia—are white by the time they begin their training at the age of three-and-a-half, and are the end result of the cross-breeding between Arabic and Iberian horses that took place in Spain during the time it was under Moorish occupation.

The stallions are the ones used for riding but in summer are taken to the countryside to graze in pastures green, so none were in evidence when the tour moved across to the school's stables. Some mares were there though, and to avoid having them take fright, taking pictures of them was not allowed. Getting too close to them wasn't allowed either. When a man of the obnoxious, rules-don't-apply-to-*me*, mindset went beyond the barrier at the end of the stables, a stableman rushed over and began yelling and pushing him. Forcing him back under the barrier, he gave him a few more healthy shoves down the walk, yelling all the while. The trespassing tourist started yelling too, and they had quite a little scene going until, finally, the tourist stomped away in high dudgeon and the stableman sullenly returned to his work.

After the tour, Ellen and I stopped by the Kalina restaurant again, eager for another good meal. It was closed, but a sign said it would be open again later. The hostel wasn't open either, so we sat in the park composing a letter to the Canadian Embassy in Le Hague to see if it was, by chance, holding the missing letter containing the reply from the Paris youth hostel.

When the hostel opened, we dropped off the day's purchases and went back to Kalina's for dinner. Pleased that we'd liked his restaurant enough to pay it a second visit, Mr. Kalina gave us some restaurant stationery, showed us the restaurant's listing in an international restaurant guide, and got us to sign his guest book.

Back at the hostel, we packed up in preparation for moving on to Salzburg, and were surprised at how much room a few extra little items took up.

Chapter Seventeen
Retracing My Footsteps

Before leaving Vienna, I got another postcard for my parents. I'd already written one telling them not to worry about the cholera epidemic as we planned to get shots, but upon reflection, thought they might not have heard that particular piece of European news, and decided against posting it. The young are very protective of their parents and don't believe in upsetting them unnecessarily.

We arrived in Salzburg about half past twelve. A mere six years had elapsed since my first visit to the place from which prince-archbishops of the Holy Roman Empire once wielded their power, so I remembered the train station quite well. I also remembered the city itself quite well. Or at least the parts of it my friend Laurel and I had explored, most of which were near the hostel our group was staying in. The hostel Ellen and I had booked ourselves into was a different one and located in territory unfamiliar to me. I did come upon some 'old haunts' en route, however, such as the place where I'd lost my tartan shoulder bag, and the police station where I reclaimed it. From there, I wasn't too sure of anything, and we walked along with Ellen complaining that she was nothing but a pack horse. This because, unable read a map and carry my gadget bag and purse at the same time, I had, in my usual high-handed, autocratic, fashion, left her to carry them, and surged ahead yelling, "Come on, Nellie!" This happened most places we went, but with me not being a great map reader, she invariably had to help me sort out where we were and where we were going. She wasn't a great map reader either, though, so, usually, confusion reigned.

The hostel was closed when we arrived, but we were allowed to leave our packs in the main hall and go shopping. We followed the road as far as it went and, as luck would have it, it went to the Salzach River, taking me into an area I knew very well. Recreating an earlier experience, I bought crusty rolls in a bakery and some bologna at a butcher's shop, and we feasted as Laurel and I had back in the day. Like most teenagers, the kids in our school group's older forms had eaten pretty much anything put in front of them. The younger ones approached 'foreign food' with every ounce of the deep suspicion typically displayed by English children, and tended to eat nothing, or next to nothing, during the evening meal our teachers took us out for when they returned from doing whatever they'd been doing all day. Most hostels only provided breakfast, and we seldom ate that, either. By Salzburg (our last stop) the head teacher must have thought he was going to take us back to England as shells of our former selves, because he asked us if there was *anything* we liked in the way of the locally available cuisine—answer: no— and said he'd try to get it for us. I don't know about the other picky eaters, but unbeknownst to him, Laurel and I dined well enough during all the hours we were left to our own devices. Even if ice cream and chocolate bars didn't constitute a balanced diet, children are fairly tough, and in Salzburg, we stuffed ourselves with bologna and rolls as well.

After eating, Ellen and I visited some more shops before making our way to the Mirabell Gardens. The palace attached to these lovely baroque gardens was built by the prince-archbishop Wolf Dietrich von Raitenau for his mistress, Salome Alt, and their offspring in 1606, and was called the Altenau Castle until his successor, Markus Sitticus von Hohenems, changed it to Mirabell (from the Italian word *mirabile* meaning admirable and beautiful).

I'd been to the Mirabell Gardens before—that being about the only other place in Austria our teachers ever showed us. Though they might well have gone there themselves, they didn't even take us to the huge Hohensalzburg Fortress that stands looking down on the gardens and the city in general. Being young, and unable to speak the language, we never managed to find our own way up to it, and I was not fated to do so on my trip with Ellen either, as we weren't in the city long enough to go everywhere we wanted. I did, however, finally get to explore this most positively worthy-of-a-visit fortress when I went to Salzburg with my son Richard in 2007.

Mirabell Gardens was one of the places in which *The Sound of Music* was filmed, and with that famed musical having made the rounds of local cinemas just a few months before my school trip, most of us had attended more than one showing. Thus inspired, some of my school chums and I amused ourselves running up and down its paths and jumping up and down its steps just like Julie Andrews had the kids portraying the Von Trapp children doing. Ellen and I were much too old and dignified to do *that*, but we did take photos of each other with a pair of stone unicorns once we were able to gain access to them. The unicorns were ideal for children to play on, and before we could take possession of the only unoccupied one, two little English girls of about six and eight got on it. Then their big brother (about nine) came along and pushed the littlest one off. She screamed and beat upon him, but he ignored her and she went away howling. Big sister remained unsympathetic, as she still had *her* place. Then big brother went away and little sister got back on. When another big brother (about ten) showed up, the girls told him there wasn't enough room for him to get on, but he said he would if he wanted to, and did. He then scampered away until their mother called them all together for a photograph of all her little munchkins. There was another brother, too (about seven), but he didn't seem inclined towards being a troublemaker. Except at picture-taking time, as I think he might have been the 'Steven!' Mummy was constantly ordering to keep still. ('Jane' proved difficult in this regard, too.) Mummy did eventually get the shot she wanted, though, and they all left. But, once again, Ellen and I weren't quick enough and had to wait as child after child clambered onto the mythical equines. Couldn't they tell the big girls wanted to play on them, too?

Our visit to the gardens was followed by another round of shopping. At that time, Salzburg was not marketing either *The Sound of Music* or its favourite son, Wolfgang Amadeus Mozart (1756-1791), to the unbridled extent it does now, and there was considerable non-Maria and non-Mozart-themed merchandise to be had. In one shop, the proprietor somehow got the idea we were looking for music boxes and wound up every one of them for us. Some were really nice, but I'd purchased a music box in Germany and couldn't afford another.

Back at the hostel, we booked in and were handed our individual bed number cards. We also each received two slips of paper, one yellow and one blue. As I was making up my bed, my slips fluttered to the floor, and the only one I could find was the yellow one. But, figuring it was probably just a receipt or something, I did not feel overly concerned.

That evening, we went back into town for supper, planning to go to the restaurant in which my school party had eaten its evening meals and the head teacher had finally managed to get something his first formers were willing to eat. Namely, fish and chips, and *Wiener Schnitzel* and chips. On the way we passed a restaurant where the fresh fish were so fresh, they were swimming in a tank in the entrance hall.

That was not the eatery I was seeking, though, so we went on until we found it. After the waiter had taken our order, he returned to say he was out of chicken and chips, our usual order. That being, along with tea, about the only thing we knew how to say in most languages, we decided to go somewhere else. I wasn't as much of a food critic at eighteen as I'd been at twelve, but with myriad allergies, couldn't afford to be too venturesome.

A little up the street we found yet another restaurant and ordered chicken and chips there. Accompanying beverages appeared after ten minutes or so, but as time marched on, we started to wonder aloud if the main course was ever going to. Members of a party of Americans who'd ordered before us said they were wondering the same thing because some of them had been served and some hadn't. We did eventually all get fed, but the meal was by no means up to Mr. Kalina's standards.

Back at the hostel we met and spoke with a number of fellow hostellers; some of them single travellers, the others with an English school group that was following the same route mine had: Innsbruck, Zell am See, Werfen, and Salzburg. Watching this group's more rambunctious members being rambunctious, I thought nothing on earth would persuade *me* to chaperone a herd of adolescents and/or pre-adolescents on a whirlwind tour of a foreign country, even if—if my own experience was anything to go by—chaperoning only occurred during evening meals and moves between cities. My school's young travellers had been fairly tame, but we'd crossed paths with some that weren't, and what a cousin told me he and his friends got up to on his—supposedly strict—Catholic school's trip to Spain that same year would have made their parents' hair stand on end.

* * *

At breakfast the next morning I learned the little slip of blue paper I'd lost was a breakfast ticket. I went back to the dorm to see if I could possibly still find it but was unsuccessful, so we got a breakfast with Ellen's ticket and shared it. What the yellow slip was for, I still have no idea.

After breakfast, we left the hostel and went to the train station. Although we'd planned to get cholera shots in Salzburg, it now seemed more sensible to wait until we got to Rome, where we were due to pick up letters from home. Not eager to get the shots anyway, we chose to believe that, if our parents had heard about the cholera epidemic, it was bad, and if they hadn't, it wasn't.

On the train, our packs started off on the empty seats beside us, but as the compartment filled, had to be moved onto the rack above. About halfway to Innsbruck, Ellen's bounced off and crashed down on her and a fellow passenger. It even caught me on the arm but we were all free of serious injury.

On the way to Innsbruck, we passed through Werfen and Zell am See, rekindling a few more memories. One reason we hadn't chosen to stop over in Werfen was that I could still vividly recall walking up to its mountain-top castle-hostel in the full fury of an Austrian summer storm with a large, and very heavy suitcase, and did not intend to do the same thing with an even heavier packsack. I could also remember accompanying Laurel to the lavatory in the dead of night because she had 'to go' and few things are creepier than a cold, dark, noiseless, castle late at night. Visible from the train, it looked friendlier minus the storm, and picturesque little Zell am See still looked as beautiful as it had before, so I must admit to feeling a little sorry we weren't stopping *there*.

Our fellow passengers varied from time to time, starting with an old lady, then a woman and a boy of twelve or so, and then, when they moved, a middle-aged couple who pointed all the sights out to each other and looked at them so conscientiously they must have thought they'd be struck down with a thunderbolt if they missed as much as one.

Built up around the River Inn, Innsbruck replaced Meran as the capital of Tyrol back in 1849, but its glory days ran from the time of Duke Friedrich IV (1382-1439)—who moved his Court there in 1420—to the time of Emperor Maximilian I (1459-1519). The latter had the three-storey royal box that became known as the *Goldenes Dachl* (Golden Roof) erected on the Old Town's central plaza in 1500 so he could watch tournaments and such without having to mix with the rabble. Intended as a commemoration of his marriage to his second wife, Bianca Maria Sforza, it features an image of Maxi between her and his first wife, Maria von Burgund (Mary of Burgundy, daughter of Charles the Bold). He reputedly liked the first one better, but even if he hadn't, he wouldn't have wanted to tick off the Burgundians by not having her likeness there too. A protective bunker was put around this famous Innsbruck landmark in World War II to keep it from being damaged by Allied bombs, and I think Laurel and I *might* have passed by it the first time I was in Innsbruck. If we did, we were unaware of its historical significance. Just like we were unaware of the historical significance of all the places in Austria we were *not* taken to on that supposedly educational tour. I remember some of the older kids talking about a building with a golden roof, so they must have visited it, but it probably didn't hold much meaning for them either.

The first place Ellen and I went to upon arrival in Innsbruck was the station's WC. I paid the woman in charge the small sum demanded and went into a cubicle. She closed the door behind me, but when I took off my pack, it fell against the door and knocked it open. I tried re-closing it, but it was an automatic type that required a key. Ellen hailed the attendant and said I couldn't close the door. The attendant said it was automatic, but she would close it—for an additional fee. I explained that she'd already closed it once, and it had come open. But, like many of the, mostly elderly, WC attendants we'd come across, she was a disagreeable old crone. She just repeated what she said and shook her head to indicate she didn't understand, reiterating that the cubicle time had to be paid for. I said I knew that. I had paid. It was fortunate I wasn't desperate to use the facilities because she refused to climb down from the stand she'd taken. Frustrated, I leaned against a wall and glared at her until Ellen was ready to leave. As we made our way out, Ellen said she hadn't got any change back from the money she'd handed over, even though she should have, thus giving both of us cause to feel mistreated.

As in Salzburg, the hostel we had reservations for was not the same hostel I'd stayed at before. The tourist information clerk from whom we asked directions said the only way to get to it was by cab, and my teachers had certainly not taken sixteen kids to it by cab. We'd walked. A bus went part-way, but it was a long hike, even from there, and the clerk thought we'd be better off going to a hostel in another area. Thinking this probably was the best thing to do, we asked him to ring up that hostel to see if they had places, and, if they did, also ring up the hostel we had reservations for, in order to cancel them. He said he couldn't do that, but someone at the post office would.

Starting out for the post office, we hadn't taken three steps when a fellow Canadian we'd met at the Salzburg youth hostel hailed us. She'd hitchhiked from Salzburg to Innsbruck and got there the same time we did, but hitchhiking was still something we were only willing to do if we absolutely had to.

I left her talking to Ellen and went to the post office to contact the youth hostels. I gave the woman there the telephone numbers from our YHA address book, but the number for one of them had changed and no one answered at the other.

I returned to Ellen and our Salzburg acquaintance, whose name, we learned, was Deedee, and we all went into the station café to have tea and trade travel stories. A twenty-six-year-old from Calgary, Deedee was looking for accommodations too, so we decided to wait until the hostel recommended to us opened and go there to see if it had places for three girls, and, if it didn't, share the cost of a cab out to the other one.

As we followed the route that had been drawn out for us on a city map, I started to think the closer hostel might be the one I'd been to before and thought, if I tried really hard, I might remember the way, but I didn't. Mostly because it wasn't that hostel, but yet another one. An interesting one, full of interesting things, among them two igloo-type structures that contained sleeping bags and were obviously used as additional dossing down spaces when the hostel was full.

And full it was close to being. We stood in a long queue feeling sure we'd never get places, and passed the time by trying to figure out who a marble monument with names, dates, and ages on it was supposed to be a tribute to, as recent dates made it unlikely that it was any kind of war memorial. We never did find out, but eventually reached the reception desk and got what we were told were the last beds to be allocated that day, Deedee's upstairs and ours downstairs.

Once we'd settled in, we met in the lobby and went back into the main part of town to obtain the Tyrolean hats Ellen and I had decided we simply had to have. As well as have supper and visit Innsbruck's Imperial Garden, the Hofgarten. The Hofgarten was floodlit on summer evenings and constituted another place the teachers had not deigned to take my school group to.

The first hat shop we tried didn't have the sizes we wanted, so we left and got to another just as it was closing. They let us in anyway and Ellen and I were able to purchase our Tyrolean hats, as well as feathers and pins to go with them. I looked at knives, too, thinking I might find a skean dhu substitute I could afford, but I couldn't.

The restaurant we stopped at afterwards had no menu outside. We all knew that, if there was no menu outside displaying a restaurant's prices, it was probably quite expensive, and didn't go in. We found a cheaper alternative and after eating went to the Hofgarten. When it was first laid out in the sixteenth century, only the fellow who commissioned it, Archduke Ferdinand II, and other members of the aristocracy were allowed to stroll around it. Commoners like ourselves were not admitted until the nineteenth century. On the way we saw a band marching down the street. It must have been going to the Hofgarten, too, because we heard it again there. Once night fell, we walked through the floodlit area, which really was beautiful. Ellen said she thought it looked like fairyland, and with that I had to agree.

Chapter Eighteen
A Memorable Train Trip

We awoke to peals from the bells of a nearby church. After breakfast, Ellen and I got Deedee to take a picture of us in our Tyrolean hats before we set off for our next destination: Venice. Deedee was again hitchhiking to, I believe, Zürich, so we said good-bye to her at the train station and waited for a train to come and transport us to Italy. In view of how long the Romans were in Great Britain, Ellen and I thought we might have at least a little Italian blood, but it would later, through DNA testing, transpire that we do not, not a drop, and can only surmise our ancestors were not amongst those who consorted with the invaders.

Knowing we'd be on the train for a long time, we stocked up on Bounty® bars before we left. After a considerable wait, a platform change was announced, and the desired locomotive pulled into it. The only non-smoking compartment with free seats within a carriage marked Venezia contained a woman and two children, a girl of about four and boy of about two. And those children were possibly the reason that that compartment was the only one with free seats. Now, me, I like children. I always have, but these two were to put even my patience with the human race's youngest members to the test. As to Ellen's, well, she didn't have much to start with.

Just after we crossed the border into Germany, the kids fell asleep, and until they woke up, it wasn't too bad. They had, even by Ellen's standards, been fairly tolerable up until then but, having restored their energy, turned into little fiends after their nap. Their names were Klara and Rudi—or so we gathered from their mother continually nattering at them. Before long, the pattern became set. Klara would get irritable because Mutti (Mummy) wouldn't let her do something. Rudi would poke Klara and make her more irritable. Then Mutti would tap Rudi on the leg and make *him* irritable. In between times, the train would stop somewhere, the kids would climb up on a window to look out, the train would start up again, and Mutti would make them get down. Each would then howl with frustration and rage—particularly Rudi. (He screamed, whereas Klara usually just whined a lot.) Occasionally both of them would go out into the corridor, usually stepping on either Ellen's feet or mine en route. When in the throes of one of his tantrums Rudi even stamped on my foot, but Mutti's only response was, "Tsk, tsk! Nein, Rudi."

With the train so packed, the corridor was full of other people they could annoy, and they did, drawing unfavourable comments from several. We only understood the ones in English, some by an American couple, although the man did also say they were 'kind of cute'. And they *were* very attractive children, particularly Rudi, with his golden curls.

By the time we hit Italy, the heat was unbelievable and being cooped up with a couple of *enfants terribles* made it worse. Besides that, their mother wouldn't let us have the window open more than a crack in case one of the kids fell through it. Ellen said she thought the idea had merit, but didn't try to help things along because, as I pointed out to her, headlines like, 'Canadian Teenager Pushes Toddlers Out Of Train Window' wouldn't be good for international relations.

In Verona the train stopped for close to an hour and a half and did nothing but shunt back and forth in the station. The heat was quite intense whenever we were stationary, and the kids were worse, too. But that was hardly surprising. Travel—especially prolonged travel—*is* hard on pre-schoolers. The poor little things were hot, tired, and bored, and their mother clearly wasn't having a picnic either. Even so, I could have sympathized more if they'd just been tetchy because of the heat, but they also had the usual pre-schooler/toddler ability to switch from joyous play to whiny misery to boiling rage. At one point, Rudi started to scream and went on screaming because he couldn't have his own way about something. I took some cookies out of my pack and, in an attempt to give him something else to do with his mouth, offered them to his mother, but she indicated that they had their own food. She didn't bring it out for them though, which left them carrying on as usual with no respite for me, Ellen, or two women who'd been foolish enough to get into that compartment at some point.

Whilst rummaging for the cookies, I noticed that our chocolate bars were melting and thought we should probably consume them before they deteriorated further. So, we did. All of them. Not a pleasant task, as they were warm, and gooey, and no one else in the compartment could be induced to accept a share of our 'Bounty'. Face and hands covered in chocolate, Ellen said she was never going to eat chocolate bars again. A false statement. Like me, she still does, whenever they come her way.

When the train eventually resumed its journey, the two women got off at the next stop and a man came into our compartment. He didn't stay in it much though. Kept getting up and going out into the corridor. I can't imagine why.

Not long afterwards, Ellen reached her breaking point, and, in view of her pre-existing antipathy towards the younger set, it was a wonder it took so long. It happened when little Klara pushed past her and trod heavily on her big toe. Before this, Ellen had been content to express her displeasure over any misconduct by muttering about the desirability of the board of education being applied to the seat of knowledge, and the only words she'd spoken directly to the children were, "Get off my pack, you little savage" (addressed to Rudi, who was standing on it). But this time, she snapped.

"I've had enough!" she shrieked, raising our phrase book. I'm sure she wouldn't actually have clipped the kid with it, but the desire was definitely there. (And here I must again assure readers that her relationship with juveniles really did change for the better with the passing of years.)

I managed to restrain her, and even though the mother didn't speak English, I think she grasped that Ellen was a little put out with her offspring. She took them to walk up and down the corridor for a while. Only for a while, though. They were soon back, screaming, whining, crying, stepping on, and pushing Ellen and me, and hitting and biting their mother—which, speaking now as a parent, I wouldn't've put up with regardless of how frazzled a kid was—until, thankfully, they got off the train at Padova.

Though now quieter, the compartment was still hot and uncomfortable, but became cooler as we drew closer to Venice. When the train stopped at Venezia Mestre we got off and went to change our money but only Ellen was able to because, as soon as she had, the cashier closed up shop without serving anyone else.

Inquiries about how to get to the Venice Youth Hostel resulted in us being told that, if that's where we were headed, we should have gone on to Venezia Santa Lucia and not got off the train at Venezia Mestre.

"Why would they add Venezia to this place's name if it's not actually Venezia?" I inquired of Ellen, not knowing, at that time, that Venice has *two* main railway stations: Venezia Mestre on the mainland, and

Venezia Santa Lucia on one of the hundred plus islands within Venice's vast lagoon.

She shrugged. "Maybe it's a suburb."

Annoyed, but resigned, we caught the next train, which proceeded to make a series of stops in the middle of nowhere, with a highway on one side of us and water on the other. When we did eventually arrive in what we regarded as the *real* Venice, we were sure the hostel had long since cancelled our reservations. These were only held until six o'clock and, thanks to the various delays we'd experienced, it was already pushing nine. Even with an hour's time change, we'd have had no trouble arriving by six if the train had not been half an hour late leaving Innsbruck and then stopped in Verona for as long as it did, but that could not now be helped and we decided to make a try for the hostel anyway.

Two hostellers who were leaving Venice told us how to get out to there and gave us the correct address, saying the one in our YHA book was out of date.

The train station was right on the Grand Canal, with a vaporetto (waterbus) station right in front of it. We bought tickets for a #5, and, on board, a girl already staying at the hostel said she could show us where to get off. Even at that time of night there was a long queue outside the hostel. As well as a sign that read 'Full For Girls', and gave directions to another youth-oriented bed and breakfast establishment that was for girls only. Unwilling to give up on the one for which we had reservations we opted to wait and see if they were still good. Happily, they were.

Chapter Nineteen
Flitting Around The Floating City

A loud alarm was pumped through some sort of public address system early the next morning and went on for about five minutes, which at least ensured that those it was summoning to breakfast would not go back to sleep.

Breakfast consisted of rolls and marmalade. Instead of putting marmalade on my rolls, I brought out a jar of Bovril® beef extract that I'd purchased. An American hosteller who was perchance only used to that sort of thing being the makings of a broth or drink couldn't quite believe I would put it on bread. His English travelling companion set him straight, shocked that anyone should have endured a whole lifetime of being deprived of 'bread and Bovril'. Hot chocolate was available, too, served in an Oliver Twist, "Please, Sir, I want some more", type bowl.

Shortly afterwards, we caught a vaporetto back to the train station, where I changed some money and Ellen went to the passenger information centre to ask where the nearest tourist information centre was. But, alas, she was told these were all on strike, which was a bit of a let-down. Our positive experience with the tours we'd taken in Vienna had made local tours seem like a practical idea for Venice, too. But how, now, to find out about them? As she stood pondering this, a young American came up to her and asked what it was she wanted to do. At first, she thought he was trying to pick her up (we were in *Italy*), but he was only trying to be helpful. He said American Express had the kind of tours we wanted and told her where to find an outlet. The travellers cheques we carried were American Express, and, we thought that was all the company dealt in, but once I rejoined her, we followed his directions and were able to book the tours we wanted: a Grand Canal Tour scheduled to leave at three o'clock that afternoon, and an Illuminated Gondola Tour for late that night.

With several hours to go before our first tour, we had some refreshments at a café and visited the souvenir shops and stands in the area. These were all by the canal and did not seem to have any counterparts when we branched off into inner streets.

Returning to the canal area, we found a souvenir shop that sold the type of charms Ellen was after. It also sold Venetian glassware and model gondolas. Unable to resist a gondola, I bought one. Carrying this somewhat fragile object around Europe promised to be a bit of a nuisance, but much to my relief, this wasn't necessary as the shop's proprietor shipped goods all over the world. After he said it would be cheaper to ship more than one thing, Ellen and I each chose some Venetian glassware and had him ship it to Canada with the gondola. His English was excellent, and this, too, was a relief. Italy was the first foreign country we'd been in that really *felt* like a foreign country. Perhaps because, aside from Holland—where several of the people we were with spoke English—Italy was the first country in which we had to contend with a language we had almost no knowledge of; 'ciao', 'arrivederci', 'per favore', 'grazie', and 'scusi', being about the extent of our vocabulary.

That settled, we started towards a park—a nice, quiet, park where we couldn't spend any more *money*—but on the way spotted some straw gondolier hats (black ones with red ribbons) and each bought one of those, too. Then we really did go to the park and sat there writing postcards, stating in some that all the stories we'd heard about the Italian male didn't seem to apply in Venice. We'd been there an evening and a morning without being approached in the type of undesirable way we'd been led to expect.

We also converted our expenditures into Canadian money and discovered we'd each spent around $25 in three hours. Good-bye Italian budget.

I was therefore not too pleased when we caught a vaporetto to the Piazza San Marco and I had to hand over even more money. The ticket taker did not seem to, or did not choose to, understand what we were asking for. He said San Marco tickets were one hundred and twenty lire, but only took a hundred lire from me and did not give me a ticket. Then he came back and demanded the full hundred and twenty lire. As in, twenty plus *another* hundred. Not being able to speak Italian, there wasn't much I could do other than pay it and accept that, like Ellen, I'd been forced to part with money unnecessarily. And be thankful my experience hadn't been nearly as expensive as her street photographer one, Italy's exchange rate then being about five hundred lire to one Canadian dollar.

At the Piazza San Marco, we went looking for Venice's main American Express office, the place from which the Grand Canal tour was due to start. The office was closed, but a sign said a tour guide would come, and to wait. Not knowing if that meant we were supposed to wait there or by the company's fleet of gondolas, we went looking for the gondolas and/or some people who might be taking the same tour. We couldn't find either, and when the time for the tour drew near, went back to the American Express office. Stationing Ellen there, I ran down an as-yet untried street and spotted the elusive gondolas. There were a lot of them, but no passengers or guides for them. Just gondoliers. Thinking it best to go back to the American Express office, I did so, and saw Ellen and a Norwegian woman talking to what turned out to be our guide. Shortly afterwards, he went off somewhere, but said he would be back and to wait for him. Being told what to do gave us security, so we sat down and talked to the woman until the guide returned. He took us to the gondolas, selected one, and got us into it. The sleek craft swayed a bit as it glided away from its mooring post, and with balance being very important, he had to move his chair to the centre to get the weight right before we set off properly.

The tour took us all over Venice's two-mile long Grand Canal—known to the locals as the *Canalazzo*—as well as down lots of little side canals, the latter of which were very peaceful. It was as though we were the only people in the whole world, floating through a deserted city. In one of the less hygienic canals, we saw a child playing half-on some steps and half-in the filthy water they went down into. The children of Venice were doubtless immune to any unhealthy microorganisms it contained, but he probably still had to have a bath later on.

Only one stop was made. This was at the Frari Church or, in full, the *Basilica di Santa Maria Gloriosa dei Frari*. The *frari* (friars) referred to are Franciscans. Their order built the first Frari Church in the mid-thirteenth century and had it remodelled twice before the last version was consecrated in 1492. A major Renaissance art repository, it houses the tombs of, among others, the eighteenth-century sculptor, Antonio Canova, and the fifteenth/sixteenth-century Italian artist Tiziano Vecellio (Titian). Two of the latter's works are there too, the *Assunta* or 'Assumption of the Virgin', and the *Pesaro Madonna*. In those days, the only paintings I could have identified with any degree of confidence were Gainsborough's *Blue Boy*, and da Vinci's *Mona Lisa* and *Last Supper*, so I can't say I paid much attention to Titian's magnificent altarpieces. But I did like a statue of Mary that was standing in a quiet area surrounded by candles.

It was at the Frari Church that the other members of our tour group caught up with us. I hadn't been aware there were any others, but when a gondola appeared with four people in it, they joined our guide.

A visit to a glass factory was in with the tour if anyone wanted it, and when we got back to the starting point, the Norwegian woman said *she* did and we went along too. Glassmaking started up in Venice in Roman times and by the late thirteenth century was the city's leading industry. So much so that, in 1271, a law came into effect prohibiting the importation of foreign glass and the hiring of foreign workers. In 1295, both the workers and the furnaces they used were moved to the Island of Murano, and the craftsmen forbidden to leave the Republic of Venice, lest they reveal trade secrets to outsiders. But having their movements restricted probably didn't perturb them all that much. They were well paid and enjoyed such high social status that their offspring were allowed to marry into the uppermost upper crust of Venice's upper crust.

In the seventeenth century, the popularity of Venetian glassware gradually started to decline. As indeed did the power and influence on the world stage of Venice itself. But its glassware never went completely out of fashion. Dedicated artisans passed their knowledge on from father to son and kept buyers interested by creating works that catered to certain trends, such as the one for little glass animals that took hold in the first half of the twentieth century. These were still popular when we were there, and it was interesting to watch a skilled workman turn a little blob of hot glass into a beautifully coloured bird. Immediately following the demonstration, the guide led us into the shop part of the factory to look around. And that was all Ellen and I did. Just looked. We'd spent enough money that day, mostly on items we didn't *really* require.

We did require film, however, and I'd used up the last of my cartridges to take a picture of the statue of Mary in the Frari Church. Luckily, the area had lots of other kinds of shops, though perhaps not as many as it did forty-five years later, when my son and I wandered around it vainly seeking a route from the Piazza San Marco to the Rialto Bridge. But we only went into one or two, as I already had Venetian souvenirs and Richard wasn't able to find anything he was willing to pay an outrageous amount of euros for. By then Venice had become even more expensive than it had been on my first visit, with gondola rides having risen to such an exorbitant sum that we, and many other tourists, eschewed them.

With my stock of film replenished, Ellen and I headed back to the hostel. It was just across the canal and a quick trip in a #5 vaporetto, but #5s didn't stop at all stations, and we had to walk quite a way.

Back at the hostel, I went to the desk to see if we could be issued late passes. The hostel's curfew time was eleven o'clock, the same time the Illuminated Gondola tour *ended*. But the warden was dealing with other concerns at the time and said no way, no late pass, not even for twenty minutes. I explained about the tour, but he still refused.

I went back to Ellen, who'd gone to the refreshment stand for a lemonade, and we discussed the possibility of leaving our dorm window open and sneaking in after hours like we had in Cork. But we were on the second floor and were pretty sure that that wouldn't work out well for girls who'd never managed to get more than a foot or so above the knot when climbing ropes in P.E. class. Another, even weightier, factor against a Cork re-play was the resident canine, a rather large Alsatian that was kept muzzled and confined in the yard in the daytime. At night there was every chance it would be unmuzzled and unconfined.

Someone told us to try the manager again when he wasn't so busy. Leaving Ellen to her lemonade, I went upstairs to write a letter home. When Ellen came up, she suggested we catch a night train to Rome after the tour if we couldn't obtain passes and it seemed the only thing we could do, even though it meant going out to the train station and depositing our bags in Left Luggage before going on to San Marco for the tour.

When we went downstairs, we again asked if there was *any* way we could have late passes. And not even very late passes, just a quarter of an hour or so. Once again, the manager refused, but then beckoned me to one side and—possibly won over by my forlorn query about a night train to Rome—said he'd let us in at quarter past eleven. But quarter past eleven exactly, not five seconds after. And only because we were British. Technically, I was the only one who was British, but was not inclined to quibble when permission to come in late had been obtained.

We got to the vaporetto station in good time to get where we were going but not as many ran at night as during the day. Worried about not making it to the tour's departure point by nine o'clock, we practically leapt aboard when one finally came, and did leap off when it docked at San Marco, where we found ourselves amidst a large crowd engaged in *La Passeggiata*, the evening stroll Italians habitually end a day with. Whenever we came to a relatively people-free area, we ran, even up and down the steps of bridges. In the side street leading to the tour departure point, Ellen called out, "Gangway!", and charged through natives, tourists, and anyone else who got in her way. (All leapt aside.) I merely followed thinking, *well, there's a historic first—Ellen leading a run!*

An unnecessary one, as it turned out. The night tour was popular, and very well attended. Many gondolas were required and the late arrival of a sufficient number resulted in a late start. Ellen and I got the couch seat of the first one and an English-speaking man and woman and their teenage daughter from an unidentified country took the remaining seats.

A large, illuminated, gondola carrying some singers and musicians set out first, and all the other gondolas followed it out into the Grand Canal, where still more gondolas joined us. They were soon all side-by-side, so close that their occupants could hold conversations with the people in the ones next to them. The traffic jam made the scene a little less grand than we'd imagined, but it was still lovely, with the illuminated gondola in front, the moon shining overhead, and the quiet sound of water lapping against our little water crafts whenever the music stopped for a moment and such sounds could be heard.

Apart from a few operatic pieces sung by a woman, the music mostly consisted of gondolier songs and romantic ballads sung by men. 'Arrivederci Roma' is the only one I can recall, possibly because it didn't seem a very fitting choice for Venice.

Even so, Ellen and I enjoyed the night tour, and would have enjoyed it even more if we hadn't been worrying about getting back to the hostel by quarter past eleven. The halfway point—where the flotilla stopped to let people just sit and listen to the music—was not reached until around five to ten. The tour was supposed to end at half past and we got quite jittery waiting for the gondolas to turn around and go back. Just before they did, I struggled up to the front of ours to get a picture of the illuminated one, and almost tipped us all in the water. Then a dog jumped into the gondola nearest dry land and proceeded to jump into each one it came to before going back ashore. Gondola-hopping dogs featured in that later visit to Venice, too, so it must be something Venetian dogs do.

Once we started moving again, I let my hand trail romantically through the water of a little side canal we entered. Of course, it would have been a lot more romantic if I'd been riding with a handsome young man instead of Ellen and some strangers, but there was a lot of flotsam and jetsam floating around Venice's polluted waters in 1971, and running into a wet paper bag was bit of a mood breaker anyway.

We got back to the departure point a little after half past ten but nonetheless hurried to the vaporetto. At the hostel, we made a point of letting the warden know we were back. He seemed surprised. Pleased, but surprised. We told him we'd run, confirming his belief that the British could be trusted.

Chapter Twenty
Rome—The Eternal City

Getting ready to move on to Rome the next day, we came up against a problem we'd already come up against in Innsbruck, where we'd had trouble packing our Tyrolean hats in such a way as to keep them from getting squashed and losing their shape. The same applied to our gondolier hats, and proved even harder to do because, being straw, there was the possibility of them cracking if they got bent too much. We finally solved this problem by stuffing our cloth hats into our packs and putting the two Tyrolean hats together, one on top of the other, and the two gondolier hats together, one on top of the other. From then on, I wore the two Tyrolean hats and Ellen wore the two gondolier hats, thus eliminating any further hat-related packing difficulties. As to what later became of those hats: Ellen has no idea what happened to either of hers. My Tyrolean one is still in its original form somewhere in my abode, and I think my gondolier hat is too, but not in *its* original form because, in 1991, I had to transform it into a Zorro hat so my four-year-old could become that famous righter of wrongs for Halloween.

When our train arrived, it did not take us long to find a carriage with a Roma sign and a compartment with only three other passengers, a man and two young women. The station sold travel food and one of the women had got herself a snack bag for the trip. At her suggestion, Ellen purchased one too. It contained bread sticks, some sort of unidentifiable meat, a chocolate-covered snack bar, and a bottle of wine. Other than the snack bar, nothing held great appeal for us and the other young woman traded us some chicken for whatever meat it was we had. Both women were teachers, the food-trader travelling solo and the snack-bag lady travelling with a group of high school kids who were staying with various continental families to learn about continental life. I told her our high school hadn't offered anything like that, and about all I and my schoolmates had learned on my earlier school trip was how to wander aimlessly around strange cities. The food-trader said that was unfortunate, as we should have been shown around them properly. As for my current European fling, she thought that, even now, travelling on our own, Ellen and I were too young to get as much out of it as we would if we were a bit older. She was sure we'd be willing to try more things at twenty-one than we would at eighteen, and more at twenty-five than at twenty-one. Looking back, I know she was right, but also know that that period between graduating from high school and going on to higher education and our respective careers was the only time slot open to us, so if we hadn't gone travelling together when we did, we probably wouldn't have taken such a trip at all.

The snack-bag lady got off in Florence. A few stops later, the man in our compartment did, too, and the those of us remaining had the compartment to ourselves all the way to Rome, which, in the heat, was a blessing. Ellen and the food-trader slept for some of it, waking only when I poked Ellen to say the train had been passing buildings for quite some time and just might be about to arrive at our destination.

As in most cities, our first order of business was to find our way to the youth hostel. Rome's tourist information people were on strike, too, but someone told us how to get there, which was via a #67 bus. The stop was just around the corner from the station, and we stood there for ages before being informed that, for the youth hostel, we had to stand on the *other* side of the street. Sighing, we went to join two American girls and an Italian boy who were also on their way there for the first time.

When the bus came, tickets were fifty lire no matter where passengers went. Since it was the rush hour, every seat was taken, forcing the five of us to stand at the back of the bus and go flying whenever it lurched or jerked forward. Lurching and jerking being the means by which Roman buses appeared to move. The initial jolt caused me to jam one poor soul into a corner with my pack and the heavy crowd made it impossible for me to move it. Pinned thus, he posed no problem, but some of the other men on that bus appeared far more eager to live up to the Latin lover image than the ones in Venice had and began propositioning us. Their intentions being clear, a knowledge of Italian was not necessary. Wondering what they could possibly find attractive about two sweaty young females staggering aboard a crowded bus with thirty-pound packs and tickets clenched between their teeth, we ignored them.

One bone-shaking half-hour journey later, we arrived at our stop, but to reach the hostel we had to get across a street with four lanes of traffic and no nearby pedestrian crossings. I found this quite disconcerting, as did Ellen and the American girls, but the Italian boy merely grinned and strode out into the middle of the oncoming streams of vehicles. In keeping with the old adage, 'When in Rome, do as the Romans do', we followed, squealing as the cars whizzed past or screeched to a halt half an inch from us.

Upon getting us to the other side of the street— unnerved, but unharmed—the Italian boy asked someone for directions. He was told the hostel was just a short walk and to keep going the way we had been.

At that hostel, guests were required to use its sheet sleeping bags rather than their own, and after getting them, we went up to our dorm to unburden ourselves of our packs before attempting to regain our composure with ice-cold drinks from a pop machine just outside the dorm door.

We then went down to the hostel's buffet to buy a meal to share. Meals were five hundred and fifty lire, regardless of what you had, and ours consisted of two pears and some pasta that Ellen ate, a sort of hamburger and some potatoes that I ate, and pop from the pop machine.

It was close to half past eleven before the dorm settled for the night. Even then the hall light remained on and that, combined with the summer heat of Italy and ongoing noise from the still-busy street outside, did not make for a restful night.

* * *

Eager to claim the letters we expected to be waiting for us in Rome, we set out for the Canadian Embassy early the next day. To get to it, we were told to take a bus back to the train station and then take another bus from there. The #67 we boarded was as crowded as it had been the day before. We again had to stand, and again found it a rough ride, but this time were at least not encumbered by packs. After a few stops, a seat became vacant, and just as Ellen was making her way to it, the bus started off with a jerk. Unable to keep from being thrown forward, she landed, kerplunk, right on top of an elderly nun. Helping hands got her back on her feet and she sat down, red-faced, beside the nun, who, with great Christian fortitude, merely smiled at her. *The archetypal little soft-spoken Italian nun from the Vatican*, I thought to myself, an illusion that got shattered a few stops on when she turned to the woman she was travelling with and, in an American accent from deep in the South said, "Say, y'all sure we weren't supposed to get off back at that ol' tunnel we just passed?"

The bus that was supposed to take us to the Canadian Embassy dropped us in the general vicinity, and we had our usual difficulty determining the specific whereabouts of our home away-from-home. This time we asked two policemen for directions, and although they spoke very little English, they managed to convey to us that we should go up the street and ask a traffic cop. (Man with big white helmet.) I was mildly surprised that Rome even had traffic cops, since everyone there seemed to drive wherever they wanted at whatever speed they wanted, but we did eventually find one and got directions from him after he got them from someone else. And I must say he was really very nice, considering that a not-so-nice little traffic jam occurred during all this.

His directions got us as far as the right street, where no one we asked spoke even a little English, so we had to resort to pointing to a suitable phrase in the phrase book. This happened to be one of the few useful ones it possessed but did not serve us in this instance because the woman we asked couldn't read, the first adult person I'd ever met who couldn't. After we said *l'ambasciata canadese* as best we could, she pointed out the way and we were able to find it and request our letters.

The receptionist asked for our passports but as this was something youth hostels kept hold of in Italy, she had to settle for our Eurail passes. Satisfied that we were who we said we were, she handed each of us a letter and we went into the lounge to read them.

As soon as I opened mine, several newspaper clippings about the Spanish cholera epidemic fell out, along with some reservation confirmations that hadn't arrived before we left home. The letter expanded on the epidemic theme, expressing concern, and urging us to get shots. Ellen's letter was from her sister, who said it had taken two television broadcasts and six radio bulletins to convince her family that we hadn't been involved in a train crash in West Germany. Their fears finally allayed only after they consulted the itinerary she'd left them and realized that that train had been travelling in the opposite direction to the one we were supposed to have been travelling in at the time.

After reading these oh, so cheery missives, we went to the American Express office near the Piazza di Spagna to book some tours. There for the, now almost laughable, sum of five thousand lire ($10) we booked two tours: one for the following morning that would take us into Vatican City, and one for that afternoon that covered almost everything we were interested in in the city of Rome itself. The exceptions were the Spanish Steps, the Trevi Fountain, and Rome's Imperial Forums. But that was okay because the first two were within walking distance of the American Express office and we were sure we could find our way to the forums.

Chapter Twenty-One
Still Rome

With our tours safely booked, we went into a nearby leather shop to inspect its wares. There were lots of lovely things to buy, but after my Venetian shopping spree I could only afford three small leather bookmarks, two of them presents for friends.

We then headed for the Trevi Fountain (*Fontana di Trevi*), which was built at the back of the Palazza Poli over a thirty-year period (1732–1762) and is considered a late Baroque masterpiece. Despite the fountain's impressive size (eighty-five feet tall and one hundred and sixty feet wide), we had a little trouble finding it. Mostly because we didn't expect it to be stuck down a little side street near a market. We looked at it and took some pictures but did not follow the custom of tossing coins into the water to ensure a return to Rome. This was not because we didn't know about it, or wanted to buck tradition, or anything. The reason we failed to act accordingly was because the fountain had been drained for cleaning purposes and there wasn't any water to throw coins into. I did perform the ritual on my second visit in 2016, sitting on the steps to do so. Something that, since 2019, has apparently been banned. The sitting on the steps bit, not the throwing in of coins bit. I don't know how much the charitable organizations that benefit from the money collected raked in on a daily basis in 1971 or 2016, but it's currently around €3,000 (over $4,000 Canadian).

The chief thing Ellen remembers about Italy is that, wherever we went, it was hot. Rome was no exception, and we consumed a couple of soft drinks and several cups of tea before returning to the American Express office for the first of our tours.

We took seats near the back of the bus and sweltered there waiting for it to start. As did everyone. When the driver came aboard, he asked the man behind us if the youngest of his three kids (a boy of seven or so) had a seat or was to be classified as a 'bambino on the lap' and not subject to charge. Daddy said he had no intention of having any bambino on his lap *that* day and assured him the kid had a ticket entitling him to a seat.

The first stop was at one of Rome's four main basilicas: the Basilica of San Marie Maggiore. As we entered it, a man came up and started muttering at Ellen and some others in the group, all of whom were clad in shorts. After he went away, still muttering, the guide told us Italy's dress codes for churches were very strict. Many foreign tourists (both male and female) failed to meet them, but compliance was advisable, because some only allowed people wearing long trousers or knee-length skirts to go in. What else he said, I don't know. Although Ellen usually stuck with the group when we took tours, I preferred to go off on my own, returning only when the guide moved on to a different area.

From there we went to another of the main basilicas. Originally a palace, the Archbasilica of St. John in Lateran was confiscated from the Laterani family when some of its members came under suspicion of conspiring against the emperor of the day, Constantine the Great (circa 280-337—his year of birth uncertain because, at the time, no one knew he was going to be Great and didn't take proper note). Constantine's Edict of Milan gave freedom of religion to all who dwelt within the Roman Empire, and having embraced the upstart Christian faith himself, he thought it would make a nice present for the hitherto much-persecuted Pope Melchiades, whose pontificate ran from 311 to 314. Damage from fires, earthquakes, and visits from Visigoths, Vandals, and other undesirables led to numerous reconstructions, but St. John in Lateran still stands and is the oldest church in Europe.

Next on the tour's itinerary: one of the hypogeum cemeteries known as Rome's Catacombs, the series of soft-rock tunnels outside Rome in which pagans, Jews, and Christians were once laid to rest. Not all of these burial sites are open to the public and, fifty plus years on, I'm not quite sure which of the Christian ones *we* visited, but think it might have been the Catacombs of St. Sebastian. Whichever one it was, the guide left us in the hands of a priest, taking pains to emphasize that we must *stay* with him. This because the catacombs ran for miles and contained many, many, passages that had yet to be recorded. Making it quite likely that people who strayed from the group would find themselves in some long, dark, *unknown*, passage.

The priest-guide took a more jovial approach. He assured us he was a very good guide and had only mislaid twenty of the last party he'd taken in, adding that there had been twenty-five in it when they started.

He then led us down in the catacombs, saying that any skeletons we saw would be those of tourists who'd got lost, as all others had been removed. As we traversed the long and extremely narrow passages— Early Christians obviously did not run to fat—he told us the catacombs were always graveyards, and all the stories about people having lived in them were myths that were probably started up to make them more interesting. Other than the bones of the departed, oil lamps and water flasks were the only things archaeologists had found, and he was sure we'd agree that even Christians couldn't subsist on just oil and water.

A little later into the tour I went down a side tunnel the priest had passed by and, upon emerging from it, frightened two girls who must have thought one of the ancient inhabitants had popped out to say hello. Further on, I went down another one, much to Ellen's horror. "Get out of there!" she yelled in a voice that everyone from miles around must have heard. "The tour's leaving! You're going to get lost!" (Unlikely, with that to home in on.) I told her I had no intention of losing the jolly man up front and, despite her fears to the contrary, made it safely back to the surface.

The last place the tour went to was the Colosseum, the huge stone amphitheatre commissioned by Emperor Vespasian in 72-74 and presented to the people of Rome six years later by his son, Titus, so that they could enjoy hand-to-hand gladiator combat, wild animal fights, the feeding of Christians to lions, and all the other bloodthirsty sporting events that represented family entertainment back then. When I tried to climb onto a wall to get a picture, a nice young man helped me up. Though I must say the nice young man had little choice as, with my purse, gadget bag, and camera case on, I overbalanced and fell against him.

Attempting to return to the tour group, Ellen and I found it widely scattered and stopped to buy ice creams before going back to the bus. Or, rather, back to where the bus had been. All we knew was that it was blue, and although there were red and green ones, we couldn't find any blue ones. At last Ellen spotted it, and since the engine had started, we ran for it with the people aboard urging us on. The guide was a bit put out with us, and probably only waited because the three kids sitting behind us noticed we were missing and their father insisted we be allowed additional time to show up.

After supper at a café near the American Express office, we climbed the one hundred and thirty-plus steps of Europe's widest and longest stairway, the *Scalinata della Trinità dei Monti*, more commonly known as the Spanish Steps because they rise from the Piazza di Spagna (Spanish Square), which took *its* name from its proximity to the Spanish Embassy. Plans for a stairway between the Piazza di Spagna and the French Trinità dei Monti church high above it were made towards the end of the sixteenth century, but only started to come to fruition in 1660, when a French diplomat, Étienne Gueffier, left enough money for their construction in his will. Even then there were delays, and work on the Steps didn't start until a relatively unknown Italian architect, Francesco de Sanctis, submitted the winning design to a competition in 1717, and they were not completed until 1725. Climbing them is a feat most visitors to Rome feel obliged to attempt, but, as with the steps of the nearby Trevi Fountain, *sitting* on them is now forbidden. It wasn't then, though, and we probably did, once or twice, in the course of *our* ascent, which heat, and weariness, had kept us from tackling when we'd visited the Trevi Fountain the day before.

Looking around for a #67 bus to take us back to the hostel, we happened upon a bookshop. The new and used books it carried were in English, so, of course, we went in, and I found several books I'd been trying to find for years. The owner said he couldn't post them to Canada for me, but the post office could. I failed to record the shop's name, but believe it was probably what is now known as the Anglo-American Bookshop started up by Englishman Patrick Searle in 1953 under the name Interbook.

Following another perilous bus ride, we got to the hostel by striding determinedly into the midst of traffic in the manner of the Italian boy the evening before. A hostel-bound girl who'd got off at the same stop looked wide-eyed at such madness, but followed when all the cars skidded to a stop. Once across, we met a young German fellow with a tiny kitten he'd found abandoned in a non-residential area and planned to take back to Germany. He asked for input on a name and liked the suggestion the girl with us came up with—Rome.

It was a very cute kitten, pure black, with ears that were just beginning to stand up and a coat that was all matted from the milk its rescuer had been trying to feed it at a nearby restaurant. Just as we all started off for the hostel, it did something unfortunate on his hand. Appalled, he said a few words in German I didn't quite catch, but that's one of the risks of holding a kitten. Or puppy, or basically any young animal.

Chapter Twenty-Two
Viewing The Vatican

When I stuck my head over the side of the bunk the next day to emit my customary cry of, "Ellen, get up!", she informed me it was a phrase she'd begun to hate, and said I always made her get up before anyone else did. And I will admit to 'often', but not to always.

On this particular day, an Italian girl must have had an early train to catch, because she was already dressed and packed. She spoke no English, but seeing Ellen awake, pointed to our food bag and whispered something in her native tongue. Ellen didn't have her glasses on and couldn't really see what the girl was pointing to, so she just nodded to indicate that, yes, it was ours, thinking that's what the girl wanted to know. Apparently, it wasn't. She sighed, picked up the bag, took it to the far end of the room, and left.

It wasn't until Ellen put on her glasses and inspected the bag that she saw hundreds of little black ants swarming all over it.

"Oh, I guess that's what that girl must have been talking about," she said.

After disposing of our insect-infested provender in an outside bin, we caught the bus into town for our next tour. Only one bus sitting in front of the American Express office was marked Tour A and, except for a few seats that weren't together, it was full. We got off and waited for another, along with a middle-aged American couple. Wanting to fill his bus and be off, the driver tried to persuade us to sit separately, but we knew another bus was coming and held firm. Which was just as well because, when the guide for the first bus came, it was the same one who'd had the honour of ferrying us around Rome the day before and would have been likely to remember us unfavourably from the Colosseum.

Tour A's principal focus was the Vatican, seat of the Roman Catholic Church since the fourth century AD, when a basilica was built over the grave of St. Peter, and a sovereign state since 1929 through the signing of the Lateran Pacts. But our new guide did point out other sights as we went along.

At Vatican City the guide procured entrance tickets to the buildings we were scheduled to view. He then went off somewhere, leaving us to wait for him. Half of us waited in the wrong place and had to go in the door all the non-tour group tourists were going in. We, of course, were in this half. Once inside, the guide retrieved his wayward charges and led us towards the lift, where we were warned against taking flash pictures in the Vatican Museum, and any pictures at all in the Sistine Chapel. He said if you took one with no guard around, no problem, but if you took one with a guard standing behind you, your camera would be confiscated. He then herded us into the lift in two droves, much to the annoyance of a non-tour group tourist, who got even more annoyed when he was told that groups always had preference.

In the Vatican Museum, we went through some of the rooms and then into the Sistine Chapel. Contrary to what is commonly thought, the Italian sculptor-painter-architect, Michelangelo di Lodovico Buonarroti Simoni (Michelangelo, for short), did not paint its famous frescoed ceiling lying on his back. He worked standing up, on a scaffold of his own design. And although he was reportedly not thrilled with the assignment—which took him from 1508 to 1512 to complete—people have been admiring the result for centuries. Despite the rigid no-picture rule, several people took them, flashes and all. None had their cameras confiscated but did get yelled at by displeased guards.

From there we went into the part of the museum that houses all the priceless artwork popes have acquired down through the centuries. Like the opulence of the museum itself, none of these impressed me much, me being of the opinion, both then and now, that if the 'priceless' treasures held by the Vatican and other religious institutions were sold, the proceeds would allow the Catholic Church to pay compensation to every remaining survivor of ecclesiastic abuses on the planet and go at least some way towards alleviating world hunger.

The library was next, but we saw only one or two books in glass cases. All the rest were locked up in wooden cabinets.

Moving on to an outside corridor overlooking the Vatican gardens, Ellen and I left the group to take pictures of the gardens with St. Peter's dome in the background. I managed to catch up with the touring party before it started down the long, winding, staircase to return to the bus but Ellen did not. Aboard the bus, I got a little nervous when boarding time came and went and there was no sign of her. Fortunately, others were missing too, and *this* guide didn't seem to mind waiting until everyone was present and accounted for.

Once they were, we were taken to St. Peter's Square, where our bus stopped to await the arrival of other buses. Everyone got off, and Ellen and I went into a gift shop for postcards and some cold drinks. But when we got back to the bus area, some of the buses' destinations had been changed. The one going back to the American Express office was not the one we'd come on, so we had to retrieve the plastic shopping bags we'd left on the first bus before finding seat on the second. Bags we were not about to abandon. Having been warned that the Sistine Chapel wouldn't admit people who were wearing shorts or short skirts, we'd wore long trousers for our Vatican visit, and the shopping bags contained the shorts we'd brought along to change into afterwards.

Mine also contained the books I wanted to post home. These were not yet wrapped, but when we got to the post office, the postmaster said I could do that in the adjoining stationery shop. The girl there didn't speak English, so I showed her the books, pointed to the post office, pointed to some large envelopes, and waved my hands about in Italian fashion until I succeeded in making her understand what I wanted to do. When dropping the package in the post office's parcel chute, I heard a passer-by mutter something to his companion about "students and their books", which suggested that that new and used bookstore did a lot of international business. Since he spoke in Italian, I briefly wondered how it was that I'd understood him, but supposed the words were probably close enough to their French counterparts for me to have subconsciously translated them.

Ellen and I then caught a bus out to the Roman Forum, which, had we taken more note of its proximity to the Colosseum, we could have visited at the end of the preceding day's tour. I'm sure the guide would have been quite agreeable to leaving us there and letting us make our own way back to headquarters.

As of March, 2008, visiting the Forum is no longer free, entry to it now being combined with a Colosseum ticket, but it was free when Ellen and I were there. Neither of us knew much about it, and therefore had no idea exactly which impressive-looking ruin stood before us whenever we stopped to rest in the shade of one. Neither did an American couple we met. For a while we traded guesses about several of them and then moved on. Going up a nearby slope, we met some more Americans. These were more knowledgeable and directed us to what they said was Caesar's Forum, so at least we knew that one when we got to it.

Before catching a bus to the hostel, we went looking for some souvenir shops, thinking one of them might have a little brass chariot for my practically non-existent brass collection, but none did. Ellen got side-tracked into clothing shops as well, almost causing me to lose her. She seldom announced her intention of going into a shop, and as she generally walked some distance behind me, I'd invariably turn around and find her gone. Despite wandering down several side streets, we were unsuccessful in tracking down a brass chariot. In fact, we wandered down so many, we found ourselves back at the place where we'd originally caught the bus out to the Roman Forum, which just went to show that, in accordance with the old saying, all roads really *did* lead to Rome in Rome itself.

Bumpy bus #67 took us back to the hostel area, where we once again played dodge-the-cars, but on this occasion most of them had stopped for a traffic light, making this street crossing not nearly as exciting as our others had been.

That evening I wrote to my brother Peter asking him to pass a message along to Mum and get her to dispatch a money order to Paris for our advance youth hostel booking. I posted the letter outside the hostel and returned to the dorm with two cups of hot chocolate, one for me, and one for Ellen. Unsweetened hot chocolate. But a girl who came in seeking a friend gave us some kind of sweetener that took the edge off the bitterness. Her friend not being present, she left again, and a different girl came in. I asked this one her name, thinking she might be the girl the other girl had been looking for, but she wasn't. When apprised of why I'd asked, she very wistfully said it would have been nice if someone *had* been looking for her. She was in Rome by herself, awaiting the chance arrival of friends, and had no firm travel plans. By then we'd met quite a few young people who had no firm travel plans, and no idea of when they were going home. Some didn't even want to go home, having, perhaps, no stable and/or welcoming home to go to. At some point in our conversation with that particular waif and stray, I happened to say I'd got a letter from my mother, which caused her to look even more dejected, and say, "I wish my mother would write to me."

I'd like to think that, at some point, she did.

Chapter Twenty-Three
Navigating Naples

Awakening with a jerk the next morning, I realized it was five after seven and we had an early train to catch. A hasty departure followed, and we learned that one sure way to make yourself unpopular with locals is to get on a crowded bus with a large pack in the middle of early morning rush hour. We got yelled at, muttered at, pushed into corners, and tipped off balance for almost the entire ride.

We got to the station a little the worse for wear and from there took a different bus to the Canadian Embassy to see if the letter with our Amsterdam response might possibly have been re-directed. There were no letters for us, but the trip wasn't wasted. Upon inquiring about the cholera shots we still hadn't got round to having, we were informed that the epidemic was over, and shots wouldn't be necessary.

Back at the train station we dragged our packs over to the Napoli (Naples) train platform and plonked them down beside a caged terrier puppy. Having missed the train we'd intended to catch, we had to wait quite a while for the next one, and various people came over to make a fuss of the little dog, which basked in the public adoration and yelped in an offended manner whenever it felt this was lacking.

The compartment we got in was empty, but soon filled. The first to enter was a man, then a woman, and another, very well-dressed, woman. When this second woman arrived, the man helped us put our packs up on the rack, but she didn't like where mine was and made me push it further along the rack so she could put her suitcase up. She could just as easily have put it in the available empty space, but I didn't argue. Then another man came in and it soon became apparent he was the pernickety woman's boyfriend. With emphasis on boy. Though older than us, he was *considerably* younger than her, and from the looks on their faces, no one else in the compartment felt any more comfortable than we did about having to listen to them whisper and giggle together, and watch them hold hands, paw each other, and otherwise behave in a sickening fashion almost the whole way to Naples. Ellen and I had heard about gigolos and felt he might have been one, but that remains pure supposition on our part.

Founded by Greeks around 600 BC, and originally known as Neapolis (New City), Naples remained a centre of Greek culture long after the Roman Empire came to power and the Romans began using it, and its environs, as a pleasure resort. As in Rome, the tourist information people were still on strike, and we had to ask two English-speaking policemen how to get to the Naples youth hostel. One of them wrote the directions on our receipt from the Rome youth hostel and gave us the bus number for going to the American Express office so we could book a tour to Pompeii.

Even though we had the right bus number, the conductor didn't seem to know where the American Express office was. No one else on the bus knew either, but everyone was very helpful. We still had our packs, but it was no longer rush hour, and people were more inclined to be tolerant. As we rattled along, the conductor, two boys on either side of Ellen, a man beside me, a woman and her husband in the middle of the bus, and the driver up front, all tried to figure out where we were trying to go and how they could best get us there. In the end Ellen wrote down 'American Express' and showed it to one of the boys beside her.

As soon as he read it out aloud, everyone seemed to know the area. As far as I could tell, he said American Express the same way we had, but I suppose there must have been some subtle difference. The man beside me said he'd tell us where to get off, and he and our other benefactors then carried on a seven-way conversation in Italian, with the only words we could follow being 'American Express'.

Upon arrival at the stop everyone agreed was the right one, we smiled, waved, and thanked them before heading down the street the man had pointed out. The American Express office was shut, but due to open again in ten minutes, so we went to a nearby café to get soft drinks, ignoring all the whistles and invitations to avail ourselves of their charms that men aimed at us along the way, a practice that seemed to become more and more common the further south we got.

Returning to the American Express office, we learned it was only an American Express bank. The office from which tours could be booked was on a different, far distant, street. We were told to catch a #140 bus, and tried to do so, but for the longest time no bus with that number came by that stop—or even one with another number. Buses *were* pulling into a stop across the street, so we went over there. Mere moments later, a bus finally came down the side of the street we'd just abandoned. A #140. We made a mad dash for it, but encumbered by our packs, got to it just as it roared off. We then watched another #140 pull into the stop across the street. As before, we ran for it, but as before, didn't get to it in time. Within a few minutes, however, another came along and we climbed aboard. Only to climb off again when the conductor said it wasn't going in the direction we wanted and pointed to the other stop.

By now, quite frustrated, we stomped over there and waited. And waited, and waited, until, at last, the right bus appeared. Its conductor didn't know where the American Express office was, but a fellow passenger—a nice helpful young man of a less predatory nature than many Neapolitans—did, and said he'd tell us where to alight. But we all had to alight before that when, a few streets on, the bus broke down. Three passengers, a short man and two rather stout women, went ballistic over this, and embarked upon a real, genuine, heated, stereotypical, Italian argument with the conductor. Throughout it, the driver quietly laughed and the young man gave us a running commentary, saying that the short man, the 'little one', was of the opinion that it was 'no possible for the engine of a bus to break down', and was accusing the conductor of just dumping us. Why the conductor should want to do this was not specified. Before long, a replacement bus came along and we all got aboard without having to buy additional tickets.

We got to the American Express office about ten minutes before it closed and booked our Pompeii tour from a clerk who was intrigued by our hats and asked why we each wore two. He was not the first to inquire. We thought it a very practical way of dealing with our hat-packing dilemma, but most people who noticed our double headgear seemed to think it—and probably us—a bit peculiar.

Our tour booked, we made to leave, but discovered the American Express office had shut up shop and the gate was down. The clerk had to lead us out a back way, opening all the doors as wide as possible so we could wriggle through them with our packs and catch a bus for the Naples youth hostel, which was on good old unreliable #140's route.

As before, we watched every number but that one come and go. When one eventually did appear, the conductor said he'd tell us when we got to the right stop. He also said we'd better take our packs off as it was a long way. We did so, but would have been better off using them as anchors, because the buses in Naples far surpassed the Roman ones in the bumping and jerking department. Neither of us had seats—Ellen being half-on a sort of luggage rack and me in a corner, huddled on the floor—but at least we didn't have a huge crush of people standing around us.

The hostel was a large, fancy, villa situated on a hill. We got to it just a little before it opened, and sat outside with other hostellers. As soon as the waiting crowd was admitted, everyone surged into the building and Ellen and I got separated. This resulted in me winding up inside and her outside. The warden dealt with reservations first, yelling out the names of those who'd made them. When he read out 'Blair', I yelled back, "Yes," but had to add, "She's back there," and get her paged down the line. Intent on the, admittedly demanding, task of signing in hordes of hostellers, the warden didn't look up from his desk when they came up to him, merely took their passports and membership cards and gave them the bed linen for their assigned billets. In handing us ours, he said B-13 to Ellen, and F-149 to me, which didn't make us very happy, as it was the first time we'd been put in different rooms. Different bunks, yes, but not different rooms.

There was, however, a reason for that. When I went next door to Dormitory F, I found that two of my roommates had beards! I tore back to the desk and said, "Excuse me," and the warden said, "F-149," and I said, "Yes, I know, but that's a *boys'* dorm. I'm a *girl*!"

Raising his head to take a proper look this time, he reeled a bit at this news and Ellen and all the other hostellers who understood English collapsed with laughter. Though saddled at my christening with Irene, I've never—mostly thanks to the song, 'Goodnight, Irene'—much cared for it, and have, from a young age, gone by Renee. In those days I signed it without the extra 'e' on the end and because of this, people often confused it with the French masculine appellation, René. (Hence the later taking on of the additional 'e'.) Granted, I did have shortish hair, but no other Italian male had had trouble recognizing me as female so, needless to say, I felt a bit miffed.

He did too, and muttered something about the picture on my youth hostel card, which was obviously all he'd been going on. F-149 was switched to B-15, and Ellen and I went downstairs to Dormitory B, with Ellen still laughing.

After settling in, we made our way to a little grocery up the hill to replace the cocoa, tea, sugar, and other foodstuffs we'd been forced to cede to the ants in Rome. On the way, we were accosted by some young Italian males who spoke to us in English, but I just said, "*Je ne comprends pas*" in French as we passed them. We actually comprehended them all too well, but one advantage to being from Canada was that, if approached in English, we could say, "*Je ne comprends pas*," and walk on, and if they then switched to French, say, "I don't understand," and walk on.

Getting tea and sugar didn't pose much of a problem but it took quite a while for the shopkeeper to grasp what we meant by cocoa. The phrase book was, as usual, little to no help, and we had to say, "Chocolate, chocolate," over and over, and make stirring and drinking motions before obtaining the desired commodity.

We then went to a fruit stand, where Ellen bought a piece of watermelon, and I inquired as to the price of one carrot. But the vendor simply handed me one and waved away my offer of payment, saying it was "a free gift from Naples". Possibly thinking that, if one carrot was all I could afford, he'd better give it to me before I fainted from malnutrition in front of his stand.

On our way back to the hostel, two young Casanovas in a car stopped and one said—accompanied by a decidedly lascivious look—"Hello! Tonight, do you think you would like to…?"

Answer: No.

After we'd prepared and eaten our evening meal, Ellen went back to the dorm to read and I stayed at the table and caught up my journal, ignoring a couple of passes made to me as I sat there.

At one point the hostel's cat walked in, and although almost every person in the room was snapping fingers at it, calling to it in a variety of languages, and otherwise trying to gain its favour, it ignored them all and jumped on me. But then, cats are like that. They always want the attention of the only person who *isn't* paying attention to them. It sat on my lap for a while, then jumped down and went into the kitchen, probably to get its dinner.

After bringing my journal up to date, I went for a wash, putting extra effort into the back of my neck in case three quarters of that deep, dark, tan was just deep, dark, dirt.

We'd decided to call it a day, but didn't get to sleep for a while, as we started to talk to two other girls in the dorm who were worried about a girl they'd recently met. They said she'd seemed upset and depressed and had not been back at the hostel for two nights. As her luggage was still there, they wondered if something had happened to her. They'd reported her absence to the warden that morning, but he hadn't seemed overly perturbed. He told them girls often didn't come back some nights, having found 'somewhere else' to stay. But her roommates didn't think it likely that she'd leave everything behind; toothpaste, make-up—everything. After talking to us, they went to see the warden again. He still refused to take their concerns seriously and there was nothing more any of us could do for this unknown, unhappy, traveller who reminded me of the girl we'd met in Rome. I wonder now if we came across more aimless and despondent young people in Italy because Italians are so very family-oriented and being there made them feel their own lack of family ties to a greater extent than they did in other places.

Chapter Twenty-Four
Ancient Ruins And Modern Hassles

Our Pompeii tour left Naples at an early hour, with the guide pointing out the city's interesting sights as we went along. When passing through its poorest sections, it was impossible to ignore how much of a contrast there was between that area and more affluent ones.

Before reaching Pompeii, we stopped off at a coral and cameo factory to learn how cameos were made. We were told the materials cost very little, and it was really the craftsman's skill that customers paid for. Receptive to this sales pitch, several people bought cameo pendants or brooches. Had I not already far exceeded my Italian budget, I would probably have too.

The first place the guide took us to in Pompeii itself was the museum, to view some of the things that had been excavated: cameos, fish hooks, utensils, paintings, statues, and, more gruesomely, molten lava-covered corpses. From there we went to what remained of the market square. Being far more interested in hunting for treasure than in preserving history, early excavators damaged Pompeii more than either the great earthquake or the volcanic eruption of 79 AD did. Today, archaeologists take much greater care, and new finds at Pompeii and its neighbouring town of Herculaneum—recently uncovered graffiti, a later-dated coin, and later-harvested fruit (specifically: pomegranates)—make a strong case for that famous eruption having taken place on the twenty-fourth of October rather than the twenty-fourth of August as was originally thought. But whenever it happened, it was catastrophic. Having since been to Herculaneum—also known as Ercolano—I personally prefer it to Pompeii, which is why I chose it for the setting of the last book in my Time Rose series.

The tour of Pompeii lasted a good hour and a half. Whenever the guide stopped to talk, everyone took refuge from the sun and heat in the nearest bit of shade, although the aspiring future archaeologist (Ellen) sometimes waived that form of respite and walked around taking pictures.

In recent years, some buildings and areas in the town have been restored to their original glory thorough The *Grande Progetto Pompei* (Great Pompeii Project) but that was still decades away from even being thought of when Ellen and I were there, so restored structures were few and far between. There were some, though. In one house the guide pointed out the kitchen and suggested the ladies go in there. And we all did, even though we suspected we were being got rid of so he could show the men something in a different room. Something he did not consider suitable for ladies.

In between stops, we walked along Pompeii's ancient streets, where, for drainage purposes, the cobblestones had been laid down all which ways and at different heights, making them ideal tourist-trippers.

At the end of the tour, most people got back on the bus to go on to Amalfi and Sorrento, but Ellen and I were part of a small group that boarded another bus and returned to Naples.

We had lunch at a restaurant near the American Express office. Chips for me and spaghetti for Ellen. From the restaurant we went to a park, stopping at a snack bar for ice creams, which we ate sitting on the grass in the shade. We'd just finished them when the man from the snack bar came up to us and told us to go and sit on some swing seats, under an umbrella. "You no pay," he said. Thinking people weren't supposed to sit on the grass, we followed him and sat down on the swing seats. He sat down on a nearby chair, shook our hands, asked our names, and said his name was Tony.

A few minutes later, he went away. Back to work, we thought. Hah! He returned with a friend who shook our hands, asked our names and said his name was Tony. Then the first Tony shooed Ellen over on the seat, sat down beside her and put his arm around her.

"What time is it?" Ellen asked.

"Five to three," I replied.

"Oh, my goodness, we've got to get going," said Ellen, hastily getting up. "Good-bye," she added as she shot down the path, followed by me, the two Tonys, and a couple of boys of eleven, or at most, twelve, who'd come along with them and were obviously there to take lessons from the old pros. And they appeared to have already picked up a few tips. One of the little lechers-in-the-making pinched my arm, and Ellen assured me later that the first Tony had pinched her lower down when he'd put his arm around her.

Fleeing back to the restaurant, we managed to while away the rest of the afternoon sipping tea at an outside table.

A couple of hours later we caught a bus back to the hostel, where we separated to get various shots of Italian villas on the Bay of Naples. After taking mine, I went and stood outside the youth hostel talking to a girl who'd been in our dorm in Rome. She agreed that Italian men's libidos seemed more active in Naples than anywhere else she'd been, and said she'd even got propositioned standing next to her boyfriend. She also had a story to match my carrot incident. It must have been common belief among locals that all young travellers were starving, because, in one restaurant she'd been in, the waiter asked her if she wanted bread. This was sometimes in with the meal and sometimes not. Since she didn't really care one way or the other, she asked if it was. He said, no, it cost extra, and she said not to bother then. A few minutes later, he returned and furtively slid her three pieces of bread, saying, "Here, you may have it." He didn't quite add, "you poor child," but it was implied.

After the hostel opened, I went in and was recording the day's events in my journal when Ellen arrived, mumbling about the Italian male and vowing that we would never walk about in Naples separately again.

In fact, she had an announcement.

"I hate all men!" she said.

I inquired as to whether this was a decision she'd come to through close observation of the species over the years, or if some specific incident had brought on this revelation and sparked her current outburst.

"All I wanted was a picture of the Bay of Naples. And what did I get? Accosted at every turn by every guy between nine and ninety!"

Whilst trying to find a good place to take her picture, all the men she saw—be they in cars, outside houses, or just walking—had said something to her or made obvious gestures. Three in a car had even followed her for a good distance as she walked along the road staring straight ahead of her as though they didn't exist.

She did get the picture she was after, but to do so had to lean over a wall and suspend herself above the Bay, a complicated enough procedure without having to worry about some local Lothario coming up behind her.

On her way back to the hostel, she ran into four more of them, one of whom said, "Hello, darling!" and moved forward, arms outstretched. She sidestepped him, walked on, made the safety of the hostel, and shook for a while.

"Don't they ever think of *anything* else?" she stormed. "No wonder Rome fell!"

After supper we spent half an hour or so trying to talk the warden into letting us out of the hostel before its usual morning opening time of half past seven so we could catch the early train to Florence. He wouldn't, which meant we'd have to take a later one and risk not getting there before our hostel reservation claim time expired.

Resigned, we got washed and went to bed. It was only just after nine o'clock, but, weary from our tour, we'd have been in bed even earlier if we hadn't had to waste time fruitlessly petitioning the warden who, unlike the Venetian one, proved immovable.

Going to bed early didn't mean getting to sleep early. The two girls we'd been talking to the night before came in and gave us an account of a ruckus that had, unbeknownst to us, been going on outside. They said a group of youths down the street had started behaving inappropriately towards some girls, and when two other girls ran into the hostel speaking rapidly in Italian, the warden had gone running out and his wife got on the phone to the police, who had apparently refused to come because they didn't think such a complaint was all that serious. But, in view of the warden's dismissiveness regarding the missing girl they'd reported earlier, these girls thought, for him to go out, it *must* have been serious.

We then traded Italian male stories with them. None of us considered ourselves raving beauties and were of the unanimous opinion that they went after any female that could walk. One of them was sure Italian men believed that all girls travelling Europe were 'loose', and, if so, that might explain their behaviour, but certainly didn't excuse it. She felt, if they were decent sorts themselves, they wouldn't even approach that kind of girl. The other said she longed to knock one of her admirers end for end but was always too shocked to do or say anything.

But that was our generation. When Richard and I were in Italy in 2016, the Italian male seemed much less inclined to harass the fair sex. Possibly because, in the interim, the fair sex had discovered self-defence courses and would-be harassers had learned that the modern girl could, and *would*, knock them end for end.

Chapter Twenty-Five
On To Florence

We breakfasted at the train station's café before boarding our train to Firenze (Florence). During the time we were there, a sad-looking woman with small children came in and went round some of the tables begging. The kids were thin, and dressed in near rags, and probably either came from the slums we'd seen en route to Pompeii, or were Romanies, the latter of whom were, and unfortunately still are, an ethnic group that is looked down on in many parts of Europe, and meets with both mistrust and mistreatment.

The cultural and scientific revolution known as Europe's Renaissance Period ran from the fourteenth century to the seventeenth, and our journey to its birthplace was long, hot, and boring; the second condition only occasionally relieved by the drinks vendor who sometimes rolled his trolley along the corridor, and the third by the spaniel from the next compartment that wandered in and out of ours from time to time.

At Florence we went to the station's passenger information desk to find out about trains to Champex in the Swiss Alps. We planned to move on to there the next day, but the clerk had never even heard of the place, let alone knew of a train going to it. I had to point it out on a map so she could determine the train changes required. The first was Milan, but there were at least three others, and getting to Champex itself involved taking a bus from Orsières.

Transportation out to the Florence youth hostel was also by bus, and even though it was crowded we got seats because two women insisted that we take theirs. No doubt fearing they'd be injured by a blow from a swinging pack if we were allowed to remain standing.

The Ostello Villa Camerata was out in the suburbs, surrounded by a large park. A lovely fifteenth-century building with pillars and frescos, it seemed more like a palace than a villa. Letters from home awaited us there, and according to mine, I no longer had to get Mum her face cream as she'd found some in our local Woolworth's.

Letters read, Ellen went to take a shower and I went down to the hostel's bar and bought a really big bottle of pop thinking that, oh, yes, I'm sure we can drink that much in this heat. Three large glasses later, I gave up. Ellen wasn't too pleased at the prospect of having to finish off the rest, but I left her to it and went and had a shower. The water wasn't hot, but wasn't cold, either, and at least I got water. By ten o'clock, when a lot of people wanted to shower, it had gone off, something it had a tendency to do at times. This hostel was also the first place we came upon truly unusual toilet facilities. Users had to stand above a basin-like thing to do what was necessary. Awkward, but according to some of the other girls, the ones in parts of France and Greece were even more rugged.

* * *

The city of Florence teems with both culture and history, but the next day was Sunday, and many places were closed. We did find a few shops open, but mostly just strolled around looking at Florentine architecture before seeking out a park and resting on a stone platform surrounding some plants. My book-buying spree in Rome having resulted in my having only a few hundred lire to get me out of Italy, I did not accompany Ellen when she went off to find out if the shops that were open had anything interesting. I still had several traveller's cheques in my possession but didn't want to cash one before Switzerland and go over my budget for *that* country.

I didn't really mind staying in the park. It was very peaceful there, watching people ride past on bicycles or take their children over to a pond to play with boats. After a while, the sun crept up on the place where I was sitting, and I moved to a bench, where a young man came and sat beside me. But he didn't get overly amorous, and we exchanged a few words. The sun later moved me on to yet another bench, and on the way to it, I saw Ellen sitting at a table outside a café having a glass of water. Unlike at home, the water had not been free, and even though a hundred lire could hardly be regarded as an excessive amount, she resented having to pay it.

Florence was reputed to have good flea markets, and she said she and some Americans had spent over an hour looking for one before being told they weren't open on Sundays. She did, however, show me two pairs of leather gloves she'd been able to purchase in a shop. She then related how she been followed by a young man in a car. When he said something to her, she just walked on—only to have him slowly follow alongside her. Approaching a row of tour buses, she ducked around behind one, but found him on the other side of it waiting for her. Trying the same tactic with the next bus led to the same result and this happened again and again until she finally went behind a bus and stayed there for a much longer period of time. When she emerged, he'd gone.

We got ourselves some ice creams and went and sat on the bench I'd earmarked, the only distraction to an onset of boredom being a couple of lizards scuttling around in the ditch behind us. Twenty minutes or so later, a middle-aged man on a bicycle came along, and even at a distance was giving us a predatory look. Ellen had been absent-mindedly tossing pebbles into the street, and when one accidentally went through the spokes of his bicycle as he went by, he took this as encouragement. He stopped his bike, got off and came and sat beside us. When he started to speak to Ellen in Italian, she said nothing, just stared straight ahead. At one point I said, "*Elle ne comprend pas,*" but it didn't deter him. He then said something to me. Glancing at my watch, I suggested to Ellen it was time to go back to the hostel.

She shook her head.

"No," she said, with icy calm. "I'm going to kill this one. I've had it. I'm going to give it to him right in the teeth."

Being as he was a rather large, muscular, person, this didn't strike me as the best of ideas. There weren't many people around, and those who were didn't look though they'd be very helpful: three young guys up ahead a bit, who would doubtless have been delighted by the spectacle; an elderly woman on the bench I'd recently left; and a few couples walking too far away to provide adequate assistance if he took exception to being attacked. Which was likely. When I pointed out these drawbacks to her plan, she grudgingly abandoned it and accompanied me over to a fruit and vegetable stand and bought a watermelon. I'd never tried watermelon before, being of the opinion I probably wouldn't like it. And I didn't, but at least it was thirst quenching.

The water was off when we got back to the hostel but began flowing again in time for us to shower before going to bed, where we drifted off to the pleasantly soporific sound of some hostellers below our window singing along to a guitar.

Since the getting to Champex involved travelling on more than one train, we had to get up at six the next morning to catch the first one, and I must have been subconsciously worrying about waking up at the proper hour because I dreamt about climbing up on something like a luggage rack that Ellen was apparently sleeping on, in order to awaken her. That could have been because I was, maybe, climbing up to my bunk after having, maybe, been out of bed. I use 'maybe' because I really can't be sure of my movements that night. I was a bit of a somnambulist in my younger years, and as I can still vaguely recall being on—or perhaps dreaming about being on—the hostel's wide, stately, staircase at some point, I might have gone sleepwalking. Not something I like to think I was doing in foreign lands, but it's possible.

    I also dreamt about Ellen and myself being asleep amidst the luggage in a post office and having to get somewhere. Frantic and confused, I flung my head over the side of the bunk and began to urge Ellen to get up. When she muttered something about it not being time yet, I got mad and then confused and then finally did what she told me to do, which was shut-up and go back to sleep.

Chapter Twenty-Six
Another Memorable Train Trip

In the usual set-back-to our-plans fashion, the train we got up early for did not leave on time. Ellen and I should have been used to that by this point, but since we had several connections to make that day, we were more than a little put out. We spent our wait time commenting on the inefficiency of the Italian railway, the probability of the train having been deliberately re-routed to miss our stop, and the likelihood that we could have walked to Milan by now. Teenage disgruntlement at its finest. But at least the delay gave us time to change some money into Swiss francs.

An hour and a half after our train was supposed to arrive, one rumbled into the next platform and a man on a loudspeaker mumbled something about Milano. This caused some people to move to the next platform so we did too. And even though the side plate said Venezia, got aboard. But only because the conductor we asked assured us it was the train to Milan.

He was mistaken. Once we were underway a man in our compartment told us we couldn't possibly get to Milan on the train we were on. Alarmed, we got off at Bologna, where Ellen stayed with our packs and I went to find out how to get to Champex from Bologna.

Here, the passenger information desk was in a separate little room. As in Florence, the clerks I approached had never heard of Champex. The first man I spoke to didn't speak English, and when I tried to explain where it was that we wished to go, all I managed to do was get us both confused and cause him to say "But Signorina," in that half-exasperated, half-pitying way I'd often heard in Italy. In Germany, Austria, and German-Switzerland it had been a frustrated, "Fräulein, Fräulein", many people having chosen to ignore the fact that, earlier in the year, this supposedly derogatory term had, at least in West Germany, been officially banned. In England I'd met with a measured, "Oh, Miss!", and in Scotland, a low, "Ach, Lassie". Now used to being addressed in such tones, I suspected that, in France I would hear a mournful, "Mademoiselle", and in Spain a sighing, "Senorita".

Still determined to serve me, the nice man found me an English-speaking clerk. She'd never heard of Champex either, but together we managed to locate it on a map. Exactly why access to Champex—and even the existence of Champex—was some kind of state secret, I could not say, but it apparently still is, because, just last year, I was at a garage sale, and in talking to the Swiss woman running it, got on the subject of Champex, which she, too, had known nothing about until she did a Google search for it on her tablet.

Once the clerk had located it, she looked up the connections. One of them was Brig, and she told me a train would be going there from Platform One in about three minutes, so I'd better run.

Run, I did. All the way around the room, going round and round in circles and jumping up and down like a lost member of the Keystone Cops as I tried to find the door that led to the stairs that led to the platform Ellen was on—which I knew was *not* Platform One. Everyone around me helpfully pointed at the right door, but I was much too agitated to follow directions, and dashed out the first open one I saw. Fortunately, there were some stairs near it. Tearing down them, I raced along a corridor, skidded to a semi-halt in front of the stairs leading to Ellen's platform, thundered up them, and ran towards my companion waving my arms and yelling, "Ellen, the train's leaving from Platform One. *Now!*" Another example of how this trip was failing to help me become mature and sophisticated.

Ellen snatched her pack up baby fashion, I grabbed mine, and we trundled down the stairs and along to Platform One. I asked some kind of railway official if the train there was the one going to Brig and he said, no, the train to Brig was on Platform Six, a platform over from the one we'd just left. We whirled around and charged down the stairs again, with mothers snatching their children out of our path. Halfway down the stairs, the gondolier hats fell off Ellen's head, but she managed to restrain herself from kicking them to the bottom and jumping on them as she later told me she'd had a strong urge to do. A kind woman picked them up and Ellen staggered after me with the hats between her teeth.

Arriving at Platform Six, I found no train for Brig—or anywhere else—sitting there. Thinking we'd missed it, I threw down my pack and turned to look for Ellen, who was doggedly making her way up the platform stairs behind the official we'd spoken to earlier. He grabbed one handle of my pack and said he'd been wrong, the train we wanted *was* the one on Platform One. He and I set off at a brisk trot, with Ellen following as best she could, her pack slipping by degrees as she went along until a man relieved her of it and carried it for her. Desperate to catch up to me and the official, she sprinted ahead in a manner none of our P.E. teachers would ever have believed her capable of and left him to follow like a faithful hound.

Much to our amazement, we did make the train, which rolled out of the station about a minute and a half after we panted aboard. When a guard came by for the tickets, he told us that to get to Brig, we'd have to change carriages in Milan, for which we were now finally heading.

In Milan, we changed carriages and got in a compartment with an elderly couple, a young Canadian woman, a young Italian man, and two French girls. The Canadian woman was heading for Geneva and told us that some sort of festival would be on when we were there, an unexpected, but welcome piece of intel.

Brig was the only Champex connection info I'd managed to obtain in Bologna, and upon arrival we still had to find out how to get to Champex. Its information clerks had at least heard of the place and directed us towards a train for Martigny. A French couple aboard said they were getting off there so, confident we could just follow their lead, we relaxed a bit and allowed ourselves the luxury of taking in the beautiful Alpine scenery in the land of Heidi, William Tell, alpine horns, army knives, cheese, chocolate, precision watches, secret bank accounts, and a long history of political neutrality.

At Martigny we were told the train for Champex would be coming in in about five minutes, but after fifteen minutes passed without a train showing up, I asked a porter, and he said ten more minutes. Ten minutes later, a train did roll in, but it wasn't the Champex train. The Champex train, someone said, was the small red one at the end of the platform. We went down to it and asked the people inside if it went to Champex. A man said sort of, as it went to Orsières and passengers wanting to go to Champex had to take a bus—adding that the last bus of the day had already left and we wouldn't be able to get there that night.

As we stood wondering what we were going to do I, for no reason at all, save boredom and vexation, recalled one of my favourite nursery rhymes from my nursery days and began muttering, "Dog won't bite pig, pig won't jump over the stile, and I shan't get home tonight."

"Oh, shut-up," said Ellen, not unreasonably, although I thought I'd summed up our talent for winding up in this now all-too-familiar predicament rather well.

But, this time, not too much of a predicament. Soon after, a guard came by and told us Martigny had a youth hostel. Not having planned to stay there, we didn't have reservations, but since it wasn't full, we were able to obtain places.

We had supper at a nearby restaurant and were served so many chips we couldn't eat them all. Feeling decidedly replete, we went back to the hostel, made up our beds, and attempted to sleep away the cares of a somewhat trying day.

Chapter Twenty-Seven
A Taste Of Mountain Air

The office wasn't open when we went to sign out of the hostel the next morning, but our cards had been left out to be picked up. A practice that, in these days of identity theft, is probably no longer followed there. Or anywhere.

If the museum honouring the large furry canines that the monks of the Great St. Bernard Hospice once used to find travellers lost in the mountains had been around in 1971, Ellen and I would definitely have visited it, but, unfortunately, it didn't come into being until 2006. The town now also has restored Roman ruins from back when it was a Roman settlement called Octoduras or Octoduram, but they hadn't been restored then, and even if they had been, we were not aware of the town's Roman history, or really anything else about Martigny, since it had not been on our original itinerary.

After stopping at the bank for some more money, we went to the train station and caught the train to Orsières. The area was full of small villages, or what would, in Canada have been called one-horse towns, and we passed through one microscopic place that didn't even have a horse. It did have some pigs, though, and what looked like a field for playing some type of sport, so there must have been enough local inhabitants to form at least two teams of something.

From Orsières we got a bus to Champex, high up in the Alps. Travelling up a narrow, winding, mountain road gave us a magnificent view of the valley below us, but the very fact that it *was* a narrow, winding, very close-to-the-edge, road made the journey somewhat unnerving. The Champex youth hostel was a bit out of Champex and the bus dropped us at the top of a road that led to it. The main hostel was a large chalet, but the room we were shown to was in a nearby building, and after we'd made up our beds, we left and went into Champex.

Originally merely a place to let cows wander, the beauty and tranquillity of the Champex Lac area started attracting summer tourists around 1892—making it seem odd that we'd had trouble finding people who'd ever heard of it, because it became popular with winter visitors as well, due to all the snow sports facilities available.

We had some tea in one of Champex's cafés, and, later on, a full meal in another. Ellen had soup and salad and I had an omelette that came with so many chips, Ellen and I together couldn't finish them. The waitress even asked *me* for the order, a rare occurrence, since, curiously, takers of orders usually chose to ask Ellen. But I rose to the occasion and requested the menu in perfect French. "*La carte de manger, s'il vous plaît.*" That being one of the French phrases I had down pat—along with "*Est-ce que le train pour...?*" At that café we saw the same small boy we'd seen at the café where we'd had tea. And he seemed to belong in both, all the cafés in the area perhaps being a family enterprise.

From there we went into a small shop that sold groceries and got a carton of milk, a container of jam, a couple of chocolate desserts, and other makings of our evening meal. We also went into another souvenir shop, but left as soon as it became clear that the proprietress was of the, 'You're not supposed to look around, you can only buy', school.

Boats and pedaloes (pedal boats) were available for hire by people wanting to go out on the lake, so we hired a pedalo and did just that. Neither of us had ever been on one before, but the woman shoved us 'out to sea' with no instruction, so we had to figure it out ourselves. For a while, we pedalled around taking pictures and then just let ourselves drift. It was peaceful out on the water, and the lake so clear, so unpolluted, that, even right in the middle of it, we could see all the way to the bottom.

Back onshore, we went souvenir hunting again. There were only three souvenir shops in town—not counting the buy-something-immediately-or-leave one—but they were well stocked, and we went back and forth between them.

About five o'clock, Ellen noticed she'd lost the one of the paper bags with our groceries in. We retraced our steps, but couldn't find it, so she went back for replacements and I waited by the lake with some food we'd got at a different shop. We then headed for the hostel, stopping on the way for a loaf of bread and some butter. Ellen was careful to put the butter on top of her paper bag, but it somehow slid down and got mashed on the bottom. A little while later that bag began to fall apart and I took the milk carton from it so she could handle it more easily. But during a rest stop halfway to the hostel, she discovered one of the chocolate desserts had come open and spilled all over the jam. Whilst trying to clean it off, she first squished, and then dropped the butter, which flopped in the dirt. At that point, she threw the now damp and badly torn paper bag away and muddled on as best she could with a loaf of bread tucked under one arm and her hands full of numerous other foodstuffs—some of them icky.

We managed to get to the hostel before anything else happened, but going into the dining room to eat some of what we'd bought we had to make our way through a number of irritating young savages—a school group of French girls aged around thirteen to fifteen, who were milling all around laughing, shouting, and pushing each other. The warden had earlier told us we had two French girls in our room, which didn't thrill us, as we thought it would be two of *them*.

After supper, the warden helped us figure out the local bus and train schedule. He was a lovely man, getting on in years. But he mostly only spoke German—not our best second language—and my German grammar and accent were apparently both atrocious. At one point I asked about buses "in the morning" in such a way that 'in' meant 'into' something, like food into the mouth, and not 'in' as in respect to a time frame. At least, that's the way he explained it. Even so, he knew what I meant, and we only got crossed up as to our destination. With my pronunciation, he thought we were going to Genoa, Italy, instead of Geneva, Switzerland. Once we'd managed to straighten that out, he asked us if we wanted breakfast in the morning, as the bus to Orsières didn't come through Champex until twenty to eleven. After saying 'yes' to breakfast, I asked what time breakfast was. He said anytime, and that we should sleep in in the morning because sleep was good for young people. Dubbing him the nicest warden we'd yet come across, we went back to our room and met the two French girls, who thankfully weren't two of the savages.

In this hostel, I had a ladder to climb up to the top bunk on, but didn't really require it, as I'd become skilled at leaping up to bed. For me to get up on a top bunk now would definitely require a ladder. Or a hoist.

Before retiring, I re-arranged my pack to fit in my most recent purchases, and once that was accomplished, leant back and scratched the hives on my arms that had appeared not long after I ate that watermelon in Florence. I'd only had a small chunk, but watermelon was the only thing I'd partaken of that

I'd never partaken of before, thus proclaiming itself yet another foodstuff I was allergic to.

* * *

The thundering feet of the savages making an early morning departure woke us at six o'clock, but we returned to slumber and did not go over to the hostel's dining room for breakfast until eight. En route, I told Ellen to "Smell that mountain air!", but she said she'd rather go back to bed. The air really was different way up there though—and we *were* way up, the morning mist surrounding the hostel having possibly been a cloud.

Breakfast consisted of bread, butter, jam, and huge mugs of hot chocolate. After eating and doing the dishes, we went out to find a typical little mountain meadow and Swiss chalet for me to photograph. On the way, we got caught between one car wanting to go one way, and another car wanting to go another way on the narrow road. The drivers finally sorted it out when we got out of *both* their ways.

Before long we found a mountain meadow with a chalet at the far end, and inspired by *The Sound of Music*, I got Ellen to take my picture running across it. *The Sound of Music* was, of course, set in Austria, but a mountain meadow was a mountain meadow, and with other mountains in the background, it looked similar enough for my purposes.

A stream ran through the meadow and, encouraged by my rare display of athleticism, Ellen tried to leap across it when we started back to the hostel. Instead, she fell in. The stream was only about a foot deep, but was still a wet, icy cold, mountain stream. I'd have loved to have got a picture of her half-in and half-out of it, with that surprised look on her face, but had regrettably used up the last picture in my camera and didn't have any fresh film with me.

Not long after our return to the hostel, the warden beckoned to us, loaded our packs, and us, into his car, and drove us to the Champex Post Office to catch the bus. I went for the tickets and made myself well enough understood in French to successfully place the request, but as the ticket seller handed them to me, he said something back to me. Being totally unprepared for this, and unwilling to ask him to repeat it, I just had to look blank, collect our tickets, and pray he was just bidding us a pleasant journey.

With a little time to go before the bus was due to arrive, I went over to a nearby souvenir stand and bought a tiny toy St. Bernard dog. I'd have got a bigger one—of which there were many—but thought it would be troublesome to pack. And I was right, as was proved on a subsequent visit to Switzerland when the child with me (Bryan) did buy himself a bigger one. I allowed that purchase, but, due to weight concerns, didn't let him get the real, authentic, boy-size medieval armour he came across in Rothenburg, or, fearful for the well-being of siblings who might get in the way of it, the real, authentic, Indiana-Jones-style bullwhip he wanted to buy in Paris.

The trip down the mountain was even more unnerving than the one going up, and when we got to Orsières, rain began to fall, which concerned us a little, as we particularly wanted good weather for Geneva and the festival we'd been told about.

Chapter Twenty-Eight
The Hostile Hostel

It was still raining when we got to Geneva, home to the European headquarters of the United Nations, and once known as 'Protestant Rome' because it was a refuge for seventeenth-century Protestants being persecuted in the parts of Europe that were predominantly Roman Catholic. In 1863, it also became the place in which Henry Dunant founded the Red Cross, and a year later, the place in which the first of the international treaties known as Geneva Conventions were drawn up and, along with subsequent ones, became the Humanitarian Law of Armed Conflicts that all signatories are *supposed* to abide by.

The youth hostel we were booked into—Geneva had more than one—was not yet open. Once it did open, opening time did not prove to be getting in time. It didn't have a very large lobby, and people were only admitted, at first, I swear, one at a time, and then in groups of ten or so. At one point, a few more than were 'allowed' managed to get in, and the old witch at the door physically pushed them out, causing them, and anyone waiting on the steps, to go flying. Two American girls who'd already spent a night there told us all the wardens were like that, and painted a pretty grim picture of the place, saying you had to re-register every day, which meant filling out lengthy question-and-answer forms every day.

Ellen and I filled in our forms outside, a somewhat difficult task when attempted in the midst of a large crowd of weary travellers and an unrelenting downpour. But it didn't seem to bother a stoical young English fellow. After filling in his form, he just stood there reading a biography of Houdini he'd shielded with a bit of plastic, and when anyone said something uncomplimentary about the hostel to him, just said, "Do they have hot water?" and, upon being answered in the affirmative, said, "That's all right, then."

No one tried rushing the door again—the aged doorkeeper hit hard and pushed harder—but one of the American girls obviously still got too close to it for the harpy's liking.

"This old woman's hitting me!" she exclaimed. (The old woman was.)

"Well, hit her back," replied her friend, who was standing near us. (The girl didn't.)

"I wonder if they ever caught all the female guards that worked for the Beast of Belsen," someone else said speculatively. "If not, I think I've got a good idea of where they could look for one of them."

That was, I suppose, a possibility, but women's suffrage came late to Switzerland, and Swiss women had only got the vote six months earlier, so this ancient specimen was perhaps still in the habit of taking her feelings of repression out on hapless hostellers. Well, most Swiss women got the vote. Not all. Those who lived in the canton of Appenzell Inner-Rhodes had to wait until 1990.

Quite some time later, I got into the building in one of the permitted droves. Ellen didn't, and I had to wait for her to come in with the next one. At the desk, we were asked—make that, commanded—to put our passport numbers on our entrance forms. As soon as we did, the man at the desk said the forms were too soggy to be acceptable and gave us others. The forms did not—to us—seem any soggier than those of any of the others being presented by people who'd filled them in whilst standing out in pouring rain for an hour, and, seething, we made our way to a table and re-did them.

Then another woman—younger than the doorkeeper, but obviously her soul-sister—came along and barked out an order for us to put our packs to one side. With the limited number of people allowed into the lobby, they weren't really in anyone's way, so this was just about the last straw as far as Ellen was concerned. With an enraged, "Damn!" that was probably heard from one end of the street to the other, she flung hers down and kicked it into a corner, glaring at the old besom by the door who stood clicking her tongue in disapproval at such a display.

We finally got our entrance forms up to the required standard of presentability and were handed our bed numbers—surprisingly enough, together, which was a lot more than we expected by this time—and dragged our packs down to our room vowing we wouldn't stay there more than one night if they paid *us*. The bed numbering system had absolutely no logic to it, but we did eventually find ours, and went to see if we had any letters in the hostel's post files. We both did, but they took a bit of finding too, as the stack wasn't in alphabetical order.

Back in the dorm we read our letters and, after sitting and talking for a bit, gradually began to feel better. We even decided to stay our reserved number of nights, since Geneva's other hostels were likely to be full at festival time and a pension would have been too expensive.

Despite all else it lacked—a friendly atmosphere and a members' kitchen being top of the list—the hostel did have hot water, so Ellen got out her sponge bag in preparation for a shower and discovered that her tube of toothpaste—the gigantic tube referred to Chapter One—had burst and oozed out all over her toothbrush, hairbrush, flannel, soap, glasses cleaner, face conditioner, and the inside of the pack pocket that all of the above had been in. I wisely refrained from pointing out I'd advised her against bringing it, and she cleaned everything off as best she could before she went to bed.

    Later that night, when I was just on the borderline of dreamland, I became vaguely aware that someone was speaking to me and opened my eyes to focus on one of the wardens (male) who kept talking about a card. All I could think of was my youth hostel card, which he already had, and *what are you doing in here, you man, you?* It then dawned on me that he meant my bed number card and I groggily fished it out of the depths of my gadget bag, which I fished from the depths of my sheet sleeping bag. He nodded and handed it back and then checked Ellen's. We had #104 and # 105, and I fully believe that if it had just so happened that we'd had the wrong card for the section of the bunk we were in, he'd have made us change around. It was that kind of place. He then went over to a girl who had mislaid her card and said he'd be back in five minutes, adding that, if she hadn't found it by then, out she went, bag and baggage—at eleven o'clock on a dark, rainy night. Leaving her understandably distraught, he moved on to the next dorm, where I heard a distinctly British female voice protest his presence with the words, "I say! I didn't think they allowed *men* in here!" Upon returning to our dorm, he inspected the poor girl's card—which, luckily, she had found—before going on with his nightly rounds.

Chapter Twenty-Nine
Festival Fun

The inhabitants of our dorm all rose at half past seven, when one of the resident she-devils came in issuing orders for everyone to do so. Hostellers didn't have to be out until ten, but they woke them long before, probably because it gave them perverse pleasure. Once up, Ellen and I went to the front desk to check in for another night, although, by then, we planned to write off the fee as a loss if we could find somewhere else—*anywhere* else—within our means later in the day. But Prince Charming at the desk said we couldn't re-register until five o'clock, so we got our youth hostel cards back, packed up, and left. Stand in that sign-in crowd again? No, thank you! The street was preferable.

We caught a bus to the train station, and as its Accommodation Bureau wasn't yet open, went and had tea. When it did open, the man in charge said he could book us a room at a girls' hotel for twelve francs ($3) each per night, which, times three, would come to thirty-six francs ($9). That was a little more than we wanted it to be—about four dollars more—but unlike the girls' hotel suggested to us in Munich, this one appeared to be known to local officialdom, so we got the address and set off.

The hotel was nearby and the woman managing it the polar opposite of the hostel harridans. We filled in forms and paid our money, which turned out to only be ten francs each per night because the room was a five-bed room. The manager then took us up to it in a lift and showed us our beds and the bathroom. Hot water and a bath. A *bath*! Then, and to this day, my preferred method of body washing, due to a traumatic experience with a shower aboard an ocean liner when I was a small child. We even had a balcony, and after the manager left, Ellen and I went out on it and were pleased to note that our new lodgings were quite close to Lake Geneva. (Also called Lac Léman, from the Roman name for it, *Lacus Lemanus*.)

Shortly afterwards, the manager came back and got me to write the English words for *Auberge de Jeunesse* (Youth Hostel), *porte avant* (front door) and *sac* (packsack), as she said she often required those words. And she probably did, as I'm sure she got a lot of asylum seekers from the *Auberge de Jeunesse* we'd been in. Then a maid came in to vacuum and Ellen and I went out on the town.

Banks are something Switzerland has no shortage of, so we had no trouble cashing some traveller's cheques before going shopping. Ellen wanted a Swiss watch and found an exquisite little pendant one that required her to change another traveller's cheque after buying it. But exquisite though this timepiece was, it didn't turn out to be one of her better purchases. Failing to live up to the high standards of clock and watch workmanship Switzerland was known for, it quit working in under a week.

We stopped at a café long enough to eat, and as I was the first to finish, I went to a nearby tourist information centre and got someone to translate a French list of the events taking place at the upcoming *Fêtes de Genève* (Geneva Festival), the city's annual folklore festival. This ten-day successor to the *Fêtes des Fleurs* (Flower Festival) started up in 1947 and for many years was Switzerland's largest festival. Financial losses sustained in 2016 and 2017 led to it being discontinued in 2018, and I think only the grand fireworks display still takes place now.

We then went shopping again, this time for stamps and groceries, the latter at a restaurant-cum-supermarket-cum-department store right near the girls' hotel. There we bought a tin of chocolate drink mix that came with some little plastic farm animals (a duck and a pig). Cute, but not as upmarket as the metal horses that came with that particular brand of chocolate drink mix when I was a child.

We got back to the hotel shortly before two of our roommates arrived, American girls with whom we talked for a while before going to bed.

* * *

After breakfast the next morning, Ellen and I got into our swimsuits and applied suntan lotion to each other before going down to sunbathe on the nearby concreted area serving as a beach. It did not take long for laying in the sun to bore us, and walking back to the hotel along one of the lake's promenades we saw fairground rides and tiered seating being put up for the *Fêtes de Genève* scheduled to get underway in just a few hours.

Returning to the lakefront early that evening, we found that some areas of the promenade were off limits without a ticket. Since those seemed to be the areas where all the action was taking place, we got tickets. Ellen bought her usual fairground fare—candy floss, which I don't happen to like—and after she'd eaten it, we went on the dodgem cars. The car we got into refused to move until we were informed the little plastic disc that we'd been presented with had to be put in the slot at the top. The car then *did* move—right out into the middle of the dodgem arena with other cars zooming in from all sides. Two boys of about twelve hit us dead centre and I got a deep cut down the side of my right knee, the scar from which I still have today.

After the ride we went to a fountain so I could wash off the blood and looked around for a tamer ride. The roundabout seemed more suited to our abilities, but it was mostly being ridden by children, so we went back on the dodgems. We should have known the car we got in was another unlucky one as soon as Ellen got her foot stuck between it and the platform. Then, as soon as she got free, the thing shot out into the middle of the platform and stalled. I hopped out and made it out of the arena with only three attempts on my life; the drivers of the other cars seemingly determined to get the 'pedestrian'. Ellen, had to manoeuvre through what quickly became a traffic jam, and was extremely fortunate to escape undamaged.

Abandoning the rides, we walked around for a bit and wound up in front of the stage where all the folk dancing was to take place. This started shortly afterwards, and we got to watch dancers from Portugal, Greece, Bolivia, and Switzerland, and listen to musicians from Romania and Switzerland.

About halfway through the show, the stage mike was appropriated by an American tourist who'd mislaid his wife in the massive crowd. "Vera!" he bellowed. "I'm over here, behind the stage. Come and get me!"

Everyone was highly amused, even if they didn't understand English, as people who did explained it to them. That was really about the only way he could possibly have found her in that crowd though, so, bright man.

The show ended just after eleven, along with our energy and we made our way back to the hotel through the happy, laughing, crowd, me a bit in front as usual.

Suddenly, behind me, I heard Ellen yell, "Stop that!".

At first, I thought she just wanted me to slow down, but upon turning saw these words were being directed at a young man with a plastic hammer who kept hitting her on the head with it. And he wasn't the only one to go for us in that manner. Such behaviour was, apparently, a festival custom. We'd seen people buying little red and yellow hammers all evening and, now aware of what they were for, made a mental note to get ourselves a couple the following night, if only for protection's sake. For some reason—possibly because I'd grown up roughhousing with older brothers and learned how to duck—Ellen (whose brother was of tamer mien and whose other sibling was a sister) got attacked more often than I did. I only got bopped twice: once on the ear (the bopper was aiming for my head), and once on an elbow (which I'd put up to guard my head).

But we managed to make it to the hotel relatively unscathed and got there just as two other girls were going in and so didn't have to use our key. We went to bed with the noise of the festival still echoing loudly from the street next to us. Along with the squeaking sounds made by the plastic hammers as they connected with the heads of unsuspecting victims.

* * *

The next day I went out and bought bananas, peaches, peanuts, chocolate bars, and some milk and sugar for our breakfast. During the course of this meal, we discovered I had made an adverse purchase in regard to the sugar. It had gelatine in it and tasted revolting. After breakfast, we threw together some washing and took it to two laundries, but found both were about to close for a half-day, either because of the festival, or because Saturdays were half-days for such businesses. Instead, we returned the washing to our room and went shopping, visiting shops on a number of side streets before we reached a huge department store and went around it separately for about an hour.

When I met Ellen by the entrance, she showed me a charm she'd bought for her collection, saying it had only been twenty-five francs.

"Twenty-five francs?" I yelped. "That's over six dollars in our money!"

After a day or two in each country, I was usually able to calculate the exchange rate for the local currency without the converter. Ellen hadn't thought to bother and was a little shaken by her own extravagance. Especially in light of the expensive pendant watch episode. But imagine trying to buy a silver charm for that nowadays!

To avoid spending more money, we went down to the lake to swim, but were stopped at various points by policemen manning wooden barriers, one of whom told us everything was closed off for the festival parade and we couldn't swim until after five o'clock.

Thwarted, we went back to the hotel, where Ellen read and I went on with a letter I'd been writing to a mutual friend, Nancy, in Canada. Later on, we sauntered down to the *Quai de Mont-Blanc* and bought tickets to see the parade. Having to part with six francs to see a parade rankled a bit because, even though we were used to events at our own city's big annual bash (the Kelowna Regatta) being expensive, we'd never had to pay to watch *its* parade. This one did have some really beautiful floats though, from all over the world.

When the parade started around a second time, Ellen went shopping for our evening meal and I made my way back to the hotel. There I packed up my belongings, which were strewn about the room, and talked to our roommates—different ones now, but still American. When Ellen came back, we went out to again try for a swim. We each had to buy *another* six-franc ticket to get past the barrier and once past it, found that, in spite of what we'd been led to believe, the swimming area was still closed off. People were allowed to swim from another area, if they could swim, but as we couldn't we had to give up the idea until the next morning when, an official assured us, it *would* be open again.

After making sure we could re-enter the festival area with the tickets we'd bought, we went back to the hotel and made our supper. And after that, I washed out my navy top and borrowed Ellen's light blue hooded top for the night. Being much the same size, we had started to borrow one another's clothes to relieve the tedium of our own wardrobes.

Before returning to the festival, we purchased two of the little plastic hammers to defend ourselves with and, gripping them belligerently, walked into the crowd, where we did get bopped, and bopped in return. Ellen's hammer broke at some point, but by then everyone was more interested in watching what turned out to be a spectacular fireworks display.

When it was over, we fought our way through the crowd and went back to the hotel. This time, we did have to open the door with our key but, try as we might, couldn't make it work. Fortunately, someone inside saw our struggles and opened it for us.

As before, we went to bed amid the joyous sounds of festival-goers, and the endless bonk, bonk, bonk of the plastic hammers.

Chapter Thirty
A Nice Day In Nice

Because our room had to be vacated by nine the next morning, we got up planning to have the hotel's breakfast and leave our packs in the office to be picked up later, when we were due to move on to Southern France. Specifically, to Nice, pronounced like 'niece'—possibly a victory name derived from the Greek word *nikē* and bestowed on the city by its Phocaean founders.

Down in the kitchen, breakfast did not appear to be being served, so we went to the office to turn in our door key and drop off our packs. But because the office was shut, and was going to be shut all day because of the *Fêtes de Genève*, we had to go to the train station and once again make use of a Left Luggage room.

After a café breakfast of tea and croissants we went down to the now open swimming area. And never before had we ever been in such *cold* water. Several brave sorts—the sort who do the Polar Bear dips on New Year's Day—ran down the slope and plunged in, but we crept in by degrees, numbing one section at a time, until we got in up to our shoulders. We didn't stay in long and went back to the side to sunbathe until a voice came across a loudspeaker telling people that the swimming area was closing to accommodate festival festivities. A message conveyed in English and about six other languages to make sure of getting through to everyone.

In compliance with this order, we wended our way back to the train station, and read some English magazines we'd bought until a man who'd been mildly bothering us for some time grew more emboldened by the beer he'd been drinking and began to look luridly at Ellen's legs. This prompted us to get up and go to sit on a window ledge outside the station until a nearby restaurant opened for the seating of supper. As we waited for this, some hostellers came by looking for the hostel we'd been at and we directed them to it, adding that they'd probably hate it. We then went for our supper, wondering if we'd have to wash dishes to pay the bill as we'd almost run out of Swiss money. Happily, it turned out to be within our collective means, albeit not by much.

Back at the train station, we got our packs and would have gone straight to the platform our train was scheduled to leave from if we had not been advised that Customs were easier to go through in Switzerland than in France. And they must have been, because a great many people were waiting to do so. Since our night train wasn't due to leave for several hours, we decided to go somewhere else until the Customs people weren't as busy. This we did, but chose an area peopled by some clods who kept crooning to us and hitting us on the head with those wretched festival hammers. Just as we were thinking about going for the police, they got discouraged and left. Besides the police, we'd seen signs for '*L'Amis de Jeune Filles*' and '*Protection de Jeune Filles*', which was reassuring in that the existence of such organizations meant there were lots of places to run to, but at the same time, disquieting, in that it made us wonder why *jeune filles* (young girls) in Geneva required so much protection.

A little later we went into the French-destination departure area to go through Customs. We still had quite a wait, but it was hammer-free in there, and we whiled away the time talking to two Canadians and two American girls from California. With a few exceptions, every American we met in Europe seemed to be from California, New York, or Georgia.

Getting through Customs only amounted to having our passports looked at. Aboard the train, all the compartments in the first first-class carriage we tried were reserved, so we got off and asked a conductor if there were any first-class carriages for people without reservations. There were, he said, and pointed one out. Inside, we found a non-smoking compartment with only one person in it, a girl from Calgary by the name of Gina. But after we sat down, a man came in and said he had a reservation for the seat Gina was in, so she moved over one. Then an American couple came in, only to have to leave again when two American boys came in with reservations for *their* seats. The conductor's claims were invalid. This carriage, like all the others, was reserved, but those of us without reservations didn't feel inclined to move until someone said we had to.

For three hours or so, all was well. We dozed, talked to Gina and the two boys and shared travel experiences. But at Grenoble, a man and his wife got on and claimed the seats Ellen and I were in, so we had to move. After a bit of a struggle through some people in the corridor, we found the door connecting our carriage to the next one locked and had to spend the next four hours sitting on the corridor floor getting stepped on by people who either wanted to use the WC or get on or off the train.

* * *

When the two American boys got off at Marseilles, we again struck up a conversation with Gina, who suggested we spend the day together on the French Riviera. At Nice, Gina went to hunt for accommodation and Ellen and I made inquiries about the night train to Carcassonne. In view of the difficulties that we'd had keeping seats on our most recent trip, we wanted to make reservations for next one, but the ticket seller didn't think it would be necessary for the Carcassonne run. Ellen then stayed in the spot in which we'd arranged to meet Gina, and I went in search of a bank. But all of Nice's banks were closed on Mondays, and this was a Monday. There was a currency exchange booth near the station, but the world and his wife appeared to be seeking its services so I went back to Ellen and we waited for Gina.

After waiting for some time, I left Ellen with the luggage and went looking for our new acquaintance, finding her, as I expected to, in that long, long queue outside the currency exchange that I'd been unwilling to join. She'd gone there because there was a lengthy queue at the tourist accommodation bureau, too, although a guy there offered to share *his* room with her. An offer she declined.

This time, I stayed with Gina, as I really did require French funds, and Ellen went to check our packs into Left Luggage and go to the accommodation bureau to get Gina a room for the night. (By then its queue was not as long.) In the meantime, I alternated between wandering up and down our queue to find out why it wasn't moving ahead with any particular regularity—mostly, I gathered because several people kept changing money for half a dozen people farther back.

Gina and I were within touching distance of the wicket when Ellen returned, and after about ten minutes or so more, we managed to get to the cashier and change our money ahead of a blonde girl who'd pushed her way to the front in such a way as to incur the wrath of all present. Because Gina and I had been standing near some other English-speaking tourists, this aggressive—from her accent, French—female must have thought we were a tour group or something, because she bleated that it wasn't fair that she should have to wait "so long when I am only one and you are so many". And being informed that we were all either travelling alone or in pairs, or, at most, trios, didn't change her attitude any. Just after I got my money changed, she did manage to push through to the counter, to the great annoyance of one and all. If she'd already had a friend in line and gone to join her, people might not have found her queue jumping so irritating, but elbowing her way in and being belligerent had endeared her to no one.

Gina then went to her hotel to put her stuff in her room, and Ellen and I went to a nearby café to order tea and colas for us and lemonade for Gina from a waiter that was (a) a very cheerful, extrovert type, (b) a little crazy, or (c) had been nipping the wine stock. When Gina came, I went to a nearby post office and got some stamps. As was my usual practice in each new country, I had a list of all the stamps I was likely to require for letters and postcards to friends and relatives back home, and always tried to buy them at the first stop, that being the most convenient way to acquire them. Convenient in regard to having them in hand, that is. The act of getting them was sometimes problematic. "I want six of such and such a stamp going to such and such a place, and two of such and such a stamp," etc. could sometimes get complicated when the stamp seeker didn't speak a country's language very well (or at all) and the stamp seller didn't speak English very well (or at all).

Here, however, I got them without too much trouble. After paying the weird waiter, Ellen, Gina, and I went across to a tourist information centre and asked the way to the beach. It was, we were told, a mere fifteen-minute walk straight down the first street on our left, but that was a dead end, and we actually had to go down some *steps* off that street.

Upon reaching the beach, all three of us were amazed, and disappointed, to find the beautiful, sunny, sandy-beached Riviera we'd always pictured, was, in reality, a rock beach. Sand, it appeared, was only available twenty or so miles away. Cannes and Monte Carlo had sand. Nice had rocks.

But the French Riviera was still the French Riviera, so we went to a private beach and hired three mattresses and a beach umbrella before wading out into the Mediterranean Sea. It was lovely and warm, so Ellen and I didn't have to do a repeat performance of inching as we had in Geneva.

Back on the mattresses, we applied suntan lotion and for a few hours lazed around in the manner of idle rich socialites enjoying an afternoon of sun-bathing.

Towards evening, we took a train to Monte Carlo in the Principality of Monaco. Ellen and I didn't feel it was right to be in the South of France and not go to Monte Carlo, even if we didn't think we were old enough to get into the famed Monte Carlo Casino that Monaco's Prince Charles III allowed to be put up in 1861 to revitalize the principality's economy and avoid an uprising of the peasantry, who were fed up with their taxes being used to keep the royals in luxury. It wasn't his idea though. His mother, Princess Caroline, had been to the spa town of Bad Homburg—then an independent territory, but now part of Germany—and taken note of how *its* ruler got enough 'licence' money from the operators of a casino there to pay for, not just royal perks, but various state expenses as well. ("That should keep the people happy, dear.")

Monte Carlo's casino entry age is now eighteen. Whether or not it was eighteen in 1971, I don't know. We simply assumed it was twenty-one. Gina *was* twenty-one, and therefore definitely eligible, but none of us were tremendously interested in going into a casino. We didn't want to gamble. We just wanted to say we'd been to Monte Carlo.

Gambling is, of course, what a lot of people go to Monte Carlo for, and many have tried their luck at the Monte Carlo Casino. With varying degrees of success. The music hall song, 'The Man Who Broke the Bank at Monte Carlo,' refers to Charles Deville Wells, an

Englishman who visited the casino in 1891. He'd hitherto pocketed a fair bit of cash from getting people to invest in non-existent inventions, and in Monte Carlo used his ill-gotten gains to fund a system that eventually netted him a million francs; a sum that would, today, be the equivalent of quite a few million dollars. Some thought his 'system' was really just a way he'd found to cheat—perhaps in collaboration with someone who worked at the casino—but this was never proved. Charlie did periodically get jailed for other scams, though, and died in penury. At the time we were in Monte Carlo, he was still the casino's biggest winner, but three years on an Italian gambler walked away with even more.

We, however, just strolled around outside the casinos, and later had a meal at a restaurant. After leaving it, we noticed we were being followed by some males displaying unsettling interest in us, and quickly made our way back to the train station to return to Nice.

The only other person in our compartment was a man on his way to Cannes. Since he spoke English, we talked about our travels, and he offered Gina his company as she would be "all alone" when we left for Carcassonne. Another offer she declined. She later told us that, when she was in Vienna, a guy had offered to show her the sights of the city and then find her a hotel. Not being as savvy to the ways of the continental male then as she was now, she'd agreed. But after assuring her there was still plenty of time for her to find a hotel, he'd driven her around until quite late and there was nowhere to stay except—surprise—his apartment. She did indeed stay there though. As soon as he went out to get something to "help them enjoy the evening", she locked him out and fled first thing in the morning. Where he spent the night, she neither knew nor cared. The apartment's manager had refused his demand to be let in with a master key and, in fact, seemed to find her way of dealing with her

Viennese 'guide's' obviously less than honourable intentions quite amusing.

Chapter Thirty-One
A Brief Stop, Then On To Sunny Spain

Ellen and I walked Gina to her hotel and then returned to the train station and found an empty compartment in a night train going to Carcassonne. It did not remain empty, and sleep was difficult once it became crowded. But we did all sleep some, though at one point everyone awoke with a start when my pack fell on top of us.

It would have been better for Ellen and myself if we had *stayed* awake, but we didn't. We woke up just before the train stopped in Toulouse, rather than Carcassonne, which it had already passed. We hastily got off and asked a porter when the next train back to Carcassonne was. He told us to follow another porter who led us to a man in an office who wrote something down on a piece of paper—probably to the effect that these two little idiots had slept through their stop and had to be got back. He told us to get on the next locomotive to show up at Platform Two and we sat on an empty luggage cart until it arrived. Luggage carts had become our favourite type of train station seat, as they could accommodate both us and our packs.

In Carcassonne, the passenger information clerk only spoke French and Spanish, but upon hearing us trying to make inquiries regarding our next day's travel plans, an American man who spoke Spanish stepped in and ascertained that in order to get to Madrid the following morning, we'd have to leave at noon *that* day. Since Carcassonne was another place where we were expecting to get letters, we realized we'd have to go out to the hostel to collect them before making a much quicker, and less thorough, exploration of Carcassonne than expected. The medieval part that is, as I can't say modern Carcassonne interested us in any way. Our interest lay in the old citadel, the best-preserved example of medieval fortifications in Europe. Or, rather, the best *restored* example of them. Carcassonne fell into disrepair after walled cities ceased to hold as much importance as they had in medieval times, and in the mid-nineteenth century, the renowned French architect, Eugène-Emmanuel Viollet-le-Duc, set about reconstructing the cathedral and ramparts—a project that took over fifty years to complete and attracted much criticism from those who didn't think his work was authentic enough. But it was authentic enough to suit us.

Swiftly consigning our packs to Left Luggage, we rushed outside, found a cab, and went to the Carcassonne youth hostel to cancel our reservation and collect our letters.

With those in hand, we paused long enough to have some breakfast before setting out on a whirlwind tour of old Carcassonne, a breakfast we regretted ordering, as it consisted of the worst tea and croissants we'd ever tasted. This did not take away from the joy of looking around the good old town itself, though. Walking through its cobbled streets gave us a definite 'medieval feeling'; a feeling that only faltered once, when we came upon a group of young people pushing themselves against an outer wall and groaning. I've no idea why. At the time, we figured it was either an ancient ritual of some kind, or they were on something. Time constraints forced us to leave shortly after that, but since motor vehicles were not allowed inside the old city, we had to go down to the entrance to get a cab to the train station.

***

The trip to Irun at the French-Spanish border had a few interesting moments, such as when Ellen hopped off the train at the first convenient still-in-France stop to post some Carcasonne postcards she'd written and almost got left behind. And when Ellen and I tried to eat semi-melted chocolate bars, à la Verona. And when I tried to get a drink from the canteen that was attached to my pack up on the luggage rack and overbalanced, knocking the pack down on some people beneath and getting water everywhere.

At Irun we went through to the Spanish side of the train station, changed some money, and tried to figure out which Spanish word on the status board stood for 'Arrivals', and which for 'Departures'. Language difficulties occurred in station's restaurant, too, resulting in communication problems with the waitress. Ellen had a tortilla and a cola, and I had a cola and tea. Ellen didn't want a cola, but the drinks order somehow got turned from two teas and one cola to two colas and one tea. But she wasn't missing anything, as my tea was nothing to write home about, other than in a derogatory way. By now we were convinced the French, and, it would seem, Spanish, just weren't able to make a good cuppa. How they could do anything to a tea bag was a mystery, but they could.

Several unreserved couchettes were available on the night train to Madrid, and we found one without difficulty. But even having a couchette did not lead to a comfortable night's sleep. Unaware that Spain got quite cold at night, we both had shorts on and, not being alone in the couchette, weren't able to change into anything warmer.

We slept in fits and starts and then finally sat up and just looked out the window until the train rolled into Madrid. Or Mayrit or Magerit, as it was called when the Iberian Peninsula was under Moorish control. It did not become a place of any great significance until well after the *Reconquista* (Reconquest) of that part of Europe, something that took Christians several centuries to achieve—possibly because they were so busy fighting each other. That happened in 1492, and in 1561 Spain's King Philip II moved his Court to Madrid and declared it the country's capital instead of Toledo, which had hitherto had that honour.

* * *

From Madrid we would be going to Lisbon and wanted to ascertain the time of the Lisbon night train before we left the station. Its passenger information booth didn't open until eight o'clock, so we sat down beside it to wait, but wound up having to stand as an officious official wouldn't let us sit on the floor.

Despite the information clerk's inability to speak English, and ours to speak Spanish, we managed to find out about the Lisbon train. We then asked him how to get to the Madrid youth hostel but he didn't know and directed us to an information booth in a different part of the station. It was closed, but someone told us about a nearby tourist information centre, and the clerk there did know. She advised us to take a cab out to the hostel but wasn't sure if it would do us any good because the address that we'd shown her indicated it was in the *Ciudad Universitaria* (University City) district. As far as she knew, the universities were closed for the summer.

This wasn't the best news, but we did have a confirmed reservation, so we went outside to get a cab. Or rather, try to. Not that there weren't any. There were, in fact, more cabs than we had ever come across anywhere. Black ones, with red stripes. But they were in high demand. Even though there were a lot of them, there were also a lot of people flagging them down, and everyone else must have waved more commandingly than Ellen and I did. All the empty cabs shot by us and went to pick up someone else until, eventually, a modern Man of La Mancha got one for us—thus proving that chivalry was not dead in the city that had erected a monument to the creator of Don Quixote.

The hostel was indeed in the city's university district, an area that, during Spain's civil war, was the scene of intense fighting from behind barricades made of books. Upon reaching it, the cab driver got lost trying to find the university we were after but got us there after asking a passer-by for directions.

The building was not what you would call a hive of activity, but neither was it as deserted as the woman at the tourist centre had supposed. Upon entering it we were told to wait by the office. A few minutes later, the same person who'd told us to wait there took us to another area. Then she went away, and after we'd waited a bit, someone else told us to move back to where we'd been. We did so and sat there for about half an hour until the hostel's warden, or perhaps, administrator, turned up. She was very nice, and very efficient. Within just a few minutes she led us to our rooms, checked us in, showed us where to catch the bus back in to town, and told us how to get to the nearest laundry, an amenity we by this time desperately required. She even handed over some letters that had arrived for me before returning to her other duties.

A short time later, we packed up our washing, changed into what few clothes we had that *didn't* require a good going-over with soap and water, and set off for the laundry. Everyone we asked seemed to have a different opinion on where it was and we got directed here, and there, and back again.

Unable to find a self-service laundry, we went into one that, as in Vienna, would do our washing for us, but found it difficult to communicate with the woman in charge. We even dragged two innocent by-standers into the conversation and had things written down for us. All to no avail because it transpired that it would take the place eight days to do it and we weren't going to be in Madrid for eight days.

After a couple of hours of fruitless wandering with the awkward bag of washing, we'd pretty much had it, nerve-wise, and, having no one else to take our frustration out on, took it out on each other. In an attempt to regain both our composure and our friendship, we went into a restaurant to fortify ourselves. No other patrons were inside, and since Spaniards eat their big meal late in the evening, I'm not sure the place was really even open. Even so the waiter took us into a room where chairs were upturned on tables, seated us at a table, and gave us a menu. We ordered chicken and chips and got a plate of...well...something. The chips were sort of identifiable but the chicken was not recognizable as such, either by sight or taste, and we doubted that it *was* chicken. Ellen guessed at dog, and I'm not sure she wasn't right. We still ate it but had to resort to using our fingers for the meat as it was impossible to dislodge it from the bone using knives and forks.

Ellen was a little worried about this, etiquette-wise, but I came up with the old English saying, "It's all right since the queen did it."

"Which queen?" she asked. "Boadicea?"

A short exchange that at least had us back on speaking terms.

Returning to the hostel, we set about washing our clothes in the bathroom. The water wasn't very hot, but sufficed, and a merry breeze blowing through the bathroom dried most of our things in record time.

Chapter Thirty-Two
Sunny Spain

Three successive night trains had taken a lot out of us. We weren't all that eager to get up the next morning and only did so because we'd bought breakfast tickets. Ellen's watch—that expensive Swiss one—had stopped at a quarter to seven, and that's what time she thought it was, causing her to feel a little put out at me waking her up "so damned early" until she checked the hostel's clock. On that occasion, the watch could have stopped because, in ancient times such as ours, watches had to be wound, and she might have forgotten to. But within a few days the stop was permanent.

Breakfast was the usual continental fare of rolls, fruit, and coffee—a first meal of the day offering that *none* of the children I would later take to Europe considered wholly satisfactory. We didn't really consider it all that satisfactory either and consumed it with indifference before catching a bus into the centre of Madrid to cash some traveller's cheques.

We went a bit past our stop and had to ask a policeman how to get back to the place where we should have alighted. Obviously used to dealing with ignorant foreign tourists, he gave us directions in sign language instead of wasting his time rattling on in Spanish.

At the bank we met with another of those interminable European waits that made us wonder if those working there were checking the political tendencies of everyone who came in. By then, we were used to it, but the extremely annoyed American woman behind us clearly wasn't. She kept saying things like, "I've never seen so many people do so little work!" and, "It's impossible for just one of them to serve you. They have to ask half a dozen others and have a big conference about it!" But Spain was a land in which life moved somewhat more slowly than it did in others, with the *'mañana'* (tomorrow will do) principle being applied to almost every circumstance, so I trust she eventually adapted.

From there we tried to find the Canadian Embassy. Ellen had not had any letters waiting for her at the hostel. To find out if there were any at the embassy, we set out on what proved to be the longest, most taxing, embassy search of our entire trip. We found the street all right, but the numbers on its buildings stopped at #78, and we wanted #88. We went over to a traffic cop and asked him, but unlike the first cop, this one *did* rattle on in Spanish. He then pointed up the street where we found the numbers started at seven. Confused, we stopped an American couple in possession of a city map and had the man ask some passers-by. Like many Americans, he spoke Spanish, but none of the passers-by he stopped knew where the embassy was.

He suggested we get in a cab and be driven to the door. This we did, but, unfortunately, the cab driver couldn't find the embassy either, making us wonder if any of Madrid's cab drivers actually knew their way around it. This one took us back to where we'd started and admitted he was at a loss.

We sighed, got out, paid the useless fare, and went over to a Pan-Am office to see if anyone *there* knew where the Canadian Embassy was, convinced it was either submerged underground, or Canada had deeply offended Spain in some way and brought about the embassy's closure.

The people in the Pan-Am office spoke English but they, too, had no idea where the embassy was. A man waiting in the queue told us to try the Hotel Plaza next door and its receptionist said the embassy was to the left of a door straight in front of us—hidden inside a hotel!

Well hidden, because, even from inside the building, we couldn't locate it. But we kept looking. And looking. And looking. The CP Air department directed us upstairs to the fifth floor. The lift didn't have a button for the fifth floor, and upon reaching the sixth floor without finding anything resembling an embassy, we went down two floors to some department or other, and people there directed us downstairs, jabbering something about a #3 lift being the one that went to the fifth floor. With no #3 lifts in the immediate vicinity, we got on one that at least had a button for the fifth floor and pushed it, but nothing happened, save that the doors opened and closed again. Ellen got out, but the doors shut before I could. Unable to find an 'Open' button, I pressed the one for the first floor and yelled at Ellen to meet me down there. But pressing *that* button re-opened the door, so we both clattered down the stairs, stopping in various departments on various floors, where we were invariably told to go up, down, or around, none of which got us to the embassy.

Back on the first floor, we finally spotted a #3 lift. We got in and pressed the button labelled with a five for the seemingly mythical fifth floor. This lift moved more rapidly than any of the others had, and when it stopped, lo, and behold, there it was: the Canadian Embassy.

"We found it!" Ellen almost sobbed. "We're here!"

"We're here!" I echoed. "It *does* exist!"

The woman at the reception desk seemed highly amused when we explained the trouble we'd had getting there. "Never mind," she said. "You're home now."

She also said that, had we but turned our gaze upward when we were still outside, there was a Canadian flag draped out the window. Looking later, we had to admit there was, but from that high up, it was rather small. Bigger than the "two-inch-by-two-inch" size Ellen claimed, but small.

She did have a letter waiting though. We got it, signed the visitor's book—after all that effort, the woman said we had to—and stepped into the lift again. This time, it proved less co-operative. We wanted to go down, and it went up. And up, and up, finally opening onto a part of the building that was still under construction, with a lot of sawdust, cement, and wooden planks lying around. We again pressed the button to go down, but nothing happened and, within minutes, our active imaginations were envisioning the scene as the people cutting the dedication ribbon on the new floor discovered our dried-up skeletons, the hand of one of them still clasping an unopened letter.

Repetitive stabs at the down button did eventually bring the desired result, and once we were back on *terra firma*, we went to find a bar that sold soft drinks, preferably Fanta® orange, as neither of us felt capable of facing another cola.

Our pursuit of this beverage took us up one street and down another until we had no idea where we were and could think of only one thing: a large, cold, sweet, orange Fanta, which it seemed unlikely we would get. The only bar with a Fanta sign was closed, and the only bar that had it listed on the outside menu, was out of it. Just when our tempers were at their flashpoints and we were ready to duel each other to the death, we saw another bar with a Fanta sign. Inside, we drained a bottle each, and ordered two more.

We drained them, too, and left the bar intending to shop. But Spain's siesta time had arrived and all the shops were either about to close or already had. Parks and squares were open though, so we made our way to the Parque De La Montaña and spent an hour or two there and another in the Plaza de España, home to the Cervantes monument. This tribute to the Spanish writer, Miguel de Cervantes (1547-1616), was commissioned by King Alfonso XIII in 1915 as a way to commemorate the three hundredth anniversary of the publication of Cervantes's *Segunda parte del ingenioso caballero don Quijote de la Mancha* (Second Part of the Ingenious Knight, Don Quixote of La Mancha), which, along with its forerunner, *El ingenioso hidalgo don Quijote de la Mancha* (*The Ingenious Gentleman, Don Quixote of La Mancha*), told of the adventures of the valiant, but delusional, Spanish knight, Don Quixote, and his loyal sidekick, Sancho Panza, both of whom appear on the monument, cast in bronze. The monument's architects were Rafael Martínez Zapatero and Pedro Muguruza Otaño, and its sculptor Lorenzo Coullaut Valera, but work on it did not begin until 1925. Still unfinished when it was unveiled in 1929, it was brought to completion in 1960 by the sculptor's son, Frederico.

After viewing it, we sat on a bench until half past three, when we thought the shops re-opened, but when we went back on the main street, none of them had. For that, we had to wait another hour and then both went shopping on our own.

In one shop I went into I asked to see some fans. Pointing to one, I asked how much it was.

"A Little cheaper, perhaps," the man said, after hearing my gasp.

I nodded, but even the cheaper ones weren't what *I* called cheap, so I didn't buy one.

At quarter to seven, I went back to the park to reunite with Ellen—who showed up at quarter *past* seven—and we went to a restaurant to eat. Crossing the communications barrier took a while, but we eventually got our order across. When it came, Ellen's sandwich meat was raw, and I'd had better chips. Unfortunately, our phrase book didn't cover "This meat isn't cooked". By then we didn't expect it to.

Following this, we caught a bus back to the hostel, shivering as we waited for it. The term 'sunny Spain' had been correct as regards sun, but not as regards warmth. A chilly breeze had been blowing throughout the day and by night-time temperatures had dropped to the point of being downright nippy.

Chapter Thirty-Three
Still Spain

The next morning, I fitted a flashcube to my camera, leaned over the side of the bunk, and took a picture of Ellen just as she turned her head to say, "I don't want to get up yet." She was not amused, saying the expression on her face was likely to have been that of a prehistoric beast emerging from a swamp saying, "Ggraghhgt!" And it was, but the possibility of being issued with a restraining order keeps me from making the photo public.

Foregoing breakfast, and lacking confidence in our cab-summoning ability, we got the administrator to phone for one to take us to the train station. After checking our packs into Left Luggage, we risked life and limb crossing a roadway with several lanes of traffic in order to reach a couple of shops and a restaurant we'd spotted. Despite our last experience with *pollo* (chicken) we decided to order it again. It came whole, as in, a whole small *pollo* each and, except for tasting strongly of garlic—which I dislike—wasn't too bad.

From there we fought our way through the traffic again and went to a nearby park. On the way we discovered stall after stall of used books and magazines, some of them in *inglés*. We got a couple of magazines, plus two ice creams, and went into the park to write letters and read until late afternoon.

If Madrid appeared to have more taxi cabs than other cities, it also seemed to have more fountains, which, I suppose is not surprising, since the city's Arabic name means 'place of water'. Re-crossing the busy roadway, I stopped by a huge fountain in the middle of it so Ellen could take a picture. As she stood across from me waiting for the cars to stop whizzing past her viewing screen, a policeman came up to me and rebuked me for standing by the fountain amidst so much dangerous traffic. Then, satisfied that he'd carried out his duty, he went away, and Ellen took the picture.

From that point, our time was taken up with spending a good bit of the money we'd allotted ourselves for Spain. But the shops in that area were more reasonably priced than the ones we'd been in the day before. This time I did get the fans I'd been after, and a Spanish shawl as well. Ellen wanted to get a belt for her brother-in-law, but that was a little less straightforward. The sizing was different and belt sizes were the one thing our money and measures converter didn't convert. Since the people in the leather shop didn't speak English, she had quite a time explaining the size she required until a man around her brother-in-law's height and build came in and she more or less dragged him over to try on the belt she'd selected. He didn't seem to mind but did give the crazy tourist an odd look.

When we'd exhausted all the funds we dared, we headed back to the train station. Trying to cross the street we got waved back by the same cop who'd told me I couldn't stand by the fountain. He pointed down the street, where we found an underground passage that got us safely across.

At the station, we retrieved our packs from Left Luggage, where all the attendants were playing with clacker balls. But this was not the first time we'd come across those noisy little plastic balls on a cord that banged together with a resounding 'clack' and resembled the South American weapon called boleadoras. Half of Europe seemed to have gone clacker-crazy that summer. And not just there, because we'd heard they'd been banned in Canada and the U.S.A. Something about them being rather dangerous, due to their nasty tendency to shatter if clacked too hard.

Unable to cram anything more into our packs in the midst of a train station, we put our day's purchases in some sturdy plastic carrier bags we'd bought. Ellen then stayed with the packs, and I went to the passenger information booth to find out when we would arrive in Lisbon.

There was, of course, a queue and as I approached, a woman in it turned and said, "Manuel? Manuel?" Finding nothing resembling this Manuel anywhere in the immediate area, she and her two daughters, aged about thirteen and eight, went charging out of the station, all shouting, "Manuel!" A few moments later, she returned, followed by Daughter #1 and Daughter #2, the latter dragging a screaming boy of about six—whom I took to be Manuel—along by the hair. Content that all her little chicks were again present, Mama placidly rejoined the queue.

Upon my return to the place in which Ellen awaited me, we read some of our recent literary purchases until the status board proclaimed the Lisbon train was in and provided the platform number. But when we tried to get into a first-class carriage, the guard wouldn't let us. We showed him our Eurail passes and argued with him for about five minutes and then went down to a second-class carriage. The guard there wouldn't let us on that, either. We argued with him and a passer-by for about ten minutes until we grasped that we had to get something put on our passes at a ticket office that was some distance off. Luckily, there was no queue. The ticket seller didn't speak much English, but gave us to understand that First Class was full. We said we'd travel Second Class, but he said we had to have a couchette, and that cost four hundred and sixty-four pesetas (almost $7). But there was no getting around it, and even though we were running low on pesetas, we got the couchette tickets.

During this discussion, an American girl near the ticket office advised us to get some Portuguese escudos before we hit Portugal, as the U.S. dollar had taken a nosedive there. This seemed a prudent thing to do, so Ellen dealt with the couchette tickets and I dashed off to cash a traveller's cheque. The train was leaving in five minutes, and I must say I have to give both the ticket collector and the exchange cashier credit, because they did hurry, our concerns over the imminent departure of our train having doubtless been made clear to them by all the fidgeting and pointing at the wall clock we did. The necessary extra tickets and funds procured, we thundered across the platform and practically ran into another guard, who urgently waved us onto a carriage, where we found an empty compartment and breathed sighs of relief.

The train set off about two minutes later. Not long after that, some type of policeman came into our compartment and demanded our passports, saying they'd be stamped in the night and returned to us at Lisbon. He then took them away. We were a little concerned, but figured it was standard procedure and decided to worry about it in the morning.

Then another man came in and asked to see our tickets and Eurail passes. But as soon as we surrendered them, he started to walk away. Well, this was different! A Eurail pass could not be replaced in the same way as a passport, regardless of how much weeping its owner did at the nearest Canadian Embassy. Oblivious to our wails of objection, he left. Ellen pursued him down the corridor but didn't catch up, leaving us with no option but to worry about that in the morning, too. Ellen vowed that, if she didn't get her pass back then, she'd sit on the train until she did.

The pass-appropriator came back a little while later, but not to return our passes. Instead, he brought us pillows and blankets, the money we'd paid in Madrid having apparently entitled us to such luxuries.

Chapter Thirty-Four
Lisbon Interlude

The next morning, a man in a white jacket came in and said, "Customs. You have anything to declare?" Not knowing what we were supposed to declare, we shook our heads and he put chalk marks on our packs and left. Shortly afterwards the man with our Eurail passes returned and gave them back to us, followed a little later by another with our passports, the latter covered with enough stamps to almost make up for not getting them stamped in other places. With these precious items restored, the world was bright again.

Founded around 1200 BC as a Phoenician outpost on what was believed to be the edge of the known world, the place the Phoenicians called *Alis Ubbo* (safe harbour) was held by Moors from 714 to 1147. They called it by a variety of names, one of them, Lisbon. When Christians finally wrested Lisbon away from the Moors, the self-proclaimed King of Portugal, Alfonso I (also known as Alfonso Henriques), became the actual King of Portugal and established his Court there. But it took over a hundred years for the city to be declared the country's capital, a designation it lost for a time. The first of several European nations to embark on the rapacious pursuit of gold, spices, and the 'righteous' imposition of Christianity on ignorant heathens, Portugal starting cutting its imperialistic teeth in 1415 with the take-over of the African port of Ceuta, and then moved on to other places in Africa and parts of South America and Asia as well. Much later, alarmed by Napoleon's 1807 invasion of Portugal, the royal family believed—rightly believed—it was in their interests to take ship for a far distant part of their now vast empire. Proclaiming Rio de Janeiro in Brazil the *new* Portuguese capital, they remained there until 1821. In 1822, Brazil declared independence from Portugal, and Lisbon regained its capital status. The royal family kept on being the royal family, but their official standing as such was withdrawn in 1910. That was the year a revolution turned Portugal into a republic, but it didn't give up the last of its colonies—Macao—until 1999.

The Lisbon hostel we were booked into wasn't actually in Lisbon. It was a few miles away in a little beach town whose name I do not recall as I didn't write it down and it was a *long* time ago. To reach it, we had to get to another train station by double-decker bus. And here, please note: trying to climb the steps of a moving double-decker with large packs on is not something to be recommended.

At the other train station, we got aboard a local train and, upon arrival in the beach town, got conflicting opinions on how to get to the hostel. None of them correct, so we spent considerable time tramping about. At one point, far up a motorway—and, as it turned out, nowhere near the hostel—we asked yet another person for directions. We must have looked quite woe begotten when he told us we'd have to go back the way we came, because he slung our packs in the trunk of his car, made his wife and three children move over in the back seat, drove us back down the motorway, and dropped us at a camping site, thinking that's where we wanted to go. It wasn't, so we asked a nearby policeman, who directed us back up the motorway. There we met another man, who took us back into the area we'd first been in and led us hither and yon, asking an assortment of people the way to the hostel until he found it for us.

Signing in, the wardens wanted to know more about us than *any* of their predecessors had. Our youth hostel card numbers, who had issued them, our passport numbers, who had issued them, the date they were issued, and more.

The dormitory we were assigned to was quite a small one, and we rested there a while before going out for something to eat and drink. The meal was okay, but the accompanying dessert (chocolate pudding) had some sort of alcohol in it, so I gave mine to Ellen, who consumed it with a readiness that would have again scandalized that aunt who belonged to the Temperance Union. But, should you be wondering, no, Ellen did *not* grow up to be a lush.

After the meal, we crossed the motorway and went up a street in search of a souvenir shop to get our Portuguese crests and some postcards. Unable to find one, we got out our phrase book and asked two girls if there were any in the area. The book actually had *that* phrase, but it wasn't required as they spoke a little English and took us to some. None were really souvenir shops, but we were able to get what we were looking for.

We also went into a couple of groceries to get the makings of our evening meal. Nothing we bought required cooking, so the fact that the hostel's members' kitchen wasn't open when we wanted it to be did not deter us. There were tables outside, and the only challenge to using one came from a brisk sea breeze that kept whisking away everything that wasn't nailed down. In contrast to Nice, this beach was a lovely sandy one, but on that day, decidedly blustery.

Later on, we sorted out our packs to make room for the Spanish souvenirs we'd just been keeping in our carrier bags, and went to bed. Rather early, but it had been a long day. And with fifteen hours to put in on the Lisbon-St. Sebastian train the next day, we knew that that was likely to be a long day *and* night. We didn't go to sleep though, as an English girl from

London came in and we talked to her for a while. She and her brother were hitchhiking around Europe—with him always sitting between her and the driver.

* * *

No great exodus from other rooms occurred when a bell was rung for breakfast the next morning. Arriving downstairs, we found we were the only people to show up, but a few more drifted in after the bell was run a little more vigorously.

After breakfast, we hoisted our packs onto our backs and walked to the train station, which really wasn't far once we were no longer doubling back on our trail like we'd been doing the day before. We took a train back to the local station in Lisbon and from there attempted to get a bus to the international station. At first, we couldn't find a stop with the right number, but even when we did, nothing showed up. We were still standing by the stop when a man who had directed us there passed by, returning from wherever he'd been heading for before. In the end we gave up and hailed a passing cab. In a repeat scenario of Madrid, the driver had trouble grasping our desired destination. By now we were beginning to suspect—but were not yet ready to admit—that, rather than the cab drivers being incompetent, the blame lay with our own poor communication skills. He eventually figured out where we wanted to go and took us there.

As soon as our packs had been safely deposited in Left Luggage, we took a bus to the city centre and dropped a letter and some postcards into a post box before leaving Lisbon.

On the train, we spent most of the day reading but at night folded down the seats, turned out the lights and settled down to sleep, trying to ignore all the people in the corridor who were laughing and talking. They stopped after a while, and we were able to sleep a bit until four young men came into our compartment. The hour was by then very late, but that did not keep them from trying to strike up a conversation with us in a manner we felt it best to ignore. The one beside me even tickled my foot to get my attention and was lucky not to get it—the foot—right in the mouth. After receiving no encouraging response to, "Do you speak English, beautiful one?" they tried *"Parlez-vous français, ma cherie?" "¿Hablas español, bonita?"*, and *"Sprechen Sie Deutsches, liebchen?"*, and other linguistic variations. Not knowing how to say, "Leave me alone," in any of the above—another phrase that useless phrase book failed to provide—we went on looking blank and they finally gave up and settled down to sleep.

Ellen and I stayed awake, wondering what the Spanish for "Guard! Guard!" was, but all but one of the young men got off a few stops later, and that one stood in the corridor for a while, so we shut the door and turned off the light again. He returned to the compartment a couple of hours later, accompanied by two more men, but this time no advances were made, and they all got off at some point during the night.

Chapter Thirty-Five
Spain Again

San Sebastian or, in the Basque language spoken by many locals, Donostia, is believed to have started out as an eleventh-century monastery that expanded into a fishing village. And that fishing village expanded into the town that was officially 'founded' by royal decree in the year 1180. The issuer of that royal decree was the Navarre region's ruling monarch, Sancho VI (1132/33-1194). Since other regions' monarchs were showing an unwelcome interest in his, he was eager to build up some defences, and fortified the place. Also known as Sancho the Wise and Sancho the Strong, he must have either been very well regarded in his time, or had a good PR department.

Centuries later, Queen Isabella II—who reigned, amid much unrest, from 1833 until she was forced into exile in 1868—made San Sebastian a popular summer retreat for people wanting to escape the heat of a Spanish summer, and its crescent shaped La Concha beach was what had attracted us there, too. Having managed to arrive unmolested, we went to the station's restaurant for tea and sugar rolls. Then, even though money was getting tight, we took a cab out to the youth hostel. There was no bus at that early hour, and the hostel was quite a long way out. Upon arrival, the meter read thirty-two pesetas, but the cab driver demanded forty-five pesetas, which, lacking the ability to argue in Spanish, we had to pay.

The hostel was not yet open, so we sat on the steps and talked to two other new arrivals who were already waiting there. American girls from, for a change, Maryland. The girls' names were Barbie and Zena. Only sixteen, they were among the few non-school party hostellers we met who were younger than us. (Most were between twenty and thirty.) They related a rather harrowing experience they'd had with a cab driver earlier on, and said we were lucky ours had only charged us thirteen pesetas over what the meter read. The driver they'd had had demanded an additional ninety pesetas, and they'd engaged in quite a shouting match with him. They didn't speak Spanish either, though, and had had to pay the money in the end.

They also related that Barbie had almost been raped in Yugoslavia. When Zena called the police, they refused to do anything because the guys involved said the girls were prostitutes who'd taken their money and not 'come through'. Luckily for Barbie, she escaped with only bruises. Another time, they were hitchhiking, with Barbie in the back seat and Zena in the front beside a friendly driver who soon got a bit too friendly. Zena promptly started yelling, "Karate! Karate! I know karate! Barbie, get the knife!"—referring to the long, vicious-looking, carving knife that was in one of their packs. Zena didn't think he really believed she knew karate, but said he must have understood enough English for the word 'knife' to cool his ardour.

Checking into the hostel, we were told we were obliged to have one meal a day in the hostel dining room. We chose breakfast, thinking it likely to be the cheapest. Barbie and Zena were in the same dormitory, so we traded travel experiences with them and an English girl before all of us walked to the now-in-service bus stop. The others got a bus for the beach and Ellen and I went to San Sebastian's main shopping area where, with most of the souvenirs in

Spain having proved to be somewhat cheaper than in other places, we planned to get the bulk of the ones we wanted for family and friends.

At siesta time we went to an English food restaurant, the Bar Miguel, that had been recommended to us by a British family that had been eating there when we'd passed by earlier. The food was every bit as 'English' as they'd claimed and we partook of good tea, excellent chips, and some lovely bacon butties.

Replete, we went and sat in a park and watched children, mostly brothers and sisters, fight over who would get the first drink from a nearby water fountain. One pair even raced for it. Little sister won and big brother actually let her have it. Then another pair started to amuse themselves by pushing each other's face into the water. This went on until big sister pushed too hard and, upon angrily aiming a kick at her shins, little brother overbalanced and fell flat on his back. It was all very entertaining.

At half past four, we went souvenir hunting again, this time along the route back to the hostel. But no shops meeting our requirements were anywhere to be found and, suddenly, in contradiction to that catchy rain in Spain falling mainly on the plain ditty, heavy precipitation started to come down—accompanied by thunder and lightning. We ducked into a grocery long enough to pick up a few provisions and made a run for the hostel, getting there just as the rain stopped.

With the dining room not scheduled to open until Spain's usual late dining hour, and eating in our dorm or the sitting room forbidden, we had to go to one of the outdoor poolside tables to have our supper. All the chairs were wet from the rain, so we ate standing up and then returned to our dorm and spoke with an American girl.

Somewhere along the line, the conversation became more of a debate. That point being when she expressed the opinion that every family should be limited to two children. She said she was the second eldest of five, which doubtless influenced her viewpoint. But Ellen and I fell further along the birth order chain and found it a rather awkward subject to discuss with someone who didn't think we should exist.

Neither side changed the other's mind.

* * *

When we went to the dining room for the breakfast we'd been forced to buy, a hostel employee told us to follow him and then sat us at different tables. I was with a group of Irish girls who cheerfully assured me that Paris was outrageously expensive. Not encouraging news for travellers whose supply of travellers cheques was dwindling.

After breakfast we signed out and, along with the girl with strong views on population control, caught a bus out to somewhere near the train station. We found it with little trouble and checked our luggage before going back to the main section of town to go souvenir hunting again. I did, however, first have to make a brief stop at a bank to change some French francs into Spanish pesetas to augment my, much diminished, monetary allotment for España.

Eventually, our souvenir search took us to a local flea market with souvenir stand upon souvenir stand, as well as stands selling just about everything else imaginable. It was there that I somehow lost track of Ellen, and she of me. Had this happened in a big, unfamiliar, city earlier in our travels, we'd no doubt have had hysterics. Now, I just went back to where I'd seen her last, saw she was no longer there, or even in the general area, and reasoned that she would, in due course, probably head for our agreed upon lunch spot—Bar Miguel—on her own. Even when I went there and found she hadn't, I figured she'd turn up eventually, and I could always contact the police if she was still a no-show by eight o'clock or so. I did go along the street a bit to see if I could meet up with her, but she happened to approach Bar Miguel from the opposite direction and was sitting outside it when I got back. She wasn't upset either, sure that I'd turn up eventually, and she could always contact the police if I was still a no-show by eight o'clock or so.

We ate at Bar Miguel as planned. The waiter looked a bit nonplussed at the size of our order, but we thought, if Paris was going to be expensive, we'd better make the most of an affordable place to eat.

During siesta time, we went down to the beach and in true, sophisticated, women travellers of the world style, took off our shoes and socks and set about building a sandcastle. This was followed by another really adult pastime, that of burying each other's hands and feet in the sand. And we were so engrossed in doing so that we didn't notice the tide coming in until it was almost upon us. Extricating ourselves from the sand, we paddled in the sea for a while before moving back to the park.

When the flea market reopened, Ellen went back to do some more shopping, but I stayed in the park watching the people there, many of them with babies, which San Sebastian seemed to have more of than any other place we'd been.

Ellen had promised to be back in the park by half past six but, as should by now be evident, punctuality was not something she was noted for in those days, and I was not surprised when she didn't arrive until seven. (Her casual attitude towards time has improved too.)

At the train station, she stayed with our packs and I went into the WC to change into my jeans. Having spent my last peseta on a car sticker for my brother—a comic one depicting a weird looking creature with the name Pedro above it—I'd had to borrow one of Ellen's few remaining pesetas to pay the woman in charge of the WC. But I didn't have to use it because she was talking to someone when I left, and didn't seem to want it. The WC attendants in Spain were much less disagreeable than in other parts of Europe and did not demand a set sum for use of their facilities, apparently content with whatever was handed over. Or in this instance, not.

Returning to Ellen, I found her in a vile rage because our tin of chocolate drink mix had come open and spilled all over her pack. My breaking into riotous laughter didn't help, and she kept muttering things like, "It's your damn cocoa!" as she scooped what was retrievable back into the container and sealed it with some sticky tape we'd bought in Geneva and used many times.

Our next destination was Paris, and to get there we had to change trains at the French border town of Hendaye. The ride there wasn't long, and throughout it, Hawaiian-type music was played. This seemed a bit out-of-place on a Spanish train, but music is international, and in later years I would ride an Israeli bus between Nazareth and Jerusalem listening to Roger Whittaker.

At Hendaye, a female voice employed six different languages to tell passengers to go up to the first carriage to disembark. We did so, and the French border guard waved us through without even looking at our passports. Someone on the platform was selling couchette tickets, and we toyed with the idea of getting one, but decided we couldn't afford it and found a regular compartment in Second Class.

Once the train was well underway, I went out into the corridor to stretch my legs. Unlike many trains we'd been on, this one's corridors were not crammed with people. Barrelling along in my usual fashion when unhampered, I pushed open the door at the end of the carriage with my usual gusto. But did so just as the train swerved, causing it to almost pitch me right out the *open* side door. Such a close shave immediately called forth an image of Ellen searching the train for me a couple of hours later, and then, in desperation, pulling the communication cord. An action that would lead to her having to try to explain herself to people who spoke little or no English as I lay bleeding in a ditch a few hundred miles back.

And my flights of fancy didn't end there. When I got back to the compartment, Ellen and I both speculated as to what might be causing a middle-aged man to throw open our door at least four times, peer in, and then depart, frowning. Was he a distraught seeker of a travelling companion that *did* fall off the train? Or an off-duty policeman who believed us to be international spies he had to keep a close watch on? Or someone who, because he'd travelled in that particular compartment as a child, wanted to do so again, and thought we might leave if he annoyed us enough?

When he finally gave up this bizarre behaviour, we turned out the light and settled down to sleep. No one else, save ticket inspectors, entered the compartment all night, but since the seats didn't pull out, and were very hard and narrow, even Ellen didn't sleep very well.

Chapter Thirty-Six
So This Is Paris

Paris was once a river town in a part of France that, sometime in the third century BC, became home to the Gallic tribe known as the Parisii. When the Romans attempted to take possession of it in 52 BC, the resident property owners burnt the place to the ground rather than surrender it to them. But, as the Romans tended to do practically everywhere, they eventually prevailed and rebuilt what they called *Lutetia Parisiorum*. And by the time Clovis the Frank made it his capital in 508, *Lutetia Parisiorum* had simply become Paris.

During our time there, we saw a newly arrived American girl sitting on a bench and heard her say, "I'm in Paris, France! I really am!"

Our reaction upon arrival at Europe's busiest train station—the Gare du Nord—was somewhat different.

Me: "Ellen, we're here."

Ellen: "Uh-huh."

But Paris might well have been that other girl's first stop. It wasn't ours, so we lacked her enthusiasm and sense of wonder.

Due to high summer demand for hostel accommodation, limits on lengths of stay were enforced more rigorously in Paris than in other places, and we were booked into two successive youth hostels. Maybe. The first one, we had a confirmed reservation for; the second, only if my parents had paid the deposit requested in that letter that had gone astray in Holland.

The first hostel was in Choisy-le-Roi, an area serviced by local trains out of another station, the Gare d'Austerlitz. As usual, the hostel was quite a distance from the Choisy-le-Roi station, but finding it was relatively easy. There were lots of signs and, when it came to asking the way, we found ourselves in the company of a young American wayfarer who had a much better command of the French language than we did.

Arriving at the hostel we were informed thievery was rife, and heeded the warden's advice to put all our valuables in the lockers that were provided free of charge. Ellen and I then got a train back to Paris and took the Métro to the Canadian Embassy, which, in contrast to Madrid, had a *huge* flag outside of it, and was quickly found. I didn't have any letters, but Ellen did. In it, her mother assured her that Duane had delivered the stuff we'd sent back with him and my brother had delivered the message about forwarding the deposit money to the second Paris hostel.

Our next stop was the American Express office, to get some money, but even though our traveller's cheques were the company's own, the rate of exchange wasn't that great. The American dollar had gone down all over Europe and travellers had to make do with what was being paid out.

We also booked a tour going out to Versailles that afternoon. When we joined it, we found that, with only a few exceptions, most of the bus's seats were occupied by people who were part of an American Tour of Europe group. At Versailles, we all trooped obediently after our guide, a young lady who kept waving a roll of pink and blue entrance tickets so everyone could see where she was. Though busy, Versailles was not, on that day, as crowded as it was when I went there in 1984. On that occasion, it was very crowded, and although adults fared all right,

Bryan claimed all he got to see of Versailles was ceiling and elbows, so when I returned to Paris in 1993 with his brother, Braden, and my son, Richard, I skipped Versailles and took *them* on a Seine cruise. Which the little ingrates said was "boring". They did, however, like the Louvre and Notre Dame Cathedral.

Versailles was originally just a hunting lodge belonging to Louis XIII (1601-1643), but the next Louis on France's king list—the Sun King, Louis XIV (1638-1715)—transformed the small château of Versailles into the huge Palace of Versailles. It was, admittedly, beautiful, but gold and marble got rather monotonous after a while, and it was easy to understand why peasants living in hovels had got a trifle miffed about their royals living in such wantonly extravagant surroundings, and decided to rid themselves of them. And, for good measure, a great many of France's other *aristocrates décadents*.

At the end of the tour the guide turned us loose until four o'clock, saying that the bus would be waiting for us in the place it let us off. Simple enough instructions, but some people still got them wrong and went to a different parking lot. This led to the bus driver having to go there to pick them up, and then go back to where he'd picked the rest of us up to retrieve a couple who'd arrived there late. Despite the delay, we were still taken around the palace's magnificent park grounds—a surprise extra not listed in the brochure—before the bus went back to Paris and dropped people off at the Eiffel Tower, Opera Square, and the hotel where the bulk of the group was staying.

Ellen and I got off at Opera Square and took the Métro out to its Rue de Montmartre station, working under the assumption that it would be close to where Montmartre and the *Basilique du Sacré-Cœur* (Basilica of the Sacred Heart) were located. It wasn't. Or at least didn't appear to be. After trudging around for a while, we asked directions and eventually got to the Montmartre area, the name derived from either

Mons Martis, a reference to a pagan temple to Mars that was there in Roman times, or *Mont des Martyrs*, a reference to Saint Denis, Patron Saint of France, and the first bishop of what would become Paris. He and a couple of other early Christian clerics named Rusticus and Eleutherius were beheaded on Montmartre around 250 for preaching their Christian belief to the town's mostly pagan inhabitants. But, according to legend, even that didn't stop Denis, who picked up his severed head and walked off, still preaching.

These religious associations aside, Montmartre was a favourite haunt of Claude Monet, Henri de Toulouse-Lautrec, Pablo Picasso, and other famous wielders of paint brushes. Artists still ply their trade there and we stopped to watch one do a chalk drawing on a stretch of pavement before moving on to climb the seemingly never-ending steps leading up to the Sacré Cœur. By the time we got to the top, we were convinced a sadist had designed the access to it as an extension of the act of penance that brought the Sacre Cœur into being. Believing France's defeat in the Franco-Prussian War of 1870 and the rise of the Paris Commune in 1871 to have been brought about by the sins of the French people, nineteenth-century philanthropists Alexandre Legentil and Hubert Rohault de Fleury sold Paris's Archbishop Cardinal Joseph-Hippolyte Guibert on the idea of atoning for these sins by building a new church dedicated to the Sacred Heart of Christ. The foundation stone was laid in 1875, but various obstacles—among them, the death of the architect, Paul Abadie, in 1884—led to it not being completed until 1914, and, thanks to the rude interruption of World War I, not consecrated until 1919.

Back at the hostel, we had a bite to eat and went up to our dorm, where it seemed the majority of our roommates were getting ready to go out for a night on the town. We, however, went to bed. Our first evening in Paris, and all we wanted to do was catch up on our sleep, well aware that *we* couldn't afford a night on the town. Except maybe the last night, when, if we still had enough francs to cover it, we thought it might be nice to dine on the Eiffel Tower and gaze out at Paris's acclaimed illuminations.

* * *

Like London, Paris was a place where travellers of limited means had to choose between eating and sightseeing. Breakfast was in with the overnight fee and consisted of coffee and as many rolls as people wanted, so Ellen and I ate several to fortify ourselves for a day of sightseeing and shopping.

One of our shopping objectives was perfume for female friends and relatives. We went up and down the famous Champs-Élysées to see what its scent sellers had offer, gasping at both the prices and the fumes. At one point we passed a café where a movie scene was being shot, but I have no idea what movie it was or who the actor and actress were.

Everywhere we went, salesclerks sprayed perfume on our hands and arms until we reeked of the stuff. Ellen was more into this than me, as exotic fragrances tended to make me feel sick and irritated my nasal passages. We eventually obtained some perfume within our monetary reach in a little shop on a street off the Champs-Élysées and turned our attention to the pursuit of a different kind of olfactory experience.

Having watched Frederic March tramping through them in the 1935 production of *Les Misérables*, and Fred MacMurray doing likewise in Disney's *Bon Voyage* (1962), Ellen and I were interested in visiting Paris's sewers. As with most cities built around a river, Paris's earliest wastewater system consisted of open-air drains that emptied out into its main source of drinking water. People kept polluting the Seine in this manner throughout the Middle Ages, and it was not until enough centuries had passed for scientific types to start making connections between raw sewage and recurring outbreaks of disease that a more sanitary method of waste disposal was sought. The first was initiated by Napoleon Bonaparte at the beginning of the nineteenth century. When not busy conquering much of Europe and harassing those nasty people across the Channel, France's industrious little general went in for home improvements, and had a few hundred miles of sewage canals built underneath his capital. But Paris's 1832 choleric epidemic made it clear that even these were not up to keeping the city disease-free, and in 1850, Napoleon's nephew, Louis Napoleon (Napoleon III), gave city planner, Georges-Eugène Haussmann (Baron Haussmann), and a talented engineer named Eugène Belgrand, the job of building an even bigger and better sewage system.

Tours of the new sewers started in 1867 and, according to a guidebook we'd consulted back home, were still conducted from the Place de La Concorde every Thursday. But when we went to an information booth there, we were told it was every Saturday. The same guidebook had talked about Paris having a lot of good flea markets, so, quickly changing plans, we went to one. Only to find that it was closed too, *its* days of operation being Saturdays, Sundays, and Tuesdays. This necessitated yet another change of plan, and since we had to do some shopping so as to know where our remaining finances stood, we consulted a map and tried to figure out which 'Bank' in town was the famous Left Bank frequented by artistic types, and which one was the Right Bank, where a lot of the city's shops were. In the end we just asked someone and were directed to a huge department store called La Samaritaine.

Catering to a less upper-crust clientele than the fancier Bon Marché and Galeries Lafayette, La

Samaritaine was, at that time, the largest department store in Paris, but was originally just a small clothing boutique run by Ernest Cognacq, who started his retail career selling ties on the Pont Neuf. In 1869, he decided to branch out a bit. Before long, he'd branched out a lot, snapping up neighbouring properties until his one little shop had morphed into four large ones and carried a variety of goods.

We spent most of our time in, I think, Shop #2, where I went to the cuff link and tie pin department to get initialled sets for my father and brother, and Ellen went in pursuit of some fancy soaps and talcum powder.

Meeting back at the entrance, we decided we could afford to eat—a little—and had a meal in a restaurant near the Gare d'Austerlitz that was, for Paris, fairly reasonably priced. When we tried to get our waiter's attention, he said, "Un moment, mes enfants." Taking this as an indication that the sophisticated world traveller image we'd been trying to project wasn't being projected all that well, we tried to remedy this by ordering in our best French when he finally got to us. But I only got as far as *"pommes frites"* before he said, "French potatoes," and we gave up. He was obviously used to people placing their orders in English.

Before going to bed that night, Ellen and I packed up in preparation for the next day's move to the second hostel, a chore I finished before she did. This was a common occurrence, but probably only because my mother had been taught how to pack by an aunt who'd once travelled the world as a lady's maid, and Mum, in turn, taught me.

Coming back from the washroom, I found Ellen in despair because she couldn't close her pack. That first hostel provided sheet sleeping bags for free, and knowing our own were the largest items our packs had to accommodate, I suggested she take hers out and transfer it to her carrier bag.

"It's not in there yet," she moaned.

She did eventually get her pack to close. But only by taking out some other items and putting *them* in the carrier bag.

Chapter Thirty-Seven
Still Paris

It was raining when we signed out the next day, so Ellen and I donned raincoats and set off for the train station. In Paris we got the Métro out to the stop we'd been told was closest to the new hostel. Unfortunately, we got mixed up between Porte d'Italie and Place d'Italie, and after getting off at the latter, had to walk quite a distance, in pouring rain. Once there, we had to stand in a lengthy queue, still in pouring rain, much like in Geneva. Here, however, the people at the other end were friendly. They couldn't find our reservation at first, but eventually did, and since Mum had posted them a deposit of twenty-four francs, we only had to part with four francs each—very helpful to the budget at that point. So was the security of a reservation. Spare places were available most nights, but some American kids told us that, due to rampant anti-Americanism in Paris, American hostellers only got beds if absolutely no one from a different country wanted them, even if the American ones were there first.

Like the other hostel, this one had theft concerns, but provided a communal locker room for the safe storage of belongings rather than individual lockers. The locker room didn't open until noon, and since the dorms were shut between nine in the morning and half past five, we had to sit on the floor of the reception hall and write postcards until such time as our packs could be safely stored. Just after Ellen had gone to get some stamps from a stamp machine, two young Frenchmen came up to me and started talking about an Arc de Triomphe postcard she'd left lying near me. I wondered if this was the usual continental come on—a female: pounce—and it might have been, but, if so, it was a polite one, and they didn't have wandering hands.

When Ellen returned, we learned their names were Michel and Sadek and sat talking to them until a janitor came along wanting to sweep the floor. This forced us to move outside, our packs carried by those nice, gentlemanly, French boys. The rain had stopped by then, and Michel pointed out several interesting places to visit on a map. At that particular moment, our energy didn't stretch to any of the places he was endorsing, but we said we'd keep them in mind.

After getting our packs secured for the day, Ellen and I went to the Louvre-Tuileries district and did some shopping. Mostly window. Eventually tiring of this, I sat on some steps in the Tuileries Gardens to wait for Ellen, who had not yet tired of it. Just as she was returning to the gardens, a young man came up to me and tried the real continental come on. He *did* have wandering hands, and had I been able to remember the French word for knee, I would have told him to remove his *main* from my *genou*, but *genou* chose to elude me until later. His hands wandered over Ellen, too, so I told him we were going to the Louvre and we left, stopping only long enough to get a picture of some children riding donkeys around the gardens. Popular with tourists and locals alike, the *Jardins des Tuileries* were once attached to the ill-fated Tuileries Palace that some members of the anti-royalist Paris Commune burned down during their brief time in office in 1871.

The Louvre Palace fared better. It was originally a sixteenth-century palace built for François I on the site of a fortress built for Philippe Auguste (Philip II) back in the thirteenth century. And then added on to, and used as a primary royal residence by a succession of French monarchs. But not by Louis XIV, who moved his Court to Versailles in 1682. A child monarch, the Sun King was kept prisoner in Paris whilst various blue bloods contested his mother's regency and wasn't overly fond of his capital. Hence the shift. By 1793 there weren't many royals left to require a residence, so France's revolutionary government turned the *Palais du Louvre* into the *Musée du Louvre*.

The glass pyramid now serving as the Louvre's main entrance was still eighteen years short of being built when Ellen and I arrived to view some of the famed museum's famed contents. With *no* kind of entrance being immediately apparent, we had to ask several people where it was. And when Ellen asked a painter (decorator variety), he told us the Louvre was closed because of a strike but would open again at ten the next morning.

Disappointed, we went back down the street to have lunch at a restaurant we'd seen that, again, for Paris, did not seem *too* expensive before returning to shopping. Another item I was looking for—make that, obsessed with finding—was a blouse or sweater that had a Paris label and was within my twenty-five to thirty franc means. I did see a blouse I liked in a clothing boutique's twenty-five-franc section, and even tried it on, but didn't take it as it turned out to be a seventy-nine-franc blouse that had been put on the wrong counter by mistake. I didn't like it *that* much.

A bit later—translation: when all the shops closed—we went back to the new hostel. It was even more security conscience than the other one, and we had to show our room tickets just to get in the gate. Once in, we retrieved our packs and extracted everything we required for the night before returning them to storage.

The new hostel was in a much busier area than the other, and we went to sleep amidst the roar of

Paris traffic. If what we'd seen during the daytime was anything to go by, the drivers were probably attempting to run other vehicles off the road or mow down pedestrians.

* * *

At breakfast, an English hosteller told us he'd had his wallet stolen from under his pillow as he slept, and his travelling companion had had a tape recorder taken. We nodded sympathetically, but privately thought it foolish of them to have not put their valuables in the locker room.

Cautiously optimistic about being able to make our remaining French funds stretch to dining on the Eiffel Tower, we went there to ascertain how much a modest meal in its least expensive restaurant would be. The Esplanade—the ground around and underneath the tower—was free to enter, and free of all the security measures that would later be put in place to keep the tower and other iconic places in France from becoming the target of a terrorist attack. But access to the tower itself was not free. I had to pay two francs to go up to the first level and check menu prices.

The Eiffel Tower wasn't supposed to be iconic. Civil Engineer Gustave Eiffel's contribution to France's 1889 *Exposition Universelle* was supposed to be a temporary construction serving as, first, a fair exhibit, and then a place for Gus and others to conduct experiments and make astronomical observations. But only for twenty years. After that the plan was for it to be taken down. And it nearly was, since much of Paris's populace had, from the very get-go, considered it a visual monstrosity unworthy of their beautiful city. But by 1909 the tower had been equipped with antennas, and its ability to relay and receive wireless transmissions made it too much of a communications asset to be dismantled.

It therefore remained standing, and is a prime example of how age and circumstances change a person's outlook. On this, my first visit to the Eiffel Tower, I merely viewed it as yet another famous structure I could say I'd been to, and did not pay much attention to its actual *structure*. On subsequent visits—with kids—I paid very close attention to that. Or at least to the height and slipperiness of the girders small children apparently viewed as a giant climbing frame, and were joyously scaling. Lattice-work girders with any number of places they could fall through. Small children were undoubtedly joyously scaling them during my first visit, too, but they weren't related to me.

There were initially four restaurants on the Eiffel Tower's first floor, but, by 1971, only two. And, to my pleased surprise, the prices in the Brasserie weren't completely out of our reach. Having learned that a meal there would cost about twenty francs—still extortion, but not as much as we'd feared—I tried to return to Ellen down on the ground. I'd taken one of the old—as in, still the original—lifts up to the first floor, but lifts going down were not, for some reason, running. During World War II, none of the tower's lifts were, as the French Resistance deliberately put them out of commission. That forced the Nazis to take the stairs and I had to do the same. The slight acrophobia I'd experienced at Blarney Castle went up a few notches, and I enlivened my spiral descent by making up possible headlines for the local newspapers. Things like, 'Paris Fire Department Rescues Canadian Tourist From Eiffel Tower Staircase'.

Relieved to get down, I rejoined Ellen and we set off for the Louvre Museum. It had indeed opened at ten o'clock as we'd been told, but until we got there, we didn't know it was going to be closing again early in the afternoon. That didn't give us much time, so we got our entrance tickets and dashed up to where the paintings were—Leonardo da Vinci's highly acclaimed *Mona Lisa* among them. If we couldn't take in everything in the Louvre in the couple of hours allotted to us—which those who speculate about such things say would take *days*—we intended to take in the most famous.

The Louvre had, and has, a lot of paintings, but could have had more if the museum's council hadn't fired its president because of suspected wartime collaboration with the Vichy government and, by association, the Nazis. Gabriel Cognacq—the great-nephew and heir of Ernest, founder of La Samaritaine—owned an impressive number of works by people such as Cézanne, Renoir, and Van Gogh, and would have left them to the Louvre in his will if it hadn't been for the scandalous accusations his friends claimed were unjustified. They said anything Gabe did during the war, he did for the sake of art, and the sanctimonious council members had obviously forgotten about things like him loaning the Louvre his La Samaritaine delivery vans so its masterpieces could be moved to the Château de Chambord for safekeeping. But bad publicity won out. He was turfed off the council, and, embittered, left not as much as a portrait miniature to the Louvre when he died in 1951, preferring that his art collection be sold at auction and the proceeds donated to the charitable Cognacq-Jay Foundation established by Ernest Cognacq and his wife, Marie-Louise Jay.

The *Mona Lisa* was the first item on our viewing agenda. Unexpectedly small though her portrait was, Ellen and I agreed that she did seem to have an air of mystery about her. We then arranged to meet at the Louvre's Métro station at half past one and went off in pursuit of our own interests. I chose to limit myself to paintings and wandered through several of the rooms housing them.

Not everyone was inclined to do that. In a long gallery containing many, many, paintings, an

American woman was sitting on a long, circular, couch watching her husband walk around oohing and aahing over everything. She, however, told me that exhaustion had greatly diminished *her* appreciation for art. And when her husband strode over demanding to know how she could possibly just sit there when there were so many important works in that room, she responded with a glare and the words, "Big Wow!"

After they moved on to another part of the Louvre—him with great eagerness and her with none—I felt a little weary too, and sat on the couch for a while before heading to the Métro to meet Ellen. It wasn't quite time, and I expected her to be late as usual, but she wasn't. Certain parts of the Louvre closed earlier than others and she'd been made to leave. Well, I knew there had to be *some* reason for her exiting ahead of time, even if she didn't think the Louvre was as good as the British Museum.

As it was now Saturday—Sewer Tour Day—we took the Métro to the Place de la Concorde and tried to find the starting point. A woman we asked spoke English, but didn't know what we meant, and we couldn't remember the French word for 'sewer' (*égouts*), if indeed we ever knew it. She either hadn't heard of them, or just didn't think anyone would be crazy enough to want to go down there—*quelle odour*. But she asked a cab driver, and he said the entrance was behind one of the statues that graced the largest square in Paris.

More of an octagon than a square, the Place de la Concorde was not called that until 1795. It started out as Place Louis XV, a place in which to showcase a statue of King Louis XV (1710-1774). The statue was put up to celebrate his restoration to health after an illness. But the leaders of the French Revolution weren't all that interested in the health of kings. Or queens, or any of France's élite. During the Reign of Terror (1793–1794), they tore down the statue, changed the square's name to the Place de la

Révolution, and set Madame Guillotine up there to do away with as many noxious nobles as they could.

The entrance to the sewers was right where the cab driver had said, and it appeared a great many people were crazy enough to want to go down there, because the queue for the two o'clock tour was of similar length to Hadrian's Wall. We joined it without any real expectation of gaining admission, as participation was limited to eighty people and there were more than eighty people in front of us. A lot more.

Sure enough, we didn't get in, and elected to go out to the flea market and come back at five o'clock for the last tour of the day. When the Métro train came into the station, the door we wanted jammed, and by the time we ran to another, I was the only one to get aboard before it shut automatically. Ellen waved good-bye as I was whisked out of the station but was able to get on another train and catch up with me at the next stop, where I was waiting for her. Basically, the Isle of Skye all over again, only in reverse.

The flea market was mostly full of junk, and expensive junk at that. I looked at some blouses and sweaters, but if I liked them, they either cost too much or didn't have the desired Paris label.

We got back to the Place de la Concorde just after four o'clock and managed to secure a better queue position than we'd had before. This time, we did gain admission, and climbed into a large barge-like boat. We'd been under the impression that visitors walked through the sewers, like in *Bon Voyage*, when Fred MacMurray's Harry Willard character was stumbling around shouting, "*Au secours! Au secours!*" A phrase he got from a book that was obviously of more genuine use than ours was. Instead, four men trudged along a stone sidewalk pulling the boat along by chains. This is no longer how visitors experience the sewers, however, as I believe there is now a sewer museum. The smell wasn't as bad as expected, but a man gave us some of his wife's perfume to sprinkle on our hands should we be overcome. The tour only lasted about ten minutes, and the guide spoke only in French, but one part of a sewer is much like another and we doubted there was much anyone *could* say about a sewer.

The tour still proved interesting and was our only underground Parisian experience. Unbeknownst to us then, Paris, like Rome, had catacombs that were open to the public. Unlike Rome, the bones of the departed were still present, some neatly stacked, others arranged into macabre displays, so I doubt they would have appealed to us anyway.

Emerging from the sewers at a different place to where we'd entered them, we had to walk quite a distance to find a Métro station. This quite surprised us, as, until we were actually looking for one, we seemed to come across them quite often. We did eventually find one, and took the Métro to a shop-filled area near the hostel with the intention of doing some shopping en route to 'home'.

About halfway down the street, Ellen expressed the opinion that we were going in the opposite direction to the hostel. I said we weren't, and we pushed on until we reached the Métro station that came *before* the one we'd just got off of. So, we were indeed going the wrong way. It was lucky we were, though. When we crossed the street to start going the right way, we found a ladies wear shop with reasonable prices and I was able to get a short-sleeved light blue sweater-blouse with a Paris label for only fifteen francs ($3).

Knowing the locker room would be shut when we returned from the Eiffel Tower, we got our night things from our packs and took them with us in our carrier bags. We got up to the Brasserie just after half past eight and ordered soup, steak, chips, and tea (Ellen) and an omelette, chicken, chips, and tea (me), the same as we often did. But this meal was *different*. It cost more.

After viewing the Paris Illuminations (fountains, churches, and other landmarks, all lit up), we had to rush to get back to our hostel before midnight, when both it and the Métro closed. The trains were not as frequent as in the day, which caused us some anxiety, but even with this unexpected set-back we managed to get back to the hostel within a quarter of an hour of closing time.

Chapter Thirty-Eight
Down-and-out In Brussels

The warden asked everyone who showed up for breakfast the next morning to either help cut bread or take apart dozens of those little plastic and tinfoil jam containers that come in packages of six. In dealing with the jam, I mislaid my breakfast ticket. *This* warden would have let me have breakfast without one, but when fellow hostellers heard about its loss, they started searching diligently for it—multiple nations united in one task—and someone found it just as I got up to the counter with my tray.

After breakfast, Ellen fetched our packs, and I went to the front desk where, upon uttering the magic words 'train to catch', I was able to take back possession of our youth hostel cards without a lengthy wait.

At the Gare du Nord we went to a café across the street and had tea and croissants. We'd just had breakfast, but felt we simply *had* to have croissants in Paris, just as we'd had to have tea, toast, and shortbread in Edinburgh.

I then left Ellen standing guard over our packs and tried to find a Can-Can dancer doll and some fancy Parisian candies. A stall outside the first souvenir shop I came to did have such a doll, but it had a purple dress and I wanted a doll with a red dress. There was one inside, but it cost more, so I pointed to the cheaper one and said, *"Mais rouge"*. The salesclerk sighed at this *'très difficile'* tourist and got me a red one from the back room. From there I went to a candy shop, bought three small tubes of fancy candies, and went back to the train station with but twenty centimes to my name.

I'm sure the history of Brussels—now the seat of the European Union as well as the capital of Belgium—is as varied and interesting as that of many a European city, but it wasn't a place we explored much as we did *not* have a good time there.

This started shortly after our arrival, when someone at the passenger information counter told us the train that we had to catch in order to make a connection to Boulogne the next day left at seven in the morning, much earlier than we'd thought.

At the youth hostel, the first person we spoke to about our early next-day train time told us no one was allowed to leave the hostel before half past seven—half an hour after the train left. She thought the warden might be willing to let us out early if we asked, but then checked our reservation card and said that, even though we had the correct address for that hostel, our *reservation* was for a hostel down the street that I suppose must have worked in partnership with it.

Unfortunately, the warden there was in no way willing to open up *his* hostel before half past seven and gave us the address of a nearby student hotel a fifteen-minute walk away. Before going to it, we went back to the first hostel to pick up some letters that had gone there, one from my parents, and another from a friend of Ellen's whom I didn't know. At the student hotel we were told we'd have to wait until supper had been served before anyone could book us in, and that the overnight fee was about thirty francs more than we had. Having it would not have helped however, as the receptionist said they never opened before half past seven either, so we went and got our packs from the waiting room where we'd left them. On the way out we saw the manager and I asked him if there was a tram stop nearby. He demanded to know if we were the girls who wanted to leave at half past six, and when I said we were, started ranting about disrupting the system, even though we hadn't made any kind of fuss about having our request refused. He also said the trams didn't run that early in the morning. A little put out, I informed him we wanted it *now*, and he said they didn't run at all on Sundays. Before we stalked out indignantly—to the extent anyone wearing a pack *can* stalk out indignantly—he asked us if we knew where we were going. I muttered something about the train station, but doubt he would have cared if I'd said we didn't have the slightest idea.

Back at the train station, I went to see what sort of journey I could work out so we wouldn't have to spend the night there. Unfortunately, any train going, or connecting, to Boulogne from *anywhere*, went early in the morning. That meant we had a choice between staying in the Brussels train station all night or in some other train station all night. As we knew what our connections were from Brussels, we decided to stay where we were—in the city that had managed to shoot past Munich on Ellen's Horrible Cities list. Unlike London and Munich, which I've since had pleasant visits to, I haven't had cause to return to Brussels, so I've no way of knowing if I'd have a more favourable opinion of it now. Without further exploration, it and Miami—a later bad experience—remain cities I'm not fond of.

For a time, we sat in the station feeling sorry for ourselves and wanting our parents to somehow show up and make everything right again. But that didn't happen, so we eventually shelved our homesickness and bitterness at the unfairness of life, and went to a nearby café. There we ordered tea, and later on, more tea, so as to drag out the time until midnight, when the place closed. We then went back into the station and wondered how to keep ourselves awake for the next seven hours. This proved unnecessary, however, as unlike Munich, stranded passengers and passengers catching early trains were allowed to sleep in the station's waiting room. Or so we assumed, since quite a few people were, and no officials came along to eject them. The seats were a bit more comfortable than the benches in Munich's Banhofsmission had been, and spending the night in the station was certainly better than spending it in a gutter or doorway. Especially since it was raining outside, so luck or providence was with us. Ellen's letter from her friend had made reference to some unnerving hitchhiking experiences she'd had that still turned out all right, and contained the quote, "...whoso putteth his trust in the Lord shall be safe." (Proverbs 29:25.) Which, being too busy railing against injustice, we hadn't, but He came through for us anyway.

* * *

The damp weather had lowered temperatures inside the station and out, and even though it was summer, the waiting room wasn't overly warm. I was wearing shorts when we settled for the night and woke up several times. About the fourth time, I found my legs had been covered by a long navy coat belonging to a man seated in a corner near us. He'd been there all night too, and had perhaps seen me shivering in my sleep or something. Surprised that such a light sleeper as myself had not woken up when he put it on me, I thought it was very nice of him. Reflecting on our experiences with the citizens of Brussels the day before, I decided he couldn't possibly be one. No, no. He was obviously someone from somewhere else, and merely passing though. I tried to sleep again, but couldn't, so gave the coat back to him, with my thanks.

A little while later, a station official came in and woke up everyone who *was* sleeping, either because people were only allowed to sleep there for a certain length of time, or because trains were starting to come in and he didn't want any of the sleepers to miss theirs.

Ours was supposed to come in at seven and leave at eight minutes past. It did neither, and at ten minutes past, I asked a man and woman if they were waiting for the Lille train. They said no, they were waiting for the one that was listed after it—which also happened to be the next one due in the station. Seeing our dismay, the man went and got a station official, who looked at the board and told us the train we wanted wasn't running that day.

That put us into a bit of a flap, because we'd been told that *that* train was the only train capable of getting us to Boulogne in time for the half-past-three hovercraft flight for which we had tickets. But the official seemed to think we'd be able to make other connections, and directed us to a different platform to wait for the next train to Lille, the place where we had to make a connection to Calais, and, from there, a connection to Boulogne.

The platform was open air, but had a shelter which, since it was raining quite heavily, we stood under, and kept a close watch on the Arrival and Departure board until 'Lille' appeared on it.

At the Belgian-French border, an official came in and asked if we had any merchandise. As usual we shook our heads, though, in actuality, our packs now contained more merchandise than clothes, the latter now mostly serving as protective wrapping for the breakable objects.

The man at Lille's passenger information counter didn't speak English and just shrugged his shoulders at Ellen, even though her French *was* up to saying, "Quand departée le train pour Calais?" No one in the station's tourist information centre spoke English, either, but at least they tried to be helpful. There was, we were told, no way we could make that half-past-three hovercraft flight. There were later hovercraft flights, though, and the clerk didn't think we'd have any problem getting our time changed. This lessened our fears to some extent, but only until Ellen started to read over the regulations on her ticket and came to the delightful little clause that stated that tickets had to be used for the flight for which they were bought. That set us back to worrying, but all we could do was cling to the possibility that none of the officials in Boulogne had read that particular regulation, or, if they had, that they'd take pity on two poor, helpless, little girls on the verge of tears. Or in them, if it were to seem as though that might help. But a young man from Liverpool that we got talking to didn't think it would. Leastways, not in any kind of metropolis. He did acknowledge the possible strategic value of girls using sympathy-generating tears in some places.

"But not in a city," he advised. "Never cry in a city. Cry at a farm."

The train arrived twenty minutes late but still got us to Calais in time to catch a train to Boulogne, where we were told to wait at a bus stop for a bus to take us out to our hovercraft, the newer, faster way to cross the Channel that started up in 1968 and was a popular means of doing so until increased fuel costs forced the operating company, Seaspeed, to withdraw its services in the year 2000.

The first bus to arrive at the stop was bluish green, and its driver said we had to wait for a red one. But then a Seaspeed minibus came along and that driver said his vehicle was the one that took people out to the hovercraft, and transportation was in with our ticket.

After all our fretting over the validity of our tickets, the people collecting them took them without a murmur and gave us our boarding passes. Try making a time change without hassle and for free nowadays!

The hovercraft was half an hour late coming in. The people getting off looked as though they were glad to be back on solid ground, and we soon found out why. The sea was *rough*, and all that kept us from succumbing to *mal de mer* was the fact that we'd taken our travel tablets. Whether it was the combination of a rough crossing and exhaustion, or just the effects of the tablet, I went right out, and knew no more until I heard over the intercom that we were coming into Dover. I sat up, blinking, beside a fellow traveller who, Ellen claimed, had been sick the entire trip. She also claimed that I talked all the way. If so, I can only hypothesize that I experienced a temporary resurgence of the fever I'd had in Wales and was delirious.

Our packs came out of the luggage chute together, with the type of decided bang that made us thankful we'd had the sense to pad our breakables. We arrived at London's Charing Cross station about half past nine, two hours after the *latest* time my relatives were expecting to meet us in West Drayton. The train ride to Charing Cross had been in with our hovercraft tickets, but further transport was not, and we didn't have enough English money to go anywhere. No official currency exchange services were available at that time of night, but someone in the ticket office gave us enough cash for some of our foreign coins and bills to get us from Charing Cross to Paddington Station, and from Paddington to West Drayton.

The second-to-last of that day's trains to West Drayton was supposed to leave Paddington just before half past ten, but didn't, although the engine did start up and then quit about three times. Passengers sat around saying uncomplimentary things about British Rail until, at ten to eleven, the engine roared yet again, and we actually got going.

Despite the late hour, Auntie Betty and Uncle Bill were still waiting at West Drayton station to convey us to Auntie Dorothy's, and said they'd call in to take us sightseeing around lunchtime the next day.

Chapter Thirty-Nine
England's Green And Pleasant Land

Ellen and I got up long before Auntie Betty and Uncle Bill were due to come for us, so I washed out some clothes and Ellen set about scraping gum residue from the place on her gadget bag where, until it peeled off, her Canadian flag had been. This took her over half an hour, but she did eventually get most of it off.

Chores accomplished, we went up to Michael and Lesley's and visited with them until Auntie Betty came for us and she and Uncle Bill took us into Windsor to cash the *last* of our traveller's cheques and go around the castle.

For the modest sum of $4 each, Ellen and I had purchased British Open To View passes before leaving home, and Windsor Castle was on the list of places to which they gained us free entry. Access to Queen Mary's Dolls' House was extra, but we didn't mind paying to view that. On display at Windsor Castle since 1925, this 1:12 scale working—as in having electricity and running water—model of a townhouse was built by British architect Sir Edwin Landseer Lutyens and was a gift from the nation to Queen Mary. The Queen Mary who was the twentieth-century consort of George V, not the sixteenth-century religious fanatic who tried to rid her realm of Protestants.

It was spectacular, and we loved it, but in the nineteen-twenties, British—and probably European—

girls didn't have to be royal to have a fancy dolls' house. Not as fancy as Queen Mary's, but fancier than what was available to later generations. My mother had quite a nice one when she was a child. She told me all about its little glass windows, and carpeted staircase, and authentic miniature furniture like a wooden chest of drawers with drawers that opened, a wardrobe with doors that opened, upholstered chairs, and countless other classy things. But regrettably, it never came into my hands, because, when she left the family home after World War II, she gave it to a neighbour's daughter. The reasoning behind this being that, at the time, she only had a little boy, Brother Ronald. This lack of foresight stuck me with a much inferior aluminium dolls' house with plastic furniture that I got one Christmas. A dolls' house that came unassembled and required my father to be up half the night putting it together. No doubt employing several words that, though spirited, were not in the Christmas spirit.

Moving on from Windsor to the spot now occupied by Legoland, we were able to walk around most, but not all, of the grounds of Windsor Safari Park. Some animal enclosures had to be driven through. We were told we couldn't because Uncle Bill's car had too soft a top to withstand close contact with the inhabitants of the lion and baboon enclosures. The lions never bothered anyone much but the baboons were another story.

Uncle Bill parked the car, and we all went off to look at a multitude of furred, feathered, and finned beings before getting tickets for the minibus that took those with soft-topped cars through the lion and baboon enclosures. It was the last tour of the day, and we were the only passengers. As we went along, our driver-guide told us about people who'd gone inside the baboon enclosure with soft-topped cars and come out minus the tops, baboons being such strong creatures that ripping the top off a car wasn't much different to peeling a banana. He also told us about the day it had taken four keepers to hold a baboon down for an injection, as well as the time some keepers had gone into the enclosure to break up a fight between two baboons and got encircled by the others, who, resenting this intervention, closed in menacingly.

All this was imparted to us before we even got to the baboon enclosure, and the minibus door on the driver's side was open. I asked him if he intended to keep it that way and he assured me he didn't. Inside, none of the baboons menaced the minibus, and I said I guessed they must know they couldn't damage a hard-topped vehicle. Laughing, he pointed out that it only had one wiper blade left, and they often helped themselves to vehicles' headlamps, L-plates and antennas, as well.

In the lion enclosure the lions were all lying around contentedly. So contently that Ellen got a picture of some that had their paws up in the air and seemed oblivious to everything. Chicken feathers lay all around, indicating they'd just been fed, so I suggested she entitle it, 'Lions After Feeding Time'.

The guide said they were like that before feeding time, too.

"It's actually quite the occasion to see a lion on its feet here. Keepers sometimes chase them in trucks, just to give them exercise."

Presumably the trucks that were stationed at intervals throughout the enclosure to help with breakdowns and rescue people dim-witted enough to get out of their cars. But a little further on, we did get to see a lion on its feet. He was using them to cross the road and all the oncoming traffic made way for him. Aside from the teeth and claws aspect, running into a four-hundred-or-so-pound lion wasn't likely to do a car any good if a collision occurred.

There was a little activity in the cheetah enclosure too. Most of them were lounging around in the shade of trees, same as the lions, but one hadn't quite finished the day's rations and was still gnawing on what might have been a rabbit.

The minibus ride brought us to the end of our Safari Park tour, after which we returned to Nan's house in Iver for tea before returning to Auntie Dorothy's.

***

Our Open To View passes also covered Hampton Court and Woburn Abbey, and those were on the agenda for the next day. We went to Hampton Court first. There, Auntie Betty and Uncle Bill waited in the car, and Ellen and I went around the opulent palace Henry VIII basically stole from Thomas Wolsey (Cardinal Wolsey) in 1529 and Queen Victoria opened up to the public in 1838. The famous maze within its grounds is the oldest hedge maze in the UK, but wasn't there when Henry moved in. Successive British monarchs inherited Hampton Court, and the maze—designed by Baroque Garden specialists, George London and Henry Wise—went in during the reign of William III (William of Orange). Many people have entered it, and spent considerable time trying to get out of it but, a bit to our disappointment, we did so relatively easily. Perhaps because we'd recently been in a lot of unfamiliar cities in which we'd had to work our way through a maze of unfamiliar streets.

After we returned to the car, we set off for Woburn Abbey, stopping at Staines on the way to do some shopping. Ellen was able to get the lady's razor and blades she'd been wanting, I got two books I'd been wanting, and we both got the small flight bags we *required* for our breakables and perishables on the aeroplane. The last because the larger ones were now stuffed with so many non-breakables/perishables they would have to be checked.

At Woburn Abbey, Uncle Bill let us off at the ticket stand, saying he and Auntie Betty would be waiting somewhere nearby. But Woburn Abbey itself was not nearby. It was over a mile up the road that people in cars used to get to the Abbey. It was possible to get there across a field as well, however, and that, the ticket seller said, was only about a ten-minute walk. We therefore took to the field, where a herd of deer decided to charge us, veering off just before making contact.

In the Abbey, we went through the treasure rooms and state apartments, the latter actually looking like people had actually once lived in them, which was not always how the rooms in stately homes looked. Woburn Abbey started out as a Cistercian abbey founded by Hugh de Bolebec, Baron of Whitchurch, in 1145. In 1547, Henry VIII lay claim to it by way of the Dissolution of the Monasteries, the enrich-the-crown side line he took up in 1536, when he noticed that a lot of religious houses were richer than he was and proceeded to rectify that by closing them down and confiscating their wealth. He gave Woburn to John Russell, first Earl of Bedford, and a few earls later, a dukedom was added to the Russell family's distinctions. This presumably added to its coffers, too, but the bank balance had dwindled a bit by the time the thirteenth duke (another John) inherited the title in 1953, and with it, a lot of debt. To solve this problem, he opened his ancestral home to the public and charged admission, a course of action a number of his peers thought a bit crass. Until they realized how much money he was taking in, prompting some of them to do the same with the ancestral homes *they* were finding hard to keep up in modern times. But the Duke of Bedford did it best. Tourists started flocking to this new attraction in 1955 and would later also flock to the safari park that was added the year before Ellen and I visited. The deer that charged us were part of that, but ignored us when we went back across the field and rejoined Auntie Betty and Uncle Bill.

On the way back to Iver we stopped off in Aylesbury to visit my cousin Bun and her family, and spent the evening visiting those of my relatives who lived in the Iver area and had not yet had the pleasure of my company. Though some of them might challenge the 'pleasure' aspect after being forced to crowd together for the large 'Gathering of the Clan' photo I wanted.

Chapter Forty
Familiar Territory

The next day, we were conveyed to relatives in the little market town of Wantage, making a few stops with others along the way.

Reading was the first such stop, and my Great-Aunt Eva gave us, and our chauffeurs, tea and biscuits. More tea and biscuits awaited us closer to Wantage when we called in at the village in which Aunt Lucy's two sons dwelt.

Then it was on to my one-time home turf.

At that time, Wantage still lay in Berkshire, but was gifted to Oxfordshire when counties were reorganized in 1974. As with many places, theories vary as to the origins of its name. Some think it was derived from the area's moles (called 'wants'), others from a West Saxon tribe called Unecungs—which I do not have the slightest idea how to pronounce—and still others from an Old English term for 'a decreasing river', the last being the most accepted.

There's no firm evidence of a Roman settlement ever having been where Wantage now stands, but there was definitely a Saxon one because the Saxon king, Alfred the Great, was born there in 849 AD and places all over town are named after him. Such as the boys' grammar school (now an amalgamation of post-primary schools), a pub, a café, a bikepacking route, and the sloped wooded area known as King Alfred's Bath that an exuberant dalmatian once dragged me through when I was walking him for a neighbour. It's unlikely the mighty monarch ever made use of it as a bathing facility, though. The bricks around the supposed 'bath' are from a much, much, later date.

King Alfred is Wantage's *good* claim to fame. The other is less reputable. In the eighteenth and early nineteenth centuries, it was known as Black Wantage because a large number of unsavoury types used it as a base for their nefarious doings. Like relieving rich people of their valuables on London's Hampstead Heath and then riding hell for leather for hideouts in Wantage around seventy miles away.

Auntie Betty and Uncle Bill had been to Wantage before, but only to our house and those of some of my great-aunts, not to our ultimate destination, the home of my mother's first cousin, Tom, and his wife Iris. As a one-time resident of Wantage—perhaps, a Wantagian (?)—I had no trouble guiding Uncle Bill to Barwell Road. Only Cousin Tom was in, and once he'd taken charge of our luggage, we went to visit my Great-Aunt Nellie, who lived in the same part of Wantage as my family had, us at #15 Naldertown, in a two-storey semi-detached brick house, and her further up the street in one of the prefabricated bungalows that were put up to alleviate Britain's housing shortage after World War II. Uncle Bill did know the way there, and we found Auntie Nellie working in her garden. Ellen and I chatted with her for a while and then, leaving Auntie Betty and Uncle Bill to go on chatting, went round an assortment of my old neighbours, some of whom said they hardly knew me now that I was "all grown up".

As a child, one of my best friends, and most frequent playmate, was also a neighbour. Her family's garden almost bordered ours from the next street, and on our way to her house, we met her mother, who was just coming back from shopping. After a moment or two of speculation—*Is that Peggy's Mum? Is that Peggy's friend?*—recognition became mutual, and we exchanged greetings. Though Peggy and I had corresponded for a while after I moved away, we'd eventually lost touch, and I was surprised to learn she was married and living away from home. But she was still in town, and her mother said she'd get her to go over to Tom and Iris's to see us.

I then took Ellen into town, conscious of how nice it was to know exactly where I was going and how to get there! Ellen merely followed, just as I had when we'd been in her childhood home of White Rock a few years earlier.

We went by way of what was locally known as the brook path because, well, because after you get down the hill, the lower part of it runs alongside Letcombe Brook. In 1971, it still had the wilderness appearance I was used to, but was later spruced up. The Betjeman Millennium Park now stands across from the section of the brook where I used to feed an assortment of colourful, wild(ish) mallards, and the large white domestic ducks that belonged to someone. I think this path is called Betjeman Lane now, but wouldn't be surprised if the town's old timers still say 'brook path'.

The path runs all the way down to the mill from which Mill Street takes its name, but we didn't go that far, instead turning onto the little bridge leading up to the Church of St. Peter and St. Paul where I once went to Sunday School. Records show there was a church on that spot as far back as 950, but the current one dates from around 1250, with several additions being made to it down through the centuries. By Victorian times it required a lot of restoration work, and received it through the efforts of its vicar, William John Butler (later Dean of Lincoln). He served there from 1846 to 1881, and in addition to his restoration blitz, founded the Community of St. Mary the Virgin, one of the first religious communities to be established in the centuries following Henry VIII's dissolution of them. After St. Peter and St. Paul's erstwhile vicar passed away in 1894, one of its south chapels was converted into a Lady Chapel in his memory, and my maternal great-grandfather (a master carpenter) was one of the local craftsmen charged with the task.

Just past the church was Wantage's library. My beloved childhood library, where I'd spent many happy hours! (The new one on Stirlings Road just doesn't hold the same appeal for me when I'm home.) The librarian was another old neighbour, so we popped in to talk to her before going on to Grove Street to visit my Great-Aunt Bess.

Auntie Bess gave us a plentiful amount of orangeade and biscuits, just like she always had whenever I called in. Her house, and that of my Great-Aunt Carr—by then, sadly deceased—were just a few doors away from each other, and both great aunts used to wave to me from their windows when I passed by on my way to Garston Lane Primary. Although they and their siblings had attended the closer-to-my-house Church School, I'd opted for the council school that opened in 1929 and closed in 1999, when the town's schools amalgamated. On my way home from that school, one or the other sometimes beckoned me to come in to talk, which I was always happy to do, because, aside from them being my favourite great-aunts—the ones who used to play school with me before I was even old enough for school, with me as the teacher, Auntie Bess as the good pupil and Auntie Carr as the naughty pupil—those Victorian-era ladies had interesting things to talk about.

We went back to Cousin Tom's via a footpath off Mill Street and Ellen rang up some cousins in Oxford to tell them she was in the neighbourhood if they wanted to drop by, Wantage being but sixteen miles from there; a journey my father had had to make every weekday in his red Morris 'Mini' to go to his job at the Pressed Steel factory that manufactured the car bodies for, not just those vehicles, but various others as well.

Ellen and I then set off to visit some of my old school chums. Four of them, lived in or near the Barwell area, but one was out when we stopped by, and another, Veronica, busy with something, so we said we'd come back later.

Another friend lived further away, in the near-to-Wantage village of Challow, so Tom and Iris's son Robert took us there by car. She and her sister happened to be en route to a dance in Wantage, but we caught up with them.

We then went back to Veronica's and visited with her. After that we went into town and got some chips (with scrumps), which we ate in the car outside the shop.

Back at Cousin Tom's we were told that Peggy had been by and was at her parents' house, so we went to visit her and her husband, as well as her father and two youngest brothers. (The family-planner girl we met in San Sebastian would no doubt have been horrified to know Peggy was the fifth kid out of eight.)

When we were at school, Peggy had been famous for getting out of it whenever she could—even to the point of drinking salt water to make herself sick. Her dad told us about how, later on, school psychiatrists had made her take a whole lot of tests, and, at the end of them, informed him and Peggy's mum that it seemed Peggy didn't like school.

"We could have told them *that!*"

Following that visit, Robert took us to the home of his sister Suzanne and her husband Roger, which was where we were to spend our nights in Wantage.

* * *

We were awakened in the morning by the thunder of tiny feet and opened our eyes to see Suzanne and Roger's two-year-old daughter, Tamasine, regarding us solemnly until Suzanne called her, and us, down to breakfast.

We later walked into town, where Ellen and I went off in different directions after arranging to meet in the market square at noon, beside by King Alfred's statue. I figured even Ellen couldn't lose such a prominent fixture as King Alfred's statue. Commissioned by Colonel Robert Lloyd-Lindsay (Lord Wantage) and sculpted by Count Victor Gleichen (who took up sculpting as a hobby after retiring from the Royal Navy), it was unveiled by Edward, Prince of Wales, and his wife on the fourteenth of July, 1877.

A school year could not pass without Wantage's young being told *something* about the only English king to have the designation 'the Great' added to his name, so I know quite a lot about King Alfred—some of it plausible, some more likely just the stuff of legends—but will try to keep it brief. In what probably falls into the legend category, I've always liked the story of how his mother, a possibly quite lovely looking woman with the unlovely sounding name of Osburh or Osburga, promised to give her Bible—and keep in mind that books of any kind were really precious items in those days—to the first of her sons who learned to read, and little Alfie was the one who did. I also liked the one about him accidentally burning the cakes of a peasant woman in whose hut he'd sought refuge from his enemies.

And he had a *lot* of enemies. Real ones, not legendary. Most notably the Danish Viking invaders who yearned to claim all of Britain as their own but found the locals violently—literally violently—opposed to that. Alfred was reportedly not very robust as a child, and not expected to reach adulthood, let alone king status. Being the youngest of the five sons of Aethelwulf/Ethelwulf, King of the West Saxons, he probably *wouldn't* have achieved that lofty position if Aethelwulf hadn't decreed that his crown was to pass from brother to brother rather than father to son, so as to avoid lumbering his people with an underage ruler in a time when crowns were held by military prowess, and grown men wielded swords better than small boys did. The crown did indeed pass down in that manner, and by 871, all of Alfred's brothers had perished and he was King of Wessex. He didn't stop with just that kingdom though. A fierce fighter and clever strategist, he made alliances with other kings, most of whom tended to bow to his proven expertise when it came to annihilating as many Danes as possible and making peace with the rest—thus paving the way for his successors to be the rulers of a united England. For which I'm sure William the Conqueror was immensely grateful when he took it over in 1066.

In addition to fighting off, or, in some instances, paying off, the Danes, Alfred brought in several legal, social, and educational reforms during his reign. These, too, contributed towards him being remembered as Alfred the Great, making him worthy of, not just the statue in Wantage, but of the monuments to him standing in Winchester and Pewsey as well. The not-to-human-scale Wantage statue has him holding an axe in one hand, in acknowledgement of his fighting skills, and a scroll in the other, in acknowledgement of his love of learning and promotion of literacy.

I don't know what Ellen did with herself after she left Alfred guarding—or studying in—the market square, but I went looking for various food items my family and I could not purchase in Canada at that time, and sorely missed. This hunt for provender took me first to Lock's Bakery where I got a Lock's chocolate roll, then to sweet shops for some jelly babies and Turkish delight, and to the International (a supermarket) for some meat paste, which it was out of. I also tried a pet shop for a jewelled cat collar for our cat, Voodoo, but the proprietor didn't have any, and started directing me to another shop until I said I'd lived in Wantage and knew where it was. He then took a closer look. Wantage being such a small town, he felt sure he should know me. And he should have, since I used to get my goldfish supplies there, but he was still trying to place me when I left.

At noon, Ellen actually got to King's Alf's statue on time, and I took her up to my Great-Aunt Nell's to visit and have tea and biscuits. Nell, not Nellie. Nellie was a different great-aunt. This one's real name was Matilda, but for reasons unknown to me was always called Nell by the family, who also called Auntie Carr 'our Sue', and my birth grandmother, Ruth, 'our Dot'. Whereas Auntie Nellie's pet name was at least a diminutive of her actual name, which was Eleanor. Well in her nineties, Auntie Nell was the erstwhile lady's maid who'd travelled the world and now lived in a little bungalow called 'Dunroamin'. Still her usual forthright self, she startled Ellen by saying, "How are you off for money?" and when we said, "Oh, getting by," said, "Do you want some?" We were almost tempted to say 'yes', but didn't.

From there we went to Cousin Tom's and not long after we got there, Ellen's Oxford relatives arrived, followed almost immediately by Suzanne. I left Ellen to her relatives and Suzanne took me into Childrey to visit an old friend of my grandmother. She dropped me by the duck pond, but as it had been five years since I'd been there, and I'd only been there once or twice, I had to ask at the local shop for directions to her thatched-roof abode, Pike's Cottage. (Ellen would have been thrilled with it.) After we had talked for a while, Miss Dorothea Riley showed me over the cottage and gave me three of her 'treasures' from her massive book collection. I still have them.

I walked back to Wantage along the field-edged footpaths I'd walked with my grandmother. I also passed by Kath Harris's house. Another of my grandmother's close friends, she hadn't been feeling well when I'd made the rounds of old neighbours. This time she was better and gave me some heather from her garden to take home for Mum to plant in our garden. Knowing that Customs officials tended to get a bit stroppy about foreign plants, I decided that, if challenged, I'd tell the Canadian ones it was to keep my clothes fresh.

Ellen was out when I got back to Cousin Tom's. Her relatives had taken her up White Horse Hill and then for tea in Faringdon, but she came back for supper. I can't recall what the others had, but I had a stack of chicken and ham paste sandwiches from one of the jars Iris had got me at Barwell's little shop, and semolina, which I hadn't had for ages.

Iris had basket weaving materials, and later on, Ellen and I attempted to make baskets. I'm not particularly 'crafty', but the result wasn't too bad. We finished around nine o'clock and went across the street to visit the friend we'd missed visiting the day before. After which it was back to Suzanne and Roger's.

Chapter Forty-One
Home Sweet Home

Much though I'd enjoyed revisiting my old stomping grounds, it was time to head back to Canada. After breakfast we went to Cousin Tom's to wait for Uncle Bill and Nan to show up and take us back to Iver.

Following lunch in Iver, Ellen and I stuffed our numerous pieces of luggage into Uncle Bill's car, said good-bye to Nan and Frank, and set off for Stanstead Airport with Auntie Betty and Uncle Bill. The car overheated en route, causing us to break down fourteen miles short of the airport. But only temporarily, and we arrived there just after five o'clock. That still gave us plenty of time to check in; the three or so hours now recommended for international flights not being necessary *then*. We also had time to change our remaining money back into Canadian money—what Ellen called 'real money'—which didn't take long because, by then, there wasn't much of it.

Ellen's relatives had come to see us off too, and they and Auntie Betty and Uncle Bill kept in contact with us with smiles and hand signals after Ellen and I passed through Security. We'd not been in the secure waiting area long when the intercom announced that our flight had been delayed for half an hour, but at least it hadn't been cancelled altogether, like some charter flights we'd heard about on the News the night before.

The delay was indeed just half an hour in duration. Aboard the aeroplane, we found someone else in Ellen's assigned seat, but the woman in it moved up one and Ellen and I sat down together. Not everyone travelling together managed that. Several seats had been wrongly assigned, and just before take-off a stewardess told everyone affected to just sit down and let other people get by. She said seating would be sorted out later, but it never was. Once they got everyone aboard and into any seat available, the flight crew was happy.

Shortly after take-off, a meal was served. There was a little more of what I could eat this time, but Ellen and I could hardly wait for the trays to be cleared away so we could put on our coats. It was *cold* in that aircraft. Ellen said if my ears were bothering me (they were) it was probably because they were frostbitten. The heat did get turned up after a while, no doubt in response to the *numerous* complaints from all aboard. After that, our only cause of discomfort was the amount of smoke the nicotine addicts were again wafting around.

We slept a bit, off and on, during the next few hours, and just before another meal was brought round, were presented with Immigration cards and Customs declaration forms to fill out. One of the Customs regulations said we had to declare any goods we'd bought that exceeded the $100 limit but, in view of the amount we'd had in traveller's cheques, and what we'd had to splash out for intercity transport, in-city transport, youth hostels, food, and other living expenses (as well as all the postcards we'd dispatched), we were pretty sure we hadn't had a hundred dollars to spend on 'goods'.

A brief stop was made in Calgary, and as soon as we were airborne again the stewardess came on the intercom to say that, in honour of the sixth anniversary of Transavia Holland, we would all be getting tickets that could win us six long-playing records, a desirable enough prize in the days before CDs and iPods®. We accepted the tickets but didn't win anything.

Soon afterwards, we landed in Seattle and went through Passport Control. Because we'd been in Italy, Spain, and Portugal, Ellen and I were handed cholera exposure cards and told to show them to a doctor if we became ill in the next six weeks. In Customs, an official pawed through a few of our things, made me dig out my meat paste (which in those pre-Mad Cow scare days, he passed) and left us to fit everything back into our packs and flight bags and place them on a conveyor belt to be taken out to the buses transporting us to Vancouver.

Going down to Seattle we'd had four buses. For the return journey, the group had, inexplicably, only been allotted two; the charter flight's organizers having perhaps assumed that half its passengers would miss the plane or like England so much they'd decide to stay. Young girls like ourselves, and families with children, couldn't manoeuvre cases and packsacks fast enough to get places on the buses, and just when it was looking like Ellen and I were going to be amongst those stranded until more buses were procured, one driver said he had eleven seats left and could take eleven people with small luggage. And, much to our amazement, our large, bulging, packs and mid-size, but still bulging, flight bags were considered small luggage.

* * *

Everyone had to get off the bus at the Canada-U.S. border and go through Customs again. I declared my meat paste and plants, but no one asked me what they were. No one asked whether we'd been in Italy, Spain, or Portugal, either, so I can only assume the U.S. government was more concerned about the nasty little bugs making the rounds in those countries than the government of Canada was.

Having expected our parents to meet us at Vancouver Airport's Bus Terminal, Ellen and I were a little disconcerted to find they weren't there when we arrived in the early hours of morning. But almost immediately a man read out a list of arriving travellers who had messages, and our names were on it. The message was that our welcoming committee had gone somewhere for coffee, and we were to sit down and *not move* until they returned. When they did, my mum got us all a cab and we went to the Alcazar Hotel. After depositing our stuff in our room, we went to my parents' room to talk, and learned that our mothers had had quite a turn when a news report they'd watched earlier said a plane going to Seattle had crashed with no survivors. That one had been going to Seattle from the Yukon, and upon paying closer attention, my dad heard that bit and was able to reassure them.

Later on, Mum rang the switchboard to send a 'safe arrival' telegram to Auntie Betty and we went down to the hotel dining room to have breakfast before catching a bus out to the PNE (Pacific National Exhibition) grounds in Hastings Park.

Canadian Prime Minister, Sir Wilfrid Laurier, opened the very first PNE—known, in those days, as the Industrial Exhibition—on the sixteenth of August, 1910. Then strictly an industrial showcase, it managed to keep going during the first world war but had to sit out part of the second when several of the buildings in Hastings Park were put to use as a place to house Japanese-Canadians before they were moved on to internment camps. After it reopened in 1947, the PNE still offered up lots of exhibits, but went on to become an annual source of family fun and entertainment as well.

Neither I nor my parents had been to the PNE before. Ellen and her mother had, but Ellen was quite young at the time and could only vaguely recall walking around some animal pens. We did that too, and also visited other agricultural exhibits and a few foreign goods exhibits before taking in a show.

The popular Canadian television series, *The Littlest Hobo*, ran from 1963 to 1965 the first time it was on, and from 1979 to 1985 the second time. At the 1971 PNE, the dogs from the first series were put through their paces by their owner/trainer, Charles P. (Chuck) Eisenmann, and were remarkable to watch. He claimed they could think, and it certainly seemed like it. The technical 'star', London, was nine-and-a-half years old, and had a vocabulary of five thousand words, equivalent to a six- or seven-year-old child. But other dogs sometimes stood in for him, and we were told that Hobo, aged four, had a thousand-word vocabulary, Venus, aged two-and-a-half, a four-hundred-word vocabulary, and Thorn, aged one, hardly any vocabulary as yet. We were also told that Venus was the one who picked things up most easily. All four were clever, however, and much more obedient than some of the children watching. Kids were constantly being told to keep thirty inches from the stage but wouldn't.

After the show, I went to a heraldry kiosk, where I paid a dollar to have our family name researched and learned that Duke was an English name that dated back to the thirteenth century, and was an offshoot of the longer surname, Marmaduke. Somewhere along the line an ancestor must have got fed up with writing out the long version and dropped the 'Marma'.

Another kiosk offered electronic handwriting analyses. Ellen and I both got one, and both of us came out as being very attractive to the opposite sex and having extraordinary abilities, attributes I suspect the thing was programmed to assign to everyone. In addition to that, I scored high on having an over-active imagination, being reticent, aloof, sceptical and sincere, and inclined to procrastinate. All of which seemed reasonably accurate. But I also scored high on being sophisticated—I think our recent travels had disproved that—as well as a lover of luxury, and having a great interest in sports, neither of which were the least bit accurate. As to whether or not I was mentally well-adjusted, disciplined and self-controlled, methodical and orderly, and artistic and creative, this mechanical judge of characters was non-committal, the indicator lines for those remaining near the middle of the chart.

After a while, Dad said he was weary and went back to the hotel, but the rest of us soldiered on, and after stopping for a meal, went shopping at some of the stalls and took in another show, this one a logging display.

At the end of the show, we went over to the PNE tower, but decided against going up it as the lift spun around as well as moving up and down. We then walked around a few exhibits, one of them a model home we all decided we wanted for Christmas. We also did more shopping. Having failed to acquire a jewelled collar for Voodoo, I bought him a toy bird on a wand. A toy bird that, until he demolished it—which did not take long—he loved playing with, even though he was not, like most of our cats, much of a predator, and once almost let a real bird sit on his head when he was outside napping in the sun.

* * *

In the morning, we gathered up our belongings and made ready to leave the hotel. A passer-by helped Dad load our stuff into the lift, which, for some reason, kept going up and down on us, and landed us back on our own floor. Undeterred, we tried again, this time with success. But the five of us, plus two packs, four flight bags, and two suitcases left little room for anyone else, so even though one person did manage to squeeze in on a lower floor, everyone else just shook their heads whenever the lift doors opened.

At the bus depot, Mum and Dad and I saw Betty and Ellen off on the Langley bus before catching our own to Kelowna. There, Mum rang for a cab, and almost before I knew it, I was home. Home with a lot more travel experience (and more still to come), memories both good and bad, lots of souvenirs to show off, close to five hundred slides to bore people with, dozens of new books to read, and, of course, two more hats, than I'd started out with.

The End

Author's Note

The names of some people have been changed, but I have called the bulk of my casually met fellow travellers by their actual first names, which were usually all I knew them by anyway. Most friends and relatives have also been properly named, and to avoid confusion regarding certain family connections, I must explain that, although my mother knew and interacted with her birth family, she was not brought up with her twin sister and other siblings. Times were hard in the Great Depression, and it was not uncommon for the parents of several children to give one to relatives with no children, especially when twins came along. That's what happened with my mother, the second twin. She was raised by an aunt and uncle and always considered *them* her parents, just as my brothers and I considered them our grandparents. Until they passed on, we, too, lived with them when we were domiciled in England as opposed to Canada. (We grew up in both places.)

Also, despite this book's title, there weren't two hats to begin with. Ellen and I each just had one hat, neither of them connected to the title. Ellen's was a small blue cloth affair much like the hats worn by fishermen standing on riverbanks. Mine was made of blue denim like the caps worn by little boys playing David Copperfield on stage and screen. Setting out on our travels, we didn't know we were going to acquire other hats, or that we'd have to find a way to get them home without crushing them.

This account of those travels is taken from my journals, and readers are asked to keep in mind that this trip took place over fifty years ago. My travelling companion was my—then and now—bezzie mate/bestie/BFF, or whatever such is called in your part of the world. We were, at that time, quite young and had led very sheltered lives. Somewhat indulged by our parents, we were used to having *them* sort out any difficulties we came up against. The attitudes and opinions of our bygone days are not necessarily the ones we hold now, and our instant-ire responses to setbacks have abated quite considerably. Like most people, we've mellowed with age.

The world is different, too. In the early 1970s, climate change, pollution, the preservation of endangered species, and various other modern challenges were beginning to be of concern in some circles, but were a long way from attaining the kind of global attention they receive today. Instead, it was the time of mini-skirts and bell-bottoms, hippies and psychedelic drugs, moon landings and the space race, bussing, women's lib, peace marches, the Vietnam War, and the slow thawing of the Cold War that has, regrettably, recently been rekindled. Society's tolerances, intolerances, and priorities have changed over the years, as have its expectations and innovations. What we regarded as scandalously high prices seem unbelievably cheap in comparison to what the same goods and services command now. Prices that we had to mentally convert into 'our' money from each country's currency rather than today's all-encompassing euro. And although souvenir shops do still carry picture postcards, members of the smart phone generation are more inclined to just zap family and friends a selfie from famous places. As for sending telegrams and picking up *hand-written* letters at embassies, well, those are sure to be viewed as positively archaic practices. Along with the use of traveller's cheques, flashcubes, and terms such as stewardess and waiter/waitress rather than flight attendant and server. But to backpack around Europe was the 'in' thing for young people to do in the seventies, and our experiences and viewpoints reflect what was happening *then*.

I have, however, whenever such comments seemed relevant, provided additional, updated, information about the places we visited, and made references to other European jaunts I've been on. Being in an ocean liner anchored off Le Havre in 1957 probably doesn't count as one, but there were others. Prior to exploring 'The Continent' with Ellen, I went to Austria with a school group in 1965, and visited Europe again in the 1980s and 1990s, both by myself and with children in tow, and also made some twenty-first-century trips in conjunction with research for my time travel novels.

Disclaimer

With us now being so much older, wiser, and more even tempered than we were then, I trust readers will find our antics amusing rather than reprehensible. If not, I personally disavow all knowledge of them.

— Ellen Blair

Also published by BWL Publishing Inc.

The Royal Yot

Side Trip Book 1: Ring Of Beom

Side Trip Book 2: Shield Of Beom

Generations Five: The Time Rose Prequel

Time Rose Book 1: The Disappearing Rose

Time Rose Book 2: The Mud Rose

Time Rose Book 3: The Spirit Rose

Time Rose Book 4: The Tangled Rose

Time Rose Book 5: The Volcanic Rose

Renee Duke grew up in Ontario/B.C., Canada and Berkshire, England. Due to a treacherous re-drawing of county lines after she left the U.K., her little English market town is now in Oxfordshire, but she's still a Berkshire girl at heart.

After qualifying as an Early Childhood Educator, she went on to work with children of all ages in a number of different capacities and settings, one of them a teaching stint in Belize, Central America as part of a World Peace and Development team, another in an OSC (Out-Of-School-Care) centre running interactive history programmes for five-to thirteen-year-olds.

Until recent years, her professional writing was mostly confined to magazine articles and stories, as it was only when she retired from teaching that she had time to turn her attention to the novels she'd been putting together in her mind for decades. But this book, *Travellers With Two Hats*, is a memoir, much of it taken from the travel journals she kept.

Mother of one son and servant to a demanding cat, she resides in Kelowna, B.C., Canada, but still likes to travel beyond it.